CONVICTIONS OF A CHEF

CONVICTIONS OF A CHEF

COOKING FOR THE COUNTERCULTURE AND THE ONE PERCENT

EVAN MARCUS-ROTMAN

IGUANA

Publisher: Cheryl Hawley
Editors: Paula Chiarcos and Lee Parpart
Front cover design: Amy Law
About the Author photograph: Michael Rauner Photography

SAINT OF CIRCUMSTANCE
Words and Music by ROBERT WEIR and JOHN BARLOW
© 1972 (Renewed) ICE NINE PUBLISHING CO., INC.
All Rights Reserved
Used by Permission of ALFRED MUSIC

ISBN 978-1-77180-657-2 (paperback)
ISBN 978-1-77180-656-5 (epub)

This is an original print edition of *Convictions of a Chef.*

To Marsea, my heart, my soul, my rock and roll.

To Cassidy, for teaching me the true meaning of unconditional love.

To my family, friends, and community, who have nurtured me for my entire life.

To food, music, and travel, for teaching me everything.

To all my relations that I have, and have yet to encounter. No meeting is insignificant.

Preface

I am a chef. I am also a brother, a cousin, an uncle, a father, a Deadhead, a burner, a writer, a traveler, a husband, a convicted felon and a trauma survivor. I've run kitchens on luxury yachts, private islands and estates, as well as in concert venues, festivals, theaters, stadiums, back alleys, soup kitchens and beyond.

I am also a recreational drug user and have been since I was a teenager. Perhaps I started a little earlier than I should have ... but I can't change the past. Maybe if there had been better drug education, I'd have been armed with the information to know that drugs are better served at a more mature age. But I am a member of the "just say no" generation and was fed the hardline view that all drug use is bad (mmm-kay), and that abstinence is the only way. And like any good teenager ... I rebelled.

Meanwhile, as I got older and looked around, I saw drugs all around me. Alcohol eased the tension in the room at family functions and religious celebrations. People I looked up to embraced drug and alcohol culture, geeking out on wine or weed. The world might have been telling me to "just say no," but "hey bud, let's party" is what was really happening all around me.

Using drugs is a personal choice. Not all users are addicts. This is in no way meant to minimize the disease of addiction.

By hiding our recreational, spiritual or personal drug use, we contribute to the stigma that makes people think drug use is only for addicts. So, in this book ... there is no hiding. I am not trying to glorify or hide. I am just telling my story, and it's one in which drugs have played a role.

That being said, this book is about a lot more than recreational drug use. It's also about food and the culinary industry, travel, music, personal and spiritual growth, ethics, culture and counterculture, and what has become … my life. In these pages, you'll meet a kid who was dealt a crappy hand and made some poor choices, then ended up paying a huge price, thanks to a cruel and senseless drug war. You'll also meet the adult that kid became — an ex-convict who grabbed at a second chance to rebuild his life, see the world and cook his way into the hearts of many.

Everyone has their own story to tell. This is mine. While my family has played a major role in my life, I won't be talking much about them. I want to honor their privacy, and I want them to have the opportunity to tell their own stories, should they wish to. Family of mine, just know that I love you all very, very much, and am grateful for the relationships that I share with my brothers, cousins, nieces, nephews, aunts, uncles and in-laws. Even the ones who choose not to talk to me anymore.

"I've opted to have fun in this lifetime."

—Jerry Garcia

Part 1

The Serenity to Accept the Things I Cannot Change...

Busted!!

June 11, 1992

My roommate and I are sound asleep when we hear banging on the door. It's a noise so loud and aggressive that it can only be cops. I stumble out to the main room and twist the lock on the door. Before it clicks open it is thrown open, and within seconds I am surrounded by screaming men breaking through the front door and the kitchen door at the same time. Before I can speak, I am face down on the ground, a knee in my back and the cold steel of a gun against the back of my head. With my cheek pressing into the carpet, I am reminded that it hasn't been cleaned in years. All I can think is, *They're going to wake Cassidy*. He's down the hall in his race-car bed, dreaming about whatever it is that five-year-old boys dream of. When I try to turn my head, the cop jams his gun against the back of my neck. There is yelling, but I can't focus on the words. I just see more of them coming in the door with guns raised, scrambling in like cockroaches when a light goes on. They're screaming about weapons. "Are there any weapons? Are there guns?" I hear my voice, choked and high, saying, "We have no guns."

At that moment, one of the cops emerges from my bedroom holding up a shotgun case. They start screaming more questions. The cop holding me down wrenches my arms harder behind my back and jams the gun into the base of my skull. My shoulders feel like they're going to pop out of the sockets.

"OPEN IT!" I say through gritted teeth. The pain in my shoulders is brutal. I hear the zipper of the nylon case being opened, and the case falls to the floor with a swoosh.

Even with my head crammed into the carpet I know what they're looking at: a four-foot purple plastic Graphix bong with a six-shooter bowl on it. There is a short silence, and they all start laughing. The gun in my neck eases up a bit, and I can feel the temperature in the room come down by a few degrees. My oppressors almost seem relaxed. But that doesn't help me. I'm twenty-three and terrified. I can feel wet heat in my eyes, and I rub the tears into the smelly carpet, hoping that nobody has seen them.

When they finally let me up, I sit next to my roommate on the old brown leather couch. My arms are still behind my back, and they're aching. I finally get a look at everyone in the room. Sheriffs and local cops, and — *oh shit* — DEA, U.S. Marshals and postal inspectors. Holy fuck, this has to be bad. Why so many cops? And what the hell is a postal inspector doing here?! In that moment, that very inspector begins to light a cigarette. I'm right on it, saying, "Please don't smoke in here. Neither of us smokes." He looks at me like I'm nuts, but he stops himself in the act of lighting the cigarette and flips it around in his fingers instead.

"We're here for Evan, not for you," the inspector says to my roommate. I quickly state that all of the drugs in the house are mine, and he shoots me a grateful glance through the anger and confusion that also swim in his eyes. We both knew that the weed in his closet was his own stash … but it's now clear that I brought the heat, and since he is a teacher, he can't have anything to do with this. He could lose his teaching credential and never see the inside of a classroom again. It's true that he's a recreational cannabis user, but he has never sold a bag of weed, or any drug, in his life. The postal inspector with the unlit cigarette and the leading marshals grab me by the arms and push me down the hall, to my room, lead me inside and close the door. It's just the three of us now. The Miles Davis CD that I'd fallen asleep to is still on continuous play, and "Bye Bye Blackbird" plays ominously in the background. The marshal leans against the wall, staring at me, while the inspector paces the floor as he plays with the unlit cigarette that was just behind his ear. Suddenly it feels like that cop is kneeling on my back again, crushing the breath out of me. I sink down onto the rumpled bed, where I had been sleeping soundly just moments before.

I remember all this like it was yesterday. Panic has a way of searing tactile information on the mind. The marshal stood there, chewing on a pen cap, while the postal cop paced the room, kicking my laundry around on the floor as if he might uncover the Hope Diamond under my smelly clothes. He stopped where

I was sitting and stood over me, his breath a toxic mix of greasy fast food and cigarettes. It literally smelled like he had eaten a Big Mac moments before he led the raid. "Tell us about the liquid that went to Fort Knox and Maui." I didn't know anyone in either of those places, so I breathed a slight sigh at the possibility that they might have the wrong guy. I looked at him and shrugged. "What about a phone call with a certain woman friend of yours earlier this evening?" At that moment my heart sank, as I knew exactly what phone call, and to what woman, he was referring. *Fuck Motherfuck!*

I knew enough to ask for a lawyer. That got them really mad. My father was a lawyer and told me many stories about clients who dug their own grave by saying too much. I guess the old man did *that* much for me. He hadn't taught me much in this lifetime, but he at least tried to instill upon me when to keep my mouth shut.

The inspectors split into teams and began tearing through everything in the house, from old boxes in the garage to the depths of the freezer. They left no stone unturned.

At some point, they called my ex. It was around 1:30 a.m. I was back in the living room on the couch when Pearly arrived. I will never forget the daggers she threw me with her eyes as she carried our sleeping son out, wrapped in a blanky. She was understandably furious.

On the ride downtown the cops kept grilling me, but I just stared out the window. One asked, "Do you know the difference between a state crime and a federal crime?" I didn't, though I would soon learn.

Processing into a jail for my first time was the single most terrifying experience that I ever had. Two cops followed me into a tiled shower, similar to a locker room. "Take all of your clothes off," the one cop snarled at me, as the other thumbed through a porn magazine. "You see that new bitch they got working in records? She's fine as fuck," he said. Once I was naked, the first cop growled, "Put your hands above your head." He examined my armpits, and then said, "Run your fingers through your hair and show me behind your ears." My red hair was down to the middle of my back, and thick and curly back then. I did as I was told. "Open your mouth all the way and stick your tongue out," he barked as he shined a flashlight inside, searching for contraband. "Now lift your dick, then your balls," he said to me, while still making small talk with his partner about the new "chick" in records. "Turn around and lift your left leg, and wiggle your toes all around," he said to me. "Yeah, I make it a point to not fuck chicks from work. Too close to home," he responded to his partner, who was barely paying attention to him, but was engrossed in some advertisement in his magazine. "Bend over, spread your cheeks and cough for me three times," he told me. I followed his instructions. Then they had me shower, while they watched.

After the shower, they took pictures of me from every angle imaginable before issuing me a khaki jumpsuit with *MDCLA Inmate* printed on the back. More pictures and countless sets of fingerprints followed.

Once I was processed in, these two thug cops escorted me to the elevator where two other cops were waiting. The four of them began chatting about nothing in particular. When the elevator arrived we all piled in, and I turned around to face the doors, as one normally does in an elevator full of people. I quickly found out that this small bit of civilian body language no longer applied to me. One of the cops looked at me like I was gum on his shoe. He spun me back around and slammed me face first into the back wall. "This is how you ride every elevator from now on, Asshole," the cop snarled. "And don't ever make eye contact with any of us," he said. I gritted my teeth and faced the back wall, trying to guess which floor we were on when I heard the door open behind me.

"Let's go." I guessed I was allowed to turn around now.

They escorted me into a locked unit and walked me to an empty cell. It had two bunk beds, each with a thin gray army blanket and a nearly flat pillow. And it was cold. The air conditioning was cranking. I took in my surroundings as I entered the cool room.

"Don't get too comfortable," the guard said as he closed the door. "Court line is in twenty minutes." I sat down on the stool that was attached to a toilet and tried to steady my breath. It was the first time I'd been alone since I'd been so rudely awakened, hours earlier. I listened to the man's keys jangle as he walked away, trying to make sense of what was happening to me. I had an awful taste in my mouth, and I was engrossed in the deepest fear that I'd ever known. I felt helpless and alone.

True to his word, he came back shortly after to take me to a common room, where we were all given a tray with a box of cereal, a grainy apple and a school-lunch-sized carton of milk. There was a thermos of coffee and I saw guys filling cups, but I was too shaken up to handle such a task. At home, coffee was a ritual that I loved. I had a Chemex glass pour-over setup, and I was so obsessed with getting the best possible taste that I wouldn't grind the beans until the water was boiling. (Even before I became a chef, I always had a love of good food, beer, coffee, etc.) We were escorted, as a group, to a giant waiting area. A lot of the guys were laughing it up and joking around with each other, and some of them even seemed to be on chatting terms with a few of the guards. I remained quiet and kept to myself, too terrified to do much else.

Slowly they began to call our names from a list. We were made to stand in a line and repeat that whole process of showing every part of our entire body that I'd done during processing, only this time it was in a line of maybe forty guys. It made my experience from the previous night seem almost luxurious in comparison. At least then I was alone. This felt more like we were cattle on a feedlot being led to slaughter. I tried not to look as we all went through the process of being examined head to toe in our nakedness, and I prayed to G-d that the others would do the same for me. We each got a colored jumpsuit or a regular suit (for the few who were going to trial). Once we were handcuffed again and shackled together, they loaded us onto a bus — and drove directly across the street, not more than 100 meters from where we just were! — to the courthouse, where we waited to be called. It could be an hour; it could be eight hours; there would be no telling how long I would have to wait. At some point they gave us a bag lunch, which was a slice of bologna between two dried-out pieces of bread, another bruised and grainy apple, and a sugary fruit drink. I realized, at that moment, that Cassidy must be awake. I wondered what he was eating for breakfast. His favorite was granola and vanilla yogurt with strawberries and bananas cut into it. He called it "Hippie Food." I wondered what Pearly was going to tell him. Not that I was in jail, I hoped. My stomach hurt, so I gave my lunch away.

Some hours later, I finally got a chance to read the indictment against me. Three counts of selling what they called sixty grams of LSD. I didn't understand at first. I'd never sold, or even seen, anywhere near sixty grams. I leaned my head back and closed my eyes. It didn't make any sense. It would take a lawyer for me to understand — they weren't weighing just the LSD. See, what I knew about LSD was this: It's the most powerful drug on Earth. One gram = 10,000 doses. And if you have enough crystal LSD on your finger that you could see it, you're going to be very, very high, so you must dilute it and put it onto a carrier of some sort. And while 1,000 hits in pure crystal form wouldn't even trigger the mandatory minimum sentence, 1,000 hits on blotter paper might weigh ten grams, and 1,000 hits dissolved in liquid weighs about, well, sixty grams. And here's how the system works: You get less than a year for that amount in pure crystal form, but you get ten years for the same amount on blotter paper, and twelve to fifteen years for — yup, the exact same amount — in the liquid. Even though they're all enough to get about a thousand people high.

I read the indictment against me maybe a hundred times in the next few minutes: *June 11, 1992. The United States of America vs. Evan Edward Rotman.* There was something incredibly final about it. Like once it was in ink with an official government seal, there was no turning back. I was beginning to grasp the severity of the situation.

Somehow, I'd managed to piss off the whole country.

Kangaroo Court

Court was a blur. Like something out of someone else's life. And even though I didn't know what was going to happen next or when I was getting out of there, after a few hours, all I could think about was how hungry I was. And I realized that the pounding in my head was caffeine withdrawal, and that at some point I'd need to use the one open toilet at the end of the cell, assuming I eventually drank some water. I glanced around at the thirty other guys sitting on the benches around the edges. With all the strip-searching, I don't get how, but some of them had cigarettes and matches. And lots of them seemed to know each other. Some even knew the guards by name. There was a sense of familiarity that I hoped to never have.

After a while, my name was called and I was moved to a small holding cell. I sat there alone for a few minutes until an older guy in a rumpled suit came in and plopped down his overloaded briefcase, catching his breath. His hair was messy and there were visible coffee stains on his suit jacket. This was the public defender (public neglecter, public pretender, let the insults fly!). He thumbed through a few files without looking at me. Then he found some papers that must have told him who I was or what he was doing in that dingy cell instead of being at home with his feet up and a beer in his hand. He looked up and adjusted his wire-framed glasses with slender fingers. He cleared his throat. "Hello, Mr. Rothman, I'm your appointed legal counsel…" I figured, *If he can't even get my name right, I'm in some trouble here.*

He gave the affidavit a quick once over, looked deeper into his stack and pulled out a few more papers, muttering to himself. "Looks like they've got you dead to rights." He smiled. Then, as though realizing this wasn't the right moment to smile, he adjusted his lips into a straight line and cleared his throat again. "They're offering you a deal. Ten years. I advise you to take it. Your guideline range is a hundred and fifty-one to a hundred and eighty-eight months. A hundred and twenty months will save you some time." One hundred and fifty-one months didn't sound like that long … until I did the math, dividing it by twelve (months in a year), and I nearly shit myself.

Now I'm no lawyer, but I knew this was no deal, and I told him so.

When it was my turn in the courtroom, I pled not guilty. A trial date was set, and I was sent back to the holding tank before the judge even looked up from his papers. I was taken back to the holding facility, strip-searched again and brought upstairs to the same unit that I'd been on that morning. Most of the guys were playing cards, laughing and sitting around the televisions in the corners of the unit. There was a small patio area with weight-lifting machines and ash cans. I found it ironic that the exercise area was also the smoking area, and the rank smell of stale tobacco wafted inside. It was the sense of ease and familiarity among the other inmates that just didn't sit right with me. I wanted to devote my energy toward getting out, not getting comfortable.

That's when life got really slow. I was housed on the seventh floor of a pretty new building. They kept it very cold, and it was surprisingly clean. It smelled of cafeteria food, Old Spice deodorant and Simple Green floor cleaner. Simple Green … somehow that smell always brought me back to my mother's house. She probably used it because it was cheap, and we were poor. It has this fake sort of ammoniated pine tree smell. She used to clean feverishly every Sunday, presumably to mask her tears and rage as my brothers and I spent an awkward day out with our dad.

But before Mom died, every Saturday, she and I would bake a special dessert. We'd then watch "our" favorite shows together — *Mary Tyler Moore* and *Bob Newhart* for her, *Adam-12* and *Emergency* for me. We also both liked *The Love Boat* and *Fantasy Island*. It was the early '70s, and those are the memories that I cherish from our short time together. My three brothers are quite a bit older and were all out of the house most of my life, so Mom and I were a team of two. We kept a strict kosher kitchen when I was young, and when she died and I moved in with my father and his wife, that was just one of many things that got lost. I missed the routine of ancient tradition, and the way my mother and I bonded over those practices. My father and stepmother halfheartedly tried to keep a kosher kitchen once I moved in, but without having separate dishes for milk and meat meals, it felt a bit hollow and meaningless to me. Little gestures like that kept my mom alive in my mind, but it wasn't enough to make up for the jarring changes that hit me after her death. With the minimal efforts that my father and stepmother were putting into parenting, and the amount of trauma that I'd already experienced, I was destined for some hard times ahead.

Days in MDCLA were pretty long, but the nights were even longer. I spent a lot of time thinking about those old rituals with my mom, which felt like they were a lifetime away from this cold, concrete existence of federal incarceration. I also thought a ton about Cassidy and what he must have been going through, with his dad suddenly torn from his life. I knew he couldn't possibly understand what had happened to me, and I couldn't count on anyone to explain to him why I wasn't there for him. He still had Pearly and her boyfriend, but we had always spent a lot of time together, so I knew he had to be confused and upset. I didn't want him to feel abandoned, as I had by my mother's death.

Cassidy and I were tight. We shared a deep bond. After researching every preschool in our area and deciding on the one that was the best fit, I taught his class how to make tie-dyes. I also brought my guitar into class and led a few singalongs. I showed up for the arts-and-crafts days and I chaperoned the field trips. I was as active in his school as a twenty-three-year-old father could be, and I loved being his dad. I couldn't stand the idea of him growing up without me.

After Mom died, shortly after my eighth birthday, I'd had to go live with my father, who I'd only ever seen on the aforementioned Sunday afternoons up until then. One of the first things he did was to pull me out of therapy, which he didn't believe in. Ethan, the youngest of my three brothers, had found a therapist for me once Mom got the fatal diagnosis — a wise and bold move for a seventeen-year-old to propose for his brother. Dad also pulled me out of my private Jewish school. While he was Jewish, he didn't believe in religious education, and he wasn't willing to pay the tuition. The school had always extended my mother a scholarship for my tuition, as she was a single mother of four. They offered to continue that scholarship after her death, but my dad wasn't the kind of guy who accepted "charity." So public school it was, and in one fell swoop, I lost my mother, my faith, my school, my diet, my home and my traditions. My brothers made attempts to spend time with and to nurture me, but they were all off to college or starting their adult lives as young men.

I cried a lot those first days at his house. My father's solution was to take me to the toy store, give me a $100 bill and tell me to have at it. After that, we never really spoke of my mother again.

In prison, I had plenty of time to think about those tough times growing up in my dad's house, and to ruminate on what my own son must be thinking about me. I'd call him on the phone, but the conversations were strained and awkward. Even at that tender young age, the feelings of loyalty and disloyalty around me and his mother and me were palpable. Kids shouldn't have to choose sides in a broken home, but how is a five-year-old supposed to understand that? He did come to visit me once; an old friend brought him. But it was understandably upsetting for him, and his mother forbade that from happening again.

During those first months in prison, my dad and Margret came to visit me a few times, and so did my brothers. They all made some time to see Cassidy as well, and they would fill me in on how he was doing. I lived for those updates. And for a while, my brother Ethan took the train up from San Diego almost every week, taking most of the day to spend one hour with me. The whole process of visiting somebody in prison is most unpleasant, and while the visits were difficult for both of us, I cherished them. Of course, I had to go through the whole strip-search process every time, but that was becoming a normal part of my life.

Other family members did what they could. My mother was one of four girls and her younger sister is my Aunt Marcia (pronounced *Ahnt Mahsha*, as the family was from Boston). Aunt Marcia and Uncle Mickey would accept my collect calls, and they'd send me a little money for commissary. But they never came to visit me. And G-d bless my cousins, who I grew up with. They were, and are, great family. But nobody in my family had ever been in trouble with the law before, and certainly not to this extent. Everyone was pissed off at me, but also trying to be empathetic. None of them knew how to handle such a serious situation, so they opted to just not handle it at all. At the time, it felt like they forgot about me. And yes, I felt abandoned. In hindsight, I realize that they were no better equipped to handle a prisoner of the drug war than I was to be one.

The drug war was in full swing in 1992, and since its inception in 1973 the U.S. prison population had continued to grow. In 1971, when Richard Nixon held a press conference to declare drugs to be "public enemy number one," there were about 200,000 people incarcerated. By 1980 that number had grown to over 300,000, and by 1992 there were over a million people incarcerated in America, making it the country with the highest-per-capita rate of incarceration on Earth. (Today that number has doubled to over two million.) In step with this growth, private prisons started popping up everywhere. With ten-to-twenty-year sentences becoming the norm for drug offenses, inmates were becoming so desperate that they had no choice but to work for prison industries for mere pennies (top pay back then was about $1.15 per hour, and it took ten years to reach that tier). Not only were the shareholders of the private prisons getting rich, but so were prison industries, competing in fair marketplaces, on the backs of underpaid prison labor.

In 1994, Nixon's own policy adviser, John Ehrlichman, let the cat out of the bag by telling Dan Baum of *Harper's Magazine* the real reason for the war on drugs. "You want to know what this was really all about?" he asked, with what Baum described as "the bluntness of a man who, after public disgrace and a stretch in federal prison, had little to protect" (*Harper's*, 2016). According to Ehrlichman, "The Nixon campaign ... and the Nixon White House ... had two enemies: the antiwar left and Black people.... We knew we couldn't make it illegal to be either against the war or Black, but by getting the public to associate the hippies with marijuana and Blacks with heroin, and then criminalizing both heavily, we could ... vilify them.... Did we know we were lying about the drugs? Of course, we did." (*Harper's*, 2016)

I used to sign all of my letters POW, laying claim to being a prisoner of the drug war. This annoyed several family members. It especially ticked off Ethan, who felt that I was a prisoner of my own mistakes. While he was not wrong about that, I also believed (and still do) that my draconian sentence was a direct result of a war on drugs that has cost billions of dollars, wasted countless lives, deepened the racial divide in America, and failed to achieve its stated objectives of making the country safer. Ethan continued to visit me and write to me in prison, and that meant (and means) a lot. But I wouldn't let go of that little symbol at the end of my letters. It was important to me.

Then there was the practical matter of how to stay healthy in prison. About a month into my incarceration, my ankles began to swell. In less than a day, they were the size of grapefruits ... and then cantaloupes. I was also getting dry, scaly lesions all over my torso, legs and thighs. The pain was tremendous, so I went to sick-call daily, but I only saw physician's assistants, and seemingly the crappy ones who couldn't get better jobs, because none of them could diagnose what was wrong. They kept giving me anti-fungal creams and ibuprofen, but that wasn't helping. Then one day I was playing cards with an accused gun dealer. He noticed my fingernails, which by now were all pitted and grooved, and said, "That's psoriasis. My brother has that."

I would learn that psoriasis is an autoimmune disorder, where your immune system works overtime, producing skin cells at a rate seven times faster than normal. The result is plaques of dry, scaly skin, with new skin being made underneath it, which will also never finish growing, as there is yet more new skin under that … and so on. It is often triggered by a stressful or a traumatic event. Go figure…

I took that information to sick-call the next day, and the PA scratched his head and said, "Maybe…" But I knew that gun dealer was right. The PA said that if it was psoriasis, there was little they could do for me, so they would make it a low priority. I hobbled out of the infirmary. The next morning, and almost every morning after that, my sheets were filled with scales and stained with blood from my scratching. To me, it was anything but a low priority. The more my stress ramped up, the worse it got. And let's just say, I was stressed to the max.

The feds gave me cortisone cream and a few topical steroids that might keep it at bay, but not by much. There is no known cure for psoriasis, however, in recent years, the science has come a long way. There are now immune-suppressing drugs that keep the skin pretty clear. Not back then though, and the prison medical system leaves a lot to be desired. I would also learn that 15 percent of people with psoriasis also get an arthritis that is connected to it, known as psoriatic arthritis. I was one of the "lucky" 15 percent, which explained the deep joint pain and swelling that I was experiencing.

My seven months at MDCLA was a serious adjustment to institutionalized living. I didn't know this at the time, but Los Angeles is the nation's leading city for bank robberies, so there were a lot of bank robbers in there. My first cellmate was a washed-up professional poker player from Vegas. After he lost everything, he robbed a bank and waited in the parking lot for the FBI to arrive. He just wanted his three hots and a cot with free health care, even if the health care was crap and the food was inedible. He told me prison was his endgame all along. That guy taught me how to play spades and pinochle, and at the end of it all, pinochle is the only thing that I've ever "missed" about prison. It's an excellent card game.

For a little while I shared a cell with an older guy who was part of a well-known East Coast organized-crime syndicate. He'd done twenty years for murdering federal informants and was back for violating his probation. It was bizarre sharing a six-by-nine cell with someone who had committed all kinds of atrocities, including murder. Funny thing was, he was a hell of a nice guy.

At twenty-three, I was six feet tall and had long red hair that I usually kept braided or in a ponytail. I grew a scruffy beard inside because I thought it made me look "meaner." My lawyer would ultimately suggest that I not cut my hair, because he said that the prosecution would show pictures of me at the time of my arrest, and he thought cutting it would make it look like I was trying to hide something or manipulate the outcome.

There was another young Jewish guy from the San Fernando Valley. Our faith, age and housing proximity were where the similarities stopped, though. This kid was a straight up gangster. He was charged with counterfeiting money and buying huge quantities of drugs (like ten kilos of coke at a time) with the fake money. He and his crew would also dress up like DEA officers and rob his competitors, leaving them handcuffed in the closet, taking all their money and drugs. So, they got him for impersonating a cop, as well as the drugs and counterfeit loot. That kid was fearless.

I really met all kinds of people inside, from all over the world. One guy was a doctor from Mexico made famous because he kept a DEA officer alive so the cartel could torture him. His defense was that under the Hippocratic Oath he had taken, he had sworn to preserve life, even if that life was preserved for the sole reason of torture. He beat the feds in an epic courtroom battle, a rare occurrence as the feds had a 97 percent conviction rate. They sent him back to Mexico, and the guys in the unit gave him a hero's send-off with nachos, sodas and candy bars for everyone.

There was a Chassidic Rabbi who was being charged with racketeering. He took bribes to certify non-kosher meat as kosher. What an asshole.

Then there were the junk bond dealers from the savings and loan crisis. Michael Milken and Charles Keating were both in the building while I was as well, though not in my unit.

Around this time, two highly significant events happened to me, that would affect both how I was serving my time and how I would ultimately live my life. I found a book called *We're All Doing Time*, by a guy named Bo Lozoff, who said everybody is doing time in the jail cell known as our bodies and this life. It taught me how to meditate, do yoga and practice kindness. It taught me that not only can spirituality be practiced in the harsh confines of a prison, but that it is actually one of the best places to practice. It's funny how one book can change everything that you think you know. I'm not sure if I would've survived prison without that book. I still follow its lessons today.

Also, I started working in the prison kitchen. I've got to be honest. I was just hoping to score some better chow. The food was shockingly bad. Everyone in prison has a hustle. Some guys cut hair, some iron clothes, others do laundry. Some guys have such a great hustle they make wads of cash. It's true, the kitchen guys usually have the best hustle. So, getting a job there meant suddenly I had access to fresh garlic, tomato and onions — and sugar and yeast for hooch. Solid game.

But the best part of working in the kitchen? No matter what, you can always eat. The knives were locked to the counters, but the food wasn't, so we'd eat or steal whatever we could. They were pretty lackadaisical about searching us when we left the kitchen, and if they did find food on us, they'd just confiscate it and make us mop the walk-in fridge or something like that.

This was the first professional kitchen I ever worked in. And even though I was in jail, somehow being there felt very "right." I immediately tuned into the rhythm of the kitchen, the hum of the fans, the steady flow of the dishwashers, the sights, smells, sounds of it all. I felt right at home, and even took a sense of pride in the preparation of the slop that we put out every day.

Everyone had a job, and everyone's job made everyone else's possible. Yeah, it was prison food. So we would cook (or reheat) it, fill trays and load them onto carts that were sent to the units where orderlies would nuke them in microwaves. But even so, this was where I fell in love with the buzz, the rhythm and the dance and magic of it all. But not the food. That would come later.

After a few weeks, I was assigned a court-appointed lawyer, who was a much better litigator than the dump truck that tried to get me to plead guilty without even knowing my name. I took my legal woes seriously. When I wasn't working, I was studying my case in the law library. Most of the evidence against me was circumstantial. They had phone records connecting me to the woman who turned me in. (She and her beau had been busted and flipped on me before they ever even spoke to a lawyer, like fools.) That didn't look good, but phone trees and the word of this woman and her boyfriend was all they really had — until a few days before my trial. That's when the feds subpoenaed everyone's bank records and found a money order for $710. I never took money orders, but I'd been pretty good friends with these folks — or so I thought. And I was 400 miles away, so I made an exception. But boy, did it cost me. I sold her acid that had cost me $550 for $700 + $10 shipping. So I made $150 on the deal that ended up costing me everything.

My lawyer advised me to give up my source or take the ten-year deal. I learned that most federal drug cases plead out and do not go to trial. The thing is, I was guilty as sin. I did exactly what they said I did. And I wasn't giving anyone up. I just couldn't do it. I knew that one way or another, there would be another way out. There had to be! I figured if I went to trial, I stood a small chance of winning on a technicality, if nothing else. Ten years with the plea or twelve and a half if I was convicted in a trial felt the same to me. It all seemed like forever. So in early November of 1992, I went to a jury trial by "my peers."

By then I knew the ropes a bit (though I still wasn't one of those guys who knew all the hacks by name) but one thing I knew for sure, during my trial, I'd be spending many hours a day waiting, and I was allowed to bring only legal documents, which I kept in a big file folder. So I devised a plan. I was reading the Hermann Hesse novel *Narcissus and Goldmund* at the time, so I took a bunch of Post-it notes and scrawled legal citations on them and stuck them all through the book, highlighting many sections as well. I stashed the book in with my legal papers, which were searched multiple times a day. Every time they came across that book, I told them, "My case involves LSD and multiple personality disorders, which this book is about. We're citing it in my defense." This was when I mastered the art of "HIPS" (hidden in plain sight). Correctional officers are not exactly known for being the sharpest tools in the box, and that's how I read *Narcissus and Goldmund* during my trial.

My brother Howard was the only one who came to the trial. Ethan had to work and Dad and Margret were on a cruise. Howard was (and is) the quiet one among my brothers. He doesn't say much, but when he does, the statement usually packs some weight. I don't know why I hadn't thought that some family support might be nice, but it was very comforting to have a brother sitting behind me. I don't know why I didn't ask Aunt Marcia and Uncle Mickey to attend. I guess it didn't dawn on me? Marcia and Mickey had tried to be there for me after Mom died … but my dad made that difficult for them, and they were raising four kids of their own. So there I sat, in a suit that didn't fit quite right, with one of three brothers behind me and my court-appointed attorney by my side. The United States of America vs. Me. The whole thing felt like a bad dream.

After four days of trial and six hours of deliberation I heard the words that nobody ever wants to hear: guilty on all charges. I just stood there. Even the pain in my swollen ankles dulled. See, no matter how bad things got, I always had a secret hope that we might cast some kind of doubt in somebody's mind ... I never thought my kid was going to be one of *those* kids. Without a dad. Just because I did something stupid when I was twenty-three years old.

I barely noticed as two U.S. Marshals took me to change out of my suit. I was halfway done when I heard them laughing. But they weren't looking at me. They were talking about what they'd be doing that weekend. I felt as if they were just glorified burger flippers; I was the burger, and they really didn't care if I got burned.

It's a New Dawn...

Before the trial, when I'd lay in my bunk at night, dreams of getting out helped me survive the aching of my joints and the constant painful itching all over my body. Now those dreams were gone. My lawyer promised we could appeal, but that was just about the last I ever heard from him.

One day, a few weeks after my trial, I was told to pack my things. They didn't know where I was going and neither did I. I learned that my lawyer had requested outside medical treatment because my health was deteriorating so quickly and MDCLA wasn't doing anything about it. They sent me to a prison maybe thirty miles away in San Pedro called Terminal Island. The name freaked me out at first, but it's better than it sounds. And just like that, I was loaded onto a bus. With the stroke of a pen, I could be moved anywhere, anytime.

After seven months in a downtown LA high-rise holding facility, my first night at Terminal Island was almost like being free. Instead of getting a sad tray of microwaved mash, there was an actual chow line with steam tables of hot and cold food. It wasn't gourmet by any means, but after eating trays of microwaved food for months, it was luxurious. After mealtime I could walk in the yard, which was right on the water in San Pedro harbor. There were just guys in gun towers and two giant fences with piles of razor wire between me and that water, maybe fifteen feet away. Close enough that I could smell it and feel the salt on my skin. And I could see stars and the moon. And I was actually walking on grass rather than concrete. The smell of the sea was intoxicating. I was overcome with the feeling of being connected to nature. It had been far too long.

I had run into a guy that I'd known from MDCLA. We had played Scrabble together a few times and had passed some time talking story. It was his day for the commissary, so he bought me a pint of Ben and Jerry's ice cream, some coffee and a few other essentials, and said I could pay him back when my funds were transferred. He even had a small joint that he shared with me near the handball courts, under the moonlight, that first night. It was my first smoke in seven months. One of the stray kitties that lived on the yard came over to say hello and bum a few bites of my Cherry Garcia. There I was, outside, smelling fresh grass and the saltiness of the ocean, sharing ice cream with a kitten. It was the closest that I'd felt to being free in a long time.

The smell of the freshly cut grass took me back to when I had run away from home at about fourteen. The more my dad tried to lay down the law, the more I rebelled. I'd been breaking into people's campers for a place to sleep, but soon found myself hanging out in Chatsworth Park at the far west end of LA County. That place ALWAYS smelled like freshly cut grass. The local hippies that I'd met there took me to my first ever Grateful Dead concert at the Irvine Meadows Amphitheatre. Before going, I knew some of the Dead's music from my older cousin, as well as from my interest in the music of the '60s. I'd fallen in love with the Beatles at around the age of ten, and had progressed into the psychedelic music scene ever since. I had even bought a copy of the Dead album *Blues for Allah* when I was about thirteen, solely because I thought the album cover was so cool. I'd also gotten my hands on the live album *Dead Set*, so I knew a little bit of the music. What I didn't know about was the subculture that followed this band around. I was about to learn.

The community was tight in '85; there were maybe 2,000 people who traveled to every show, and we all knew each other. I hitch hiked across the country by myself, catching almost every show on that tour. It began a wanderlust in me that is still going strong. Back then, out in the world, if you saw a Dead T-shirt or sticker on a car, you smiled with a knowing nod. People threw the word "family" around a lot, and it was really a home for the misfits that needed community. I fell into that category. It didn't hurt that the music was amazing, the band was playing as well as they ever had (some GD pundits rate summer tour '85 as one of the top tours in their thirty-year history). It was a special moment in time that was soon to end. Within a couple of years, the band's popularity grew to a point that the traveling circus that accompanied them was no longer sustainable. They shut down the camping, and even some of the vending.

It was also the Reagan years, and the war on drugs that officially began in 1971 under Nixon was in full swing. And yet there was still this subculture of hippies. The '60s were only a few years prior, the acid was still clean, strong, cheap and flowed like water. From dirty parking lot kids to the college students and taper geeks that preserved the music and the gray-haired old timers, Grateful Dead tour was the closest thing to riding the rails, or joining the circus, that one could do. I went from reading *On the Road* to living it.

My first Dead show was not the best time of my life. I'd run away from home several times and had recently taken to living in a cave above the park. Yeah, you read that right. I was sick of my dad throwing shit at me — a bowl of cereal, a vacuum cleaner, a telephone. Whatever was at hand when he was angry. I think throwing things seemed less abusive to him than the idea of hitting me, which was also sometimes on the menu, though most of his abuse was verbal and emotional. Once, he threatened me with military school, but we both knew he was too cheap to shell out the big bucks for that. He was just sick of my stealing. I started out with the quarters from his change dish, then graduated to taking cash out of his wallet, booze out of his cupboards and porn mags from under his bed. A couple of times I even took his car. I was also getting in trouble at school, so he sent me to Tough Love meetings at a local church. It was around that time that my delinquency progressed to criminal levels. The kids I met at those meetings were far more adventurous in their shenanigans than I'd been, and the experience dragged me to new lows. We broke into houses, mostly stealing booze, money and bicycles. Before Tough Love, I'd only been ripping off my parents. They taught me how to rip off the general public.

Once, in junior high, I got caught stealing cash out of my drama teacher's purse. I was sitting in the Dean's office waiting for him as other kids came and went. The news was all over the school. Dad came in and, without saying a word, back-handed me right across the room. He went to kick me when I was down on the floor, but the Dean pulled him off me. In today's world, Child Protective Services would've been called immediately, but back in 1983, the Dean told my father that he empathized with his frustration, but he could not hit me on the school grounds (wink wink, nudge nudge).

As I got into more trouble, most of my friends turned their backs on me. I was too young to know it at the time, but I was suffering from depression and developing a fear of abandonment. My father had abandoned me at birth, my mother by dying, my brothers by just living their lives and now my small handful of friends were turning their backs on me. My behavior only made things worse.

I was incorrigible and, no matter what the adults around me tried, I was on my own destructive path. To be honest, I'd have wanted to kill me, too, if I were in dad's shoes. But in my defense, I was a broken child, and his actions did nothing to ease my pain. In fact, they made it worse. Rather than do anything to nurture me, he used to lecture me about "pulling myself up by the bootstraps" and other such nonsense, without ever addressing what I had experienced with the loss of my mother, my home and everything else that I knew.

I hadn't wanted to live with him when mom died. I was only eight years old, and Mom was perfect in my eyes. She did make two glaring mistakes in my upbringing, though. She was in so much pain, and my dad screwed her on child support so badly, that she couldn't help but bad-mouth the old man at every opportunity … which was every time a bill came, or when we had our weekend outings with him. Then, when she got sick, she told me that when she died, I would have a choice of where I would live: Marcia and Mickey, one of my three brothers or Dad and Margret. I just kind of figured that I'd go and live with my aunt, uncle and cousins. I thought I had a plan.

My brothers clearly were not cut out to raise a sad little eight-year-old, as they were just college-aged. Marcia and Mickey were prepared to take me under their roof, but Dad would have no part of that, and to be honest, my presence would have been challenging for their family, since they had teenage kids of their own. Dad's pride kicked in, and even though he wanted no part in raising me, he insisted on taking me in, even threatening to fight my aunt and uncle in court over it. He was pissed, and I was more pissed, but I had the angst and the righteous indignation of adolescence on my side. No matter what he did, I retaliated tenfold.

When I first ran away, I would either crash with friends or I would break into people's camper trailers. But once I found Chatsworth Park, I moved into Art's old cave in North Park. Art — or Artful Dead, as we called him — had lived in there for years. It wasn't very big, but it was well hidden and had a natural chimney inside, so you could have fires, and it was directly over the railroad tracks, which was handy for getting rid of garbage (I'd throw bags onto passing trains). A few friends from school lived in the condos nearby, and I finagled a key to the pool area, which of course had hot showers, a Jacuzzi and laundry facilities. I stayed there for about six months. It wasn't a bad life. I even had a dog, given to me by a girl in the park who could no longer care for it. I don't know why she thought I could care for this animal, especially since the dog came to me with medical issues. To be honest, I don't recall giving the seizure medicine that much thought. I was just into the image of me, living in a cave with a dog. It seemed cool at the time. Maybe that was the acid, which I was taking a lot of.

That first Dead show altered my life forever. As soon we pulled into the parking lot, I knew I'd landed somewhere I was meant to be. It was a psychedelic circus of wondrous amazement. Tie-dyes everywhere, and thousands of people selling everything under the sun, in most cases for a dollar. There were veggie burritos, earrings, T-shirts, stickers and posters. There was original art. There were people trading tapes and people selling bongs, pipes, balloons of nitrous oxide, drugs, drugs and more drugs. There were people drinking beer and eating phatty eggrolls, grilled cheese sandwiches and a veritable culinary smorgasbord of gastronomic hippie delights.

I couldn't believe the commerce, the buying and selling of psychedelics, out in the open, with total disregard for laws or anything resembling normalcy. It was crazy the way the same dollar bill might change hands twenty times in a day, or in an hour, without ever leaving the parking lot. And the vibe was good. Everyone was getting along and having a great time.

I'd planned on sneaking in, but of course I lost my friends … and then the acid kicked in. I climbed a fence at the neighboring Lion Country Safari and ran through the swamp. I am fairly certain that the rhinoceroses (rhinoceri?) I saw in the swamp were real, but I have never been entirely certain of that. I trampled across the mud, squeezed through a narrow fence opening and made it into the show to the opening notes of "Why Don't We Do It in the Road?" Having been such a die-hard Beatles fan, I was ecstatic to hear a song that I knew so well as an opener. The gentle music wafted from the speakers and through the air, intermingling with the incense, sage, weed, patchouli and hippie funk that permeated everything in a scene of pure synesthesia. Yes, I was tripping my young face off. I danced around in total amazement, watching everyone — some totally blissed out, dancing their asses off, others whirling dervish-like spinners, twisting and contorting to the rhythmic jolts of the music. I spent some time studying the guy who fluttered his hands with every note of Garcia's wailing leads. One couple told me this was their hundredth show, and they'd met and gotten together at their first. From old hippies to middle-aged businessmen and scrappy teenagers like me, it felt like the full spectrum of society was there, but without conflict or divisions. We were all grooving together and having a blast.

Everyone, band and crowd alike, seemed to be in on this big cosmic joke, this giant psychedelic secret of how to have the best time ever. It felt like we had all figured out how to have more damn fun than everyone else. And the so-called leaders of this big secret, the guys on stage, didn't seem to give a shit. They were just the minstrels, if you will. The hired help. They didn't even talk to the audience; there was no need to, as the conversation was between the music and the listeners. The music really DID play the band. And the crowd was part of this telepathic loop. The more the crowd cheered and danced, the harder they would play. The harder they would play, the further into a frenzy we would dance. It was this incredible symbiotic relationship, and I "got it" pretty much immediately. They closed the show with "Sugar Magnolia," and encored with "Gloria." I had found my tribe — and it's one that I'm still a member of to this day.

But that feeling of bliss was short-lived. When I got back to our camp in the parking lot, I found that my dog, Nikea, was foaming at the mouth and in convulsions. She'd been sick for a while, but suddenly she was so much worse. I gave her seizure medicine and got her to drink some water. I finally got her to sleep in my tent, and I laid with her for most of the night.

I woke before dawn and took a walk. By the time I got back, Nikea was awake again and in worse shape than before. Some of the older guys in our camp told me that she wasn't going to make it, so we gathered her up and walked to a field near the Lion Country Safari. We found a big hole, and a guy that I'm going to call Douche Bag Mark took Nikea from me and set her in the hole. It was about nine in the morning, and the sun was beginning to blaze. I was still high on the acid from the night before, and Douche Bag Mark handed me a small pistol and told me to put the dog out of her misery. I'd never shot a gun, let alone killed an animal. And did I mention that I WAS ON ACID? I began to shake and cry.

I really wanted to be the fifteen-year-old guy that could shoot his sick dog next to a Grateful Dead parking lot in extreme heat while high on LSD … but that just wasn't the case. I handed Mark the gun back. I had to get away. I was probably about 100 feet from the hole when I heard the pistol fire. I stumbled back to where Mark and the other guys were standing, staring down. And I just knelt there and began to bury Nikea with rocks and dirt. Nobody said a word; they just watched me bury my dog. And just 100 yards away, the psychedelic circus carried on, with nobody the wiser to this tragic affair.

I didn't realize it then, but this was the first in what would become a lifelong series of dichotomies with the Grateful Dead. It's kind of like being in India, where you can go from smelling the best smell in the world to the worst smell in the world in a matter of seconds. Some of my experiences with this band and the communities around them have gone from roses to shit equally quickly, and this was just the first of those times.

Terminal Island

In every prison I was in, there was always a group of older white guys, baby boomers (I'm a Gen X-er), who were in for growing and smuggling weed and often money laundering. At Terminal Island, I clicked with that group, and I felt lucky they accepted me. While being a loner in prison does have some merit, I wouldn't recommend it. It turns you into low-hanging fruit.

I was first invited to the Attitudinal Healing group by these stoner-boomers. Attitudinal Healing is based on the principle that it is not other people or situations that cause us to be upset, but rather our own thoughts, attitudes and judgments about those people that cause our distress. This had all been outlined in the book that I mentioned, *We're All Doing Time*.

As I walked in to my first meeting, an older man welcomed me and handed me a business card that read, "Dan Millstein: Holy Man with Heartburn." Dan had flowing white hair and piercing blue eyes that gave him the level of austerity and wisdom that he appeared to deserve. "Hey, young buck, how could such a nice-looking kid as yourself get locked into a federal joint?" he asked me.

"LSD and the Grateful Dead," I replied.

He shook his head in sadness and said, "LSD should be considered sacrament, not a felony. How much time did they give you?"

"A hundred and fifty-one months," I said flatly.

His beautiful blue eyes filled with anger and sadness all at the same time. "What the fuck??" he exclaimed. "There are real criminals out there, and they break that much time off for a kid like you? Did you have a lot? Were there weapons involved?" he asked, knowing that there probably weren't.

Before I could reply, one of the two gray beards sitting in the corner answered for me. "Dan, I bet this kid has never even held a gun, let alone used one in an acid deal. Besides," he continued, "who uses guns in acid deals?" It was then that I looked over and saw what he was working on. He had a wooden frame with silk fabric pulled tightly over it, the Buddhist deity Vajrayogini drawn on it in pencil. He was sewing small glass beads into the blank spots on the silk. That piece of art took him two years to complete, and he ended up sending it off to His Holiness Dalai Lama as a gift. The attention to detail was mind boggling.

I was about to comment on its beauty, when the guy sitting next to him said, "The feds don't give a crap about who they lock up, and for how long. It's just a numbers game. Why else am I doing twenty years for one small freighter of weed?"

"Yeah, but it's your third time … and you're old," Dan chortled. "Anyway, let's move these chairs in a circle, and get started."

I looked forward to those weekly meetings for the duration of my stay at Terminal Island.

My sentencing day came and went. The judge denied my motion for a reduction due to "lack of youthful guidance" and actually told me I was lucky he wasn't tacking on time for being the ringleader in a conspiracy. I stood with only my attorney by my side as the judge read off my sentence like he was ordering off a menu. A hundred and fifty-one months in custody and five years of probation. Then I'm guessing he went out for a lunch of chicken Caesar salad and an iced tea and never gave me another thought.

My lawyer informed me that my trial had cost the taxpayers $300,000. It was estimated at that time that it cost $35,000 a year to house an inmate, and another $10,000 a year in probation costs. So should I do all of my time, I would have cost the taxpayers $770,000. All on a deal totaling $710, dear reader.

For the seven months since my incarceration began, I'd felt numb, like the life I was living wasn't my own. I hadn't seen a blade of grass, my diet changed, my body changed, nothing was as it had been. But I never for a minute believed I would serve all my time. I wasn't sure what was going to happen, but I knew there was no way I'd spend twelve and a half years locked up. It just wasn't going to happen. And then it did. Or so it appeared.

Better to Be Smoking Fat Joints Than Walking on Swollen Joints

My health continued to deteriorate. I would learn that psoriatic arthritis is triggered, and fed, by stress. Hence it was no surprise that both conditions continued to get worse and worse. Shortly after my sentencing, I was hobbling around with the cane. One of the guys from the Attitudinal Healing group, Woody, was a certified massage therapist, as well as a pot grower, from Hawaii. Woody worked out a lot, and was well respected at the weight pile, as well as at his job in the bakery. He was also a Deadhead like me, so we'd sit and listen to Dead shows on public radio on Friday nights and he would massage my feet and ankles. This is an uncommon occurrence in prison, and at first I was nervous at this display of physical interaction. It made me feel vulnerable. But Woody didn't give a fuck. He did deep tissue work on my feet many nights. It was a rare display of kindness and generosity that I'll never forget.

A rabbi came once a week, and I'd go for Shabbat with him in the chapel. I also meditated with the Buddhists, chanted with the Hare Krishnas, and became friends with some of the Native Americans and was invited to their sweat lodge ceremonies. These took place on Saturday mornings, and the lodge leader burned sage, tobacco and sweetgrass, making offerings to the four directions. He encouraged us to look deep within and to pray to the Great Spirit for healing the parts of us that only we knew needed healing. We would strip down to our underwear and enter the lodge on our knees. Aside from the fire tender, a few guys would stand by to provide for our safety. This was another act of vulnerability in a place where that is frowned upon and, at times, preyed upon. It was a tricky situation, and I always felt grateful for those guys who stood watch over the lodge, ensuring our safety and privacy. At this point, one might say that I was shopping at the spiritual supermarket. It's pretty common to grasp for spirituality in prison. The options were spirituality, gang life, junkie life, thug life or the life of a recluse.

My first winter in prison, my knee began to swell even worse than my ankles. I went to the nurse and was diagnosed with a Baker cyst, which is a fluid-filled growth behind the knee. It needed to be drained, so I had to spend a few nights in the infirmary. There weren't many people there, so I was able to commandeer the remote control and watch whatever I wanted, which is a rarity in prison. I generally avoided the televisions at all costs, as they were the source of many squabbles. But on this night, I watched a really cheesy reality-style cop show where a film crew tailed cops who made three busts in the half hour. This episode was entirely on the LSD trade, and the third segment was about a bust made in Santa Cruz. To my amazement, it was about Socrates, my old friend, the guy the feds had questioned me about, whose phone number was in my journal when I was busted. The undercovers on the show did a couple of controlled buys, and then they busted him as he was leaving the house on his bicycle. It was brutal; the terror in his eyes as they threw him on the ground struck an indelible chord in me. There's something truly awful in seeing someone you care about having their whole life crumble in an instant. The drug war had way too many casualties, and Socrates was now one of them. When they questioned him, it was clear they had a lot on him and they were leaning on him to give up names. He kept tight-lipped for about a minute … and then, on national TV, it appeared that he gave them the name of one man and one woman, Walter and Gina. In later years, when Socrates and I were able to speak, he swore that he didn't give names. He ended up getting a life sentence, and people who give information don't usually get life sentences … but that part of the story comes later.

I had now been incarcerated for about a year, and one thing I learned is that when people are facing exceptionally long prison terms, they almost always give up names. I wouldn't have called myself a strong person at that point in my life, but to this day, I still feel proud that I didn't give anyone up and chose to go to trial instead. About 25 percent of federal drug cases are solved through cooperation. I had mixed feelings seeing Socrates appearing to flip on people.

I'd kept quiet in order to protect myself and live up to my own beliefs — my own sense of ethics — not to protect him or anyone else. Now that I'd seen this show, I had some misgivings about my decision to go to trial, but I'd made my choice for me, not for anyone else. And I had to live with that. And, as I said, I wasn't sure how, but I knew I wasn't going to do the whole 12.5 years (151 months), or as I started thinking of it, the 604 Mondays.

After a few days in the infirmary, I was back in my unit and feeling better. I signed up for classes with a local university. I was still deep on my spiritual path. Ethan was still taking the train up a few times a month to see me. Dad and Margret came to visit a couple of times. The visits were always strained and awkward, but I appreciated the effort. My dad, a lifelong conservative, did a radical flip on his views on the drug war once I got caught up in it. He went as far as to write his legislators, but that was about it. A small smattering of friends also made the journey, the ones that could pass the legal rigamarole that was required of visitors.

I had a few friends inside, and I could smoke a little weed pretty easily. Drugs were surprisingly accessible inside, thanks mostly to crooked guards, adding to the incongruity of the drug war and my sentence. How can we expect to keep drugs out of the country when we can't even keep them out of our prisons? I loved getting high, putting on my radio and walking the track, looking out at the water through the razor wire. I liked doing that while not high, too, but … weed.

It took me a full year to realize that my life had not ended — it had just radically altered course. I lived in relative peace for a few short months, until the day I was called to the counselor's office. I'd been sentenced to a low-security facility, but Terminal Island was a medium-to-high-security prison, and I'd only been sent there for medical evaluation. Now that I was evaluated, the powers that be decided this facility was no longer appropriate for me. Even though my psoriasis was still out of control, and I still used a cane. But none of that mattered, and I was informed that I would be transferred to Springfield, Missouri. Springfield also happened to be a medical facility, but as I had an illness with no cure, that's not why they sent me there. They sent me there solely because they had room for me there, and Terminal Island was overcrowded and my security level didn't fit. It made no difference that I was from Southern California. I was being sent to the work cadre portion of Springfield, which was meant to be low security, but as they had a psychiatric hospital on site, they ran it with all of the rules of a high-security prison. It made no sense, and I was powerlessly entangled in a bureaucratic nightmare.

I begged the counselor to reconsider and filed all the appropriate paperwork to stop the transfer. I also got the rabbi, Dan from Attitudinal Healing, the chaplain, my senators and my family to all write letters, saying that I was thriving at this facility. But there's no fighting the red tape that runs the Bureau of Prisons, and a couple of weeks later, my number was called to leave the following morning.

Missouri Loves Company...

I was awakened well before dawn, as is always the case with the feds, and brought to R&D (receiving and discharge) for the usual processing procedures, where I was strip-searched, photographed, fingerprinted and paper-worked. Somewhere in a file box in a basement of a federal building, there must be a massive collection of all things Evan from that era. A handful of other guys were being transferred as well. We were not only handcuffed and shackled, but shackled together with a long chain and brought to a big airfield on a military base to wait for the plane. It was a little chilly, and the cold metal was rough on my arthritis. To this day, when I change the strings on my guitar, the smell of metal reminds me of being cuffed in the cold. They wouldn't allow me to travel with a hair tie, or any personal items for that matter, so my long thick red hair was blowing in the wind, and the cuffs and chains left me unable to push it out of my face.

We sat silently in the van, waiting for the plane to land. Once it did, it taxied down the runway, escorted by a U.S. Marshal and armed cops, the back hatch opened, and we were instructed to stand out on the airfield where the jet engines were still whining. I could taste the jet fuel in the air and feel it lining my throat as the warm Santa Ana winds blew across the tarmac. The head marshal made sure that all our faces matched our pictures. It reminded me of a drug deal, or an arms deal going down, but in this instance we were the goods being traded.

They removed the chain that bound us together and loaded us onto the plane, still cuffed and shackled. They showed us to our seats, and connected our ankle shackles to a lock in the floor. Should this plane go down, we were all going with it. They gave us all the usual sack lunch that I despised, and the plane took off. It flew all afternoon, making a several stops. At each stop, the plane would be surrounded by armed marshals, and prisoners would be loaded on and off. Nobody talked much.

The final stop of the day was El Reno, Oklahoma. As soon as the back hatch opened, an icy breeze filled the plane. Combine that with the frozen chains that bound us together and my arthritis, and the fact that we were not even allowed ibuprofen or any other meds whilst in transit, and I was not having the best of days. We were escorted off, and once again inspected by marshals now wearing big wool parkas while we stood shivering in our cotton pants, T-shirts, thin tube socks and what amounted to plastic slippers on our feet, reciting our numbers and birthdays. They took no chances on Con Air.

The holding facility they brought us to was like something out of the movies. It was a very old building with tiers of barred cells. This place was so overcrowded that on the bottom floor, in the "common area," they had removed tables and chairs and filled the area with bunk beds. The windows high above this area had been busted out, so there were birds flying around, shitting indiscriminately on the bunks. I made it into one of the tiered cells, so I did not have to suffer through the bird shit, though the cells were old and worn out. The five flights of concrete stairs were rough on my arthritic legs, though. I pulled the thickest books I could off the book rack and settled into a bunk. Over the following week, I kept to myself, and kept my mouth shut, went to the chow hall three times a day, and the rest of the time I had my nose in a book or I walked the recreation yard when we were allowed. Every morning at 4:00 a.m. they would call people for transfers. I prayed to hear my name, but I didn't for seven long days. Thankfully, on the eighth day they called me and I was processed out and loaded into a van for the six-hour ride to Springfield, Missouri.

As we arrived at the Medical Center for Federal Prisoners of Springfield, Missouri, "Let It Be" was playing on the radio. It seemed fitting. Arriving there was the opposite of arriving at Terminal Island. No friends, no weed, no ocean smells and no nature.

The prison itself was red-brick construction from 1933. Even though it was a low-to-medium-security facility, it housed a psychiatric ward, so this prison was run like a super max, which meant life there was just a little bit more challenging. One example is something they called "controlled movements." It sounds like a weird poop thing, but it really means you're only allowed to move around the facility (from the unit to the yard, the yard to the rec center, etc.) from five minutes before the hour to five minutes after the hour. You had to plan accordingly, or you could get stuck somewhere for an hour.

As it was in the heart of the Bible Belt, the correctional officers were all corn-fed local boys. Prisons don't attract the highest caliber of staff on a good day — most of the guys barely made it out of high school and failed at getting into the police academy or the military, so they took a job at the local prison — and this place was one of the worst. While all prisons have a dark energy, the walls in this place were permeated with the tortured souls they'd housed over the years. The medical center only added to its darkness. Sick and dying prisoners drooped at the tables. Many had deep psychological issues or were so heavily medicated that they would just walk the track in circles, all day long, drooling and talking to themselves, or talking to no one.

I was assigned to a twenty-six-man open dorm. I managed to secure a lower bunk in the corner, which allowed me a small space behind my desk where I would practice late-night meditation and yoga. The guy in the bunk next to me was a hustler whom everyone called DC. He was up to all kinds of shenanigans that included gambling, selling drugs and pimping out the three transgender inmates who shared a dorm with us. Sometimes, late at night, we would tell each other stories of life outside. DC was even more of a gangster outside than he was inside, but he always had a good sense of humor, and we generally looked out for each other. He never understood why I did meditation, and when I did some of my yoga poses, he would say, "You just doing that shit so eventually you might be limber enough to suck yer own dick." He was not entirely wrong about that.…

I got a job in the recreation department and was earning $5.25 a month. But more than anything, I wanted to get into the kitchen. To get back to that rhythm and buzz. But all those guys had been there forever, and with the best side hustle in the place, they weren't leaving anytime soon.

It took a couple of months, but the evening librarian finally left and I was offered his position. This was a sweet gig and had a lot of perks, including a pay raise up to $16 a month. Also, I got to go to chow early so I could open the library. This meant there was no line, the chow hall was much quieter and the kitchen hadn't run out of anything. And in the library, not only did I have access to newspapers from all over the country as soon as they came in, but I also had a typewriter, which was not only convenient for my own needs, but I was able to work a hustle by charging 75 cents per typed page.

Now I mentioned that this was a psych ward as well, so there were some people walking around that may have been a few beers short of a six-pack. One guy paid me to type a very lengthy legal brief for him based on the premise that Hillary Rodman (*sic*) Clinton had something to do with his sentencing, the Illuminati and a bunch of other far-fetched shit. The funny part was that he dialed it all in with some numerology based on the spelling of the former first lady's name … but he had her name spelled incorrectly, so his whole theory was dead in the water before it ever started. But for 75 cents a page, I just quietly typed it.

I had many pen pals during this time. One of them was a woman who was a Reiki master. She asked me to send her some personal affects, so that she could do some long-distance Reiki (cosmic healing, for lack of a better explanation) on me. I put a toothbrush and a lock of my hair in an envelope with a letter that I'd written to her and dropped it into the postbox on our unit, unsure if they would let me send it. Sure enough, I was called to the lieutenant's office the next day, and questioned about these odd items that I was trying to send to the outside. I did my best to explain what Reiki is … let's just say it didn't go over that well. They weren't sure what I was up to, but they seriously thought I was up to something. In the end, they let me send the lock of hair, but not the toothbrush, and I'm surprised I didn't get piss tested for odd behavior.

I made friends with a small crew in my dorm. One guy was an older Vietnam veteran who used to tell us war stories about packing body bags with heroin alongside the bodies to be shipped back to the States and sold. Another was a former marine who'd been involved in the Iran–Contra affair, and he'd tell stories of flying loads of guns into Nicaragua to be unloaded and traded for kilos of cocaine that he would then fly back to America, under the security of the CIA. I saw drug-war hypocrisy everywhere I looked.

We began creating meals together when the chow was inedible, which was often. We turned the procuring and transportation of our ingredients into a *Mission Impossible*–style caper. This meth cook, Sparky, worked in the kitchen, and it was his job to load the food carts. He'd stash a bunch of stolen food, which would be unloaded at the hospital unit by our boy Dwayne, who was in for bank robbery. Dwayne would then stash it in the hospital fridge. Later, he would intentionally break something, usually plumbing related, but sometimes carpentry. It really didn't matter because we had a guy in just about every department. Whoever came to repair the break would take the food and drop it in the book drop closest to our unit. That's when I, Mr. Librarian, would retrieve the goods and deliver them to the unit. Anyone that helped in the mission got fed.

We got to be pretty masterful in our creations. One of our favorites was a jailhouse classic called Commissary Ramen Nachos. First we'd cover a card table with a brand-new plastic garbage bag. Then we'd add just enough hot water to a Cup o' Noodles to cook the noodles while creating little to no broth. When that's ready, you add a whole jar of jalapeño cheese spread and let it all melt into a cheesy, noodly spread. (Best if you can add some diced summer sausage or spam, which are sometimes sold in the commissary.) The noodles make the cheese go a long way. You then cut up a few tomatoes, an onion, a bell pepper and whatever other veggies you were able to steal that day, and heat up a can or two of chili. Next, pour four to five large bags of corn chips over the table, and load them up with all the toppings. Sometimes we'd even wash it down with a few glasses of hooch! There's always a group of guys that cook a little more elaborately than the rest … and that was my crew at Springfield.

I swore off ever stealing again after my first acid trip (which I will tell you about in a bit, dear reader), but I never considered it theft when we took food from the kitchen that was meant to feed us. It was just re-appropriation of our own allocated supplies. Life in prison is all about basic survival. One has to improvise and be creative when it comes to getting enough to eat, getting things done or just getting by. The basics that they provide are just not sufficient.

During the days of our elaborate meals and food allocation scams, the 1994 Northridge earthquake happened. Cassidy and Pearly lived just two miles from the epicenter. The quake was all over the news, but the phone lines were all down, and this was pre-internet. Several days went by and I was worried sick. Nothing but terrifying images on the TV, and no news to squash those images. I knew better than to try and commandeer a TV. The remote control is one of the most sought-after and fought about communal items that inmates are expected to share, and it becomes a right of might. Being that the prison was in Missouri, most of the inmates were from other areas around the country, so nobody really gave a crap about an earthquake in the San Fernando region of LA, even if the tremors were felt as far as Phoenix. They were more interested in the OJ trial, which was set to begin soon.

I finally was able to get through to them about four days after the quake. While their house sustained some damage, they came out unscathed. I spent a lot of time reflecting on what it meant for me to not be there for this significant event, what I had lost and how foolish I had been to risk everything in a deal that netted me a measly $150.

Prison was a constant lesson in non-attachment. Whenever you made a friend, they'd get transferred. If you were comfortable somewhere, they'd move you. If you finally got a pillow you liked, they'd take all the pillows in for cleaning and you'd get some shitty one back. If the menu said French toast, it might just be scrambled eggs and fried bologna. It was a constant reminder that you have to make your own happiness. You can't depend on circumstances, like a friend or a good pillow. If you accept responsibility for your own happiness, then good circumstances just become icing on an already good cake. I was about to put this lesson to the highest test. Being so far away from family and friends was a very different and difficult experience. Not having visits hurt a lot. In fact, I went for over a year without a hug.

The Bardo Realm

The thing that sucked about my library job was the officer in charge, Officer Godt. He was — and I don't say this lightly — the world's biggest prick. It was rumored that he used to hold the rank of lieutenant, which is pretty high up the ladder of prison staff. Many years prior, he had learned that his wife, a secretary inside of the warden's office, had been having an affair with an inmate. When Godt learned of the affair, he made a botched suicide attempt, then took an extended leave of absence and came back divorced and with the demoted position of Recreation Specialist. Not the happiest of people, and he certainly did not love his job.

One day, we got a big shipment of donated books. I wanted to inventory, catalog and get them on the shelf as soon as possible, but the boss said that he wanted to box them up and save them until Christmas. (A little Shawshank, anyone?) I explained that the shelves were pretty empty, and that we needed the books. I made my case about it a little bit, but I wasn't that attached to the outcome, so I left to box up the books. All of a sudden, six guards rushed into the office, threw me against the wall and cuffed me. I didn't even know what hit me or why this was happening. I was put in solitary confinement (the hole).

In the hole, the lights came on at 6:00 a.m. And it's not like there was any reason to get us up that early. I'm pretty sure it was just done as a form of torture. I wanted to block out the glare, but there was no escaping the intense fluorescent bulbs that hung high above. Eventually I'd slide off my bunk and onto my swollen ankles. The damp of the basement seemed to seep into my bones. Even the ridiculously high levels of ibuprofen I was on barely touched the pain. Have you ever wanted a hot bath so bad you actually fantasized about it?

The six-by-nine-foot cell had a set of bunk beds attached to one wall and a metal sink and toilet connected to it. There was a stained sheet, a wool blanket that felt like sandpaper, a rock-hard pillow, if you were lucky … and not much else. Thankfully, I did not have a cellie. I spent my days staring at the red-brick walls, my head pounding from lack of caffeine. I don't know if it was the old mattress or the one scratchy sheet, the thin wool blanket or the sheer misery that I was living, but my psoriasis was out of control in there. I'd pick at my skin for hours and then sweep up all the dry plaques with a dirty T-shirt. By the end of the first day the sheets were bloody from my scratching. And it's not like there was anything to take my mind off it. You don't get much in there — a pencil, paper and envelopes, legal materials. But I still got mail, so a couple of weeks into my stay, I finally received some books, which helped. They came around with a book cart (one that I used to stock from the library!) but whoever was stocking it wasn't doing a very good job, because I was reading the usual crappy Westerns, mystery and spy novels. Jackie Collins and Danielle Steel were popular because they were hot and racy — no chance I was getting those. And Michener books were like gold, because they were so long. I cherished my copy of *Centennial*, and savored every word of it, twice. I spent my time reading, meditating, writing, waiting for meals to arrive and then being disgusted with said meals, masturbating, thinking about food, about better times in the past, and daydreaming about the future.

Twice a week, I was ordered to slide my hands through the slot in the door. They'd cuff me and take me down the hall to a cage door with a slot in it. They locked me in and we went through the same routine: Arms out, cuffs off. Then they'd give me a chunk of what looked like slime mixed with sand that I think was soap, and a small gray towel that I knew must have been white once — before it was used to wipe the balls of a thousand other convicts. "Five minutes," they'd say. After my shower, they'd go through the same routine with the cuffs to get me back to my cell. The irony was I'd look forward to showers as a change of pace, but they were so demeaning that they were always a letdown. They used that same routine again to walk me to the outdoor kennel for humans, where I'd be locked in so I could pace for an hour, twice a week. Each pen was about thirty by ten feet, and there were six of them. They'd put a guy in every other cage so (in theory) nobody could pass each other anything. They called that one "recreation and exercise" or "reck 'n' ex" for short.

A lot of the time I thought about Cassidy and those days when *I* got to decide what time the lights were turned on and off. I was pretty sure I'd lost my library job, and I'd definitely lost my corner bunk.

One day, the nurse was walking by with meds, but she skipped my cell. I went to the door, and asked her about my ibuprofen (800 milligrams, three times a day). "Hmm … it appears that your script has run out. I'll look into it," she told me as she walked off. You know how it feels when you're looking forward to something so badly and then it doesn't happen? I begged her for just one more ibuprofen. She said she'd look into it. For twenty-four hours I lay in my bunk, my ankles feeling like watermelons weighing down my legs. It was cold but I couldn't stop sweating.

The next day I heard her returning. I called. No answer. Her footsteps got closer and I imagined they wouldn't make me get up. They'd open the slot in the door, and she'd hand me the pills with a glass of water. Maybe she'd even ask how I was doing. But then her footsteps began to drift away. I pushed myself up. I called again. Slid off the bed and almost cried when my feet accepted the weight of my body. Pain shot all the way up legs and through my spine. Somehow I made it across the damp cement and slammed my fist against the door. She stopped walking, though her eyes were focused on the chart in her hands.

"Please! You got my ibuprofen? I'm dying in here!"

She was still looking at her chart when she finally spoke. "The doctor hasn't called back yet." She started walking again.

I pulled myself up off my knees and banged the door again. "Wait! Please. Just one pill. To hold me over." Keep in mind this is ibuprofen we're talking about, not morphine. The pain was overwhelming, and I was feeling desperate and helpless.

"I'll call the doctor again," she said over her shoulder as she walked away. It was a long hallway, a long walk. When I couldn't see her anymore, I listened for the soft squeak of her running shoes against the tile. Don't ask me why. Maybe I thought she'd sneak back and slip me an ibuprofen. You have some crazy fantasies when you're in a place like that.

The following day she came around again. It was like a placebo to see her walking toward my cell. I'd crawled across the floor and was lying in front of the door when she — walked by. "Wait! My ibuprofen! Please!"

"Still haven't heard anything," she said over her shoulder. *Squeak, squeak, squeak* down the hall. In a moment my body turned from aching ice to fire. I pounded the door. "You fucking heartless bitch! What the fuck is wrong with you?" I yelled every obscenity I could think of until my energy gave out and I collapsed in a sweaty heap, crying.

"You need to learn to contain yourself." I hadn't heard her come back, but there she was, peering in the little window on the door with her flip chart in her hand, and a scowl on her face. "I'm writing you up for this little incident."

"Fuck off, you fucking poor excuse for a human. Who are you, Nurse Ratched?!?" I sobbed. What was she gonna do? Put me in the prison within the prison within the prison?

I crawled back to the bed and struggled to pull myself into it. The lights were buzzing over my head, inescapably. I just wanted darkness, but they wouldn't be turned off until 10:30 p.m. Just one more way they let you know: You have no control.

On day nineteen in the hole, I finally got my hearing. Officer Godt claimed I'd "refused a direct order" and raised my cane in a "threatening and intimidating manner." There'd been a rec hall full of guys, inmates and staff, and nobody saw anything like that go down. Even his coworkers didn't back him up! So the charge was dropped from "threatening an officer with bodily harm" to "most like attempting insolence" (I swear that was the actual charge). However, for the incident with the nurse, I was charged with insolence. I'd gone from most like attempting insolence to being insolent. At least I was progressing at something. I was sentenced to thirty days in the hole (bet you're going to sing that song all day long now!) not counting the nineteen days I'd served. So a total of forty-nine days in the hole. I had also lost fourteen days of good time (every inmate earned fifty-four days a year of what was called "good time," as long as they/we behaved).

I had just read that the bardo realm in Buddhism lasts forty-nine days. That's the period between death and reincarnation, where the soul is lost until it finds a new home. I was certainly feeling like a lost soul.

Another thirty days to stare at the bricks and think about Cassidy, though I tried not to, because it would get me really down. I felt so ashamed. I'd really had no idea how much trouble I could get into as a first-timer.

Often, I'd meditate very late at night. I'd been reading about the monks who would meditate in the Charnel Grounds, which were basically mass graves left at old torture sites. The monks figured that if they could have a spiritual practice in the Charnel Grounds, they could have one anywhere. I tried to think of the hole as my own Charnel Grounds, working through the tortured energies of decades gone by. I liked meditation better after lights out because it was quieter. Even though I was alone, I had neighbors, and they were always up to something. People were trading pills for cigarettes, coffee for stamps, food for sodas and other people's meds for who knows what. They'd have full yelling conversations with their homies down the hall. They had the orderlies doing all kinds of things, which, of course, was their hustle. Everyone had a hustle, even in the hole.

One night, I heard the guards bring in a new guy. Through the slot in my door, I saw six big corn-fed thugs carrying a large white guy as he kicked and screamed at the top of his lungs.

"Fuck you, ya nigga pricks!" he yelled in a thick, New England accent to the group of all-white guards. "I'll fucking kill all ya. I'll bust out of here and fuck all you motherfuckers, right up the ass!!"

Let's just say they were not gentle as they got him in the cell and strapped him to the bed. "I'm gonna bust outta here and kill all youse and ya families!!" They pumped him full of Thorazine and he was out … for a while.

In the morning, they unstrapped him for breakfast, and it started all over again. "FUCK YOU, YA GREASY NIGGA PRICKS." He began throwing food around his cell.

Well, none of this went over well with the other inmates. "Do your own time" is an old prison saying. It means, don't drag me into your fucked up world; I've got my own time to do. This guy was not doing his own time, and was the ultimate test of my spiritual practice. I had recently learned of a meditation technique called Tonglen. This is where you try and take on all of the pain, suffering and dark energy of those around you, and beyond, and treat it with love and healing light, and put it back in into the world. You become a filter of sorts. It's a counterintuitive practice, but a powerful one. This guy was really putting me to the test.

Late night was the worst because he would try to sleep, but the voices in his head must have been at their craziest. "Mama … Mama … Help me, Mama … I'm so sorry, please help me, G-d help me!!!" Then, from all the other cells: "Shut the fuck up!" "Shut up, you little bitch!" "Not so tough now, are you, motherfucker?"

And every day, at some point, the cops would get tired of him and the goon squad would bum-rush his cell, strap him down and pump him full of drugs.

Through all of this, I sat in (mostly) silent meditation. I even sat through hearing that he'd swallowed a pair of nail clippers. I continued meditating when they put him in there with nothing but a bucket, in hopes of getting those clippers. I sat through every time he'd shit them out and swallow them again, covered in his own shit, with no water to wash them down. He'd brag about swallowing shit-covered nail clippers to anyone who would listen. This all went on for about five days until, one day, he was just gone. I have no idea where he went and I never saw him again. I hope he finally managed to find his peace. I was certainly trying to find mine.

I was finally released from the hole. Forty-nine days without human contact is a long time, and I was a bit shell-shocked, but I was happy to see my friends again, to eat enough food and have a cup of strong coffee. I mean, it was only Folgers instant, but compared to the brown water they gave us in the hole, it was some gourmet shit. (We used to call the mixture of Folgers, real milk and hot chocolate mix, a Cadillac.) It also turned out that shortly after the incident with my library boss, he had a nervous breakdown and took an unspecified amount of leave, so I didn't lose my job after all.

What I did lose was my Pell Grant. In a shortsighted "tough on crime" stance, Bill Clinton's disastrous crime bill of '94 eliminated college grants for prisoners. I could finish my semester with my correspondence courses, but after that, there would be no more funding. The drug war marched on and, once again, I was on my own.

1,185 Feet per Second

There was some talk about the LSD carrier weight law being amended to reflect the purity of the drug rather than the gross carrier weight. "Weighing the carrier to determine sentencing makes about as much sense as weighing the defendant" was one of the quotes that the Sentencing Commission made as they delved deeper into this issue. The problem came with the Mandatory Minimum statutes. They decided that rather than weighing the carrier to determine sentencing, they would assign an arbitrary number of 400 micrograms per dose and multiply the number of hits to determine sentencing. This sounded reasonably fair, until I read the last sentence of the statute. "Carrier weight will still be used in determining mandatory minimums." This would have brought my guideline range down from 151–188 months to 33–36 months … but would have kept my mandatory minimum at ten years, and the only way out of a mandatory minimum was to provide information to the government. It was a classic example of federal fuckery to only halfway fix this travesty of a statute.

One morning I was woken up at 4:00 a.m. By four thirty I was processed out and in a van with belly chains, handcuffs and shackles, the cold metal once again searing my arthritis. I had no idea of where I was going, or why. We made the six-hour drive back to the transfer station in El Reno. Another sack lunch, more uncertainty and instability. They led me through a hall and back into the unit that housed the transfers, such as myself. Back to the packed hell hole, with the busted out windows, birds and bird shit. On my first day back there, I got into a small skirmish in a chow line over an apple that was stolen off my tray, and it landed me in the hole, which was not actually a bad thing. I now had a solo cell, bad books to read and no drama. A newly constructed building, it was a step up from the 100-year-old transfer station.

After about a week and all of the usual pictures and fingerprints and strip searches, two U.S. Marshals escorted me outside to a van. It was just the three of us. One of them looked at me with a little smile. "Any chance you can run 1,185 feet per second? Because that's how fast the bullets from my gun travel, and I won't hesitate to shoot you if you run." Again, I was in belly chains, ankle shackles and handcuffs. I'm not really sure where he thought I'd go. Come to think of it, I didn't actually have a clue where the hell we were going.

We made a stop at McDonalds drive-through, which felt like a treat. Later, we stopped at a rest area to pee, and they walked me in to use the bathroom with their guns in hand and me all chained up. A family was staring at me from a picnic table. I tried to convey to them with my eyes that I wasn't the menace that these fuckers were trying to make me out to be. They looked terrified, though, and to be fair I was in a prison jumpsuit, my arms and neck were covered in scales and lesions from psoriasis, and my wild long hair hadn't been combed in days. I was definitely not at my best.

By sunset, we made it to a small county jail, a dingy, gray and far dirtier place than anywhere I had been. County jails are much more difficult to be in than federal prisons. A lot of people are in there for DUIs, domestic violence or shoplifting, and there's a lot more petty bullshit. In a prison, people have less to lose, so great violence is a threat that keeps the petty jailhouse bullshit at bay. I could tell immediately that this was gonna be rough, and I still didn't know why I was there.

The first morning, I walked out of my cell and looked down the hall, through the windows to the adjacent unit (the units being separated by the guard station). I saw Socrates, and he saw me. He and I had not spoken since before I was busted, which had been around 100 Mondays. He had aged a lot. His long, dirty-blond hair had turned gray, and his tall frame was hunched over. He was facing a life sentence, and if that doesn't age a man, then I don't know what does. We locked eyes, with shock, sadness, fear, and empathy for the overall plight that we were in. On my side, there was also a lot of curiosity about how we had managed to be tied together. I mean, this wasn't just a coincidence that we were both in a small county jail, was it? And then it hit me like a freight train. I wasn't sure why or how, but it was clear that they had linked our cases together, on some level, and they were going to try and get me to flip on him. As we stared at each other in disbelief, the whole story was revealed to both of us, all in the breath of a moment.

Socrates

I had met Socrates early on in my Deadhead career. He was nice guy, with a very dark and sarcastic sense of humor. He was sardonic, sharp-witted, quick with a quip and never shy to speak his mind. He was significantly older than I was, but so was damn near everyone that I hung around with. He always had a book with him, and he stayed with me in LA once or twice for some Garcia Band shows. He never came empty-handed though, usually arriving with a six-pack of his beloved Bass ale, and he was quick to grab the check at dinner.

Through notes that we managed to transport across the units, I found out that after Socrates was busted on that TV show, he'd skipped bail and was hiding out in the northwest. A neighbor had seen and recognized him from the TV show and called the cops. He was looking at a life sentence. Life in prison … for LSD. I couldn't (and still can't) believe it.

"Are you here to testify against me?" he asked in one of his notes. I wrote back to say: "I've already been through a jury trial, taken my sentence and never said a word. I don't plan on changing that now." Neither one of us knew how they'd linked our cases. He asked me if I'd heard of operation Dead End, which I had not. It turned out to be a DEA operation that targeted Grateful Dead followers, and the psychedelics trade in general. I didn't even know that I'd been a part of it, and now Socrates was as well.

Later that morning, they brought me downstairs and into a cold bare room with just a table, a couple of folding chairs and a TV and VCR player on a rolling cart, like the kind in schools. And there was the postal inspector who had spearheaded my case. That fucking dick who'd tried to light a cigarette in my living room.

"Hello, Evan," he said, as he walked in and closed the door. With him was the U.S. Marshal who had also been there the night of my bust. Without saying a word, he reached over and pushed play on the VCR. "Guessing that you saw this, or at least heard about it?" the postal inspector asked me. I stayed quiet. When it got to the part where Socrates said the names of his alleged sources, the marshal hit stop, rewound it and played that part again, as if for affect. He did that one more time, hit pause and stared at me. I shrugged and said nothing. "Imagine how surprised I was to find your phone number in Socrates's phone book, and his in yours. I always knew that Santa Cruz number was going to be relevant," he chuckled.

"Get fucked! We already played this game," I said. "I maintain my innocence and have some solid appeal issues that I'm working on," I lied. (My lawyer and I hadn't spoken in months.)

"How's your roommate doing, Evan? Did he end up losing his teaching credential? Because that sure would be a shame." He reached behind his ear and removed the cigarette that he had tucked back there. He played with it in his fingers … but he didn't light it. "Why are you still protecting Socrates?" he asked me, slowly and thoughtfully. "He clearly wouldn't have done the same for you." He motioned to the TV, which was still playing, now with the sound turned down.

I smirked at him and said, "Look, man, I'd really like to get back upstairs. I'm in the middle of a gripping novel, and I have nothing to say to you."

He leaned on the table, and put his face close to mine, stinking like stale tobacco. "Look, smart-ass," he said, "you are getting one fucking chance here, and so far, you haven't had many chances thrown your way. Admit that you got the liquid from Socrates, and the California portion of our case is tied together. To be honest, we have enough against him already to give him life. Your testimony just locks in one small portion. You saw it on TV, the deals that we did are enough to lock him up forever."

I sat quietly, trying to hold back the tears welling up in my eyes. "Why are you even fucking with me right now?" I asked through gritted teeth. "I already made my decision, which is why we went to trial."

"And you lost at trial. Don't look this gift horse in the mouth, Evan. Socrates doesn't give a fuck about you, or your family. He gave us names. It's what people do, dumbass. But then he skipped bail, so any cooperation points that he once had are now off the table. Play the fucking game. This is your golden ticket out of here. You'd be a fool to not take it. Think of your kid. Think of your family. Consider this offer really fucking well. You know damn well there is only one way out of a mandatory minimum sentence. This is a chance-in-a-million deal … and it's off the fucking table tomorrow morning. I strongly urge you to take it." He gathered his papers, placed the cigarette back behind this ear and opened the door, motioning to the guard that we were finished. My face was flushed, my eyes were red and my head was spinning as they brought me back upstairs.

Back on the unit, I went straight to my cell, avoiding the day room. That place was a gladiator pit, and several fights had broken out since I'd been there. I was terrified of just being in this county jail, let alone dealing with all this really heavy shit. I couldn't believe that after fighting my case for all those months, and being firm and proud in my conviction (pun intended) to not tell the feds a thing, now I was back in the face of all that. The convict code around snitching is clear. You don't do it, ever. "Snitches get stitches." That code of honor is talked about every single day in jails and prisons around the world, and yet, a majority of cases are solved with the testimony of another. But if you listen to the rhetoric on the yard, nobody does it. I was terrified for my own safety as well as my sanity.

I wasn't afraid of Socrates. I didn't believe he would hurt me. Deadheads are not exactly known for being violent. The word "family" is thrown around a lot, and that same code runs through the parking lots of shows like it did in prison. The difference is, in prison you had to fear for your safety. In Grateful Dead land, you feared being shunned for life.

I finally got through to my lawyer and found out they couldn't come back and re-indict me for the weed garden, mess with my family or seize the house, the things the inspector had hinted at in his threats. But he encouraged me to cooperate with them. He agreed that this was a rare situation for something to come up like this, post-conviction, and the opportunity to get below the mandatory minimum was indeed a good one. I needed some outside perspective, but I had to be careful; not only were the calls all tapped, but if word got out in this hellhole that I was even considering giving testimony, my safety would have been in serious jeopardy. But I needed to hear something from those who loved me. One of these people was Campbell.

Cam was about twenty years older than me. He rode an older Harley-Davidson and smoked so many hand-rolled cigarettes that there was always one dangling off his yellow-stained fingers. He drank espresso like it was water, and played beautiful flamenco guitar. I was drawn to his wisdom, though I think that while I considered him to be a bit of a spiritual father to me, he saw us more as brothers.

It was back on Thanksgiving 1989 that Pearly and I split for good. Cam and I had gone camping, and when we returned, she was gone, off to a new relationship that still exists today. Cam had been through two divorces with two kids from each, so he was well versed in the art of self-pity and wallowing in sadness. He was able to talk me off the ledge all those years ago, and we had made quite a few memories since then. So, it was him that I called. While he was one of the wisest men that I've ever known, I would not say that compassion was his strongest skill. He was an early teacher of radical self-reliance in my life.

So when I called him in a quiet panic from prison, he talked me down again. "Sounds like one fucked up situation," he said into the phone. I could hear his Zippo light as he took a long drag from his cigarette. "Look, man," he said, "it's clear that you were honorable. You pleaded not guilty and went to a jury trial. But now everything is different. I'm not sure what went down with that TV show … but it was clearly something. Be 110 percent sure that you can live with any decision that you make. It doesn't mean anything to anyone but you. You have to look in the mirror every day. Fuck anyone that tells you otherwise. Maybe this opportunity is just that — an opportunity. Seeing that you've not had many recently, you really need to consider this, and choose wisely." Then he shared one of his favorite metaphors — "No shit, no strawberries" — and with a grin so big that I could hear it through the phone, and a drag off his cigarette, he said, "and I LOVE strawberries!" I could almost see him raising his finger in the air for the punchline, the way he'd done so many times before. While it was nice to hear his perspective, it didn't really help much. The decision was mine and mine alone … and I'd never felt so isolated in my entire life.

I tossed and turned all night. I grabbed the thickest book on the rack, which happened to be *The Tommyknockers* by Stephen King. A lovely little story to take your mind off things in normal times, but there was no way I could focus on a book.

My psoriasis was, by far, the worst it had ever been. My arthritis was flared to the max, and any possibility of sleep was out of the question. I lay there all night, running my options over and over in my head. Psoriasis was causing my body to work like a skin factory in overtime, and no matter how much I picked away at the plaques, there were always new ones coming in behind the old ones. Was this all part of the feds' goal to break up our community by turning us all against each other? I thought about all the people that loved me, and wondered what they'd have done in my shoes. I thought about Cassidy. I thought about my health. I thought about the feds, and about how dirty and conniving they were. If I didn't testify, was Socrates still going to get a life sentence? (The answer, according to my lawyer, was yes.) If the answer was yes, and they didn't need my testimony for the conviction, then why was I even here? All of these questions, and then the most pressing one: Would I be able to sleep at night if I did give testimony? Could I live with myself? And if I did testify, and found out that I couldn't live with myself, then what? The damage would already have been done, and the outlook was not good. It was a long, miserable, lonely, sleepless night. The idea of ending my life in that cell crossed my mind. I wasn't sure if that would have been the strong way out or the weak way out, but I'm grateful, in this moment, to Be Here Now.

Right after breakfast, I was called downstairs to meet with the marshal and the postal inspector. I walked in the room, and those two dicks just stared me down. (Can you tell I'm still just a little bit angry, dear reader?) With a deep sigh, I told them I bought the liquid LSD from Socrates in March of 1992, and the rest had gone down just as they'd figured. I signed a confession and stood up. The postal inspector put his hand out to shake my hand, and I looked him in the eye and shook my head no.

"You're really not going to shake my hand, Evan?" he asked.

"Your drug war has done way more destruction than LSD ever has. You broke apart my family over a seven-hundred-dollar deal, and then, as if to gloat, you drag me across the country in chains, and through fear, threats and intimidation, you coerce me into giving you information that you already fucking had. The drug war is a farce. What kind of country declares a fake war against its own citizens? People have gotten high since the beginning of time, and prohibition has never stopped them. How is society being served by giving a first-time, nonviolent drug offender a twelve-and-a-half-year sentence? Psychedelic drugs have helped way more people than they have hurt, and someday they will be seen as medicine that can change the world, mark my words. So yeah … forgive me if I don't want to shake your fucking hand." He shrugged and gathered the papers on the table. Fuck that guy then, and fuck that guy now.

The uniformed officer that had been standing outside escorted me back to the holding cells. They opened a door to a cell where I saw a slender Black man with skinny gray dreadlocks sitting quietly in the back. We eyeballed each other, sizing each other up. I could tell by his puffy face and swollen eyes that he had been crying. "Are you part of Socrates's case?" he asked me. I nodded yes.

I introduced myself as Evan, and he shook my hand and said his name was Walter. I froze, as I realized that this was the Walter who Socrates had named on the TV show. "Did Soc really give you up on that show?" I asked.

"He sure as hell fucking did," the stranger told me. "I got twenty fucking years, and I never even really dealt with him. I think he gave me up because … he wanted to protect his actual sources," he said. "The only reason he got bail was because he gave me and Gina up, and then he skipped bail. That's why they are trying to give him a life sentence."

Now my mind was really racing. Could this be true? Walter and I spoke for a while, and he told me a little about his case. He had a twenty-year sentence and was hoping to shave it down to ten with his testimony. I told him about my trial, and how I didn't even know why they had dragged me here, until I arrived and saw Socrates in person.

Suddenly, I felt vindicated. Maybe what I was doing was not the wrong thing after all … but as much as I told myself that, it still didn't sit well with me. Walter and I talked for a while about the ethics of what we were both about to do, before we heard a meek voice from the neighboring cell. "It's all a lie, Evan. Don't believe him." It was Socrates. Unbeknownst to us, he was sitting in the cell adjacent to the one we were in, but we couldn't see him because the walls went all the way to the barred door of the cell. This could not just be a coincidence. The feds were fucking with all three of us.

"The TV show was make believe," he continued, "and Walter is a liar."

"Fuck you, you racist prick," Walter said.

They exchanged a few more words before we heard a guard come and open Socrates's cell. "Back to court," the cop said to Soc. Before he walked down that hallway, he said, "Evan, I know you are going to do what you will … but just know that my integrity stays intact. I am going to die behind these walls."

Walter had plenty of things to say to counter this view, and he accused Socrates of lying and told him to go fuck himself. "I'll see you from the stand, motherfucker," he was yelling, as Socrates was being led away, "and I'll give zero fucks about returning the testimony that you made against me, motherfucker!"

My head was spinning and my face was numb. It was all so confusing, and a clear case of he said, he said. Why would Walter lie? Who should I believe? So much grief, so much pain. Walter and I were sitting there, quietly assessing what had just gone down, when we heard the jangling of the keys as a guard approached our cell. "Let's go, Walter," he said, as he opened our door.

Walter turned to me and said, "Evan, you seem like a nice kid. Don't have any hang ups about what you're about to do. This whole situation is a mess, and Socrates should have never dragged me and Gina into it." Then he wished me the best of luck as he walked out of the cell.

I sat there for a long while, stunned and shaken. Soon the postal cop accompanied the guard to open my cell. "This is your moment of truth," he said. "Don't fuck it up." We stood by a closed door for a few minutes, until it opened unexpectedly to reveal a court of law in action. A bailiff escorted me to the stand by my elbow. I was told to place my right hand on a bible that I didn't believe in, and I swore to tell the truth, the whole truth and nothing but the truth. I was then motioned to sit down.

The prosecution began by saying, "Good afternoon. I need to ask if you are here today under your own free will. Has anyone coerced you into making the testimony that you are about to give?"

"Well, I was brought here against my will with no explanation as to where or why I was being moved. I am away from all of my belongings, books and school materials, and the postal inspectors, while not actually threatening me, did indicate that they could make my life worse by not testifying. So while I am here under my own will, there is a little more to the story than meets the eye."

My head was spinning, my lips were tingling, and I felt like I was outside of my body, witnessing this awful scenario.

"Sir, in a yes or no answer, has anyone coerced or threatened you into making your testimony today? Yes or no?"

"No," I said flatly.

"Thank you," he replied and continued. "You were convicted of selling sixty grams, or one thousand hits, of LSD. You have maintained your innocence until this point. Is that position changing here today?"

"It is," I replied.

"And now that you admit to the LSD deal for which you have been convicted, can you tell this court where you acquired the LSD in question?"

"I got it from Socrates," I said.

"Let the record reflect that the witness had indicated the defendant. Had you purchased LSD from him before?"

"No, this was a one-time thing," I lied, with a lump in my throat. "I have nothing further, your honor." I glanced over at Socrates, who's eyes were fixed on the floor in a dead-eyed stare.

Socrates's defense attorney stood up. "Mr. Rotman, have you been promised a sentence reduction for your testimony today?"

I reflected a moment before speaking in a shaky tone, fighting to hold back the tears welling up in my eyes. "While I have not been promised anything, I have been told that the prosecution would recommend a time cut to my sentencing judge, and how much of a cut is up the judge," I replied. "It's the only reason I am here," I finished.

"Why didn't you give this information before? Why did you go to a jury trial if you were guilty all along?" he asked.

"Because the feds didn't offer me any incentive to plead guilty, and I do not believe in cooperating with you."

"Then why are you on the stand today?" he asked.

"Because I am worn down, I am ill and I am tired," I replied. "Prison has destroyed my health, my family and my sanity. I don't want to see Socrates get life, and I don't even want to be here. But I am beat down."

The defense attorney approached and asked, "Why should the court believe you today when you pleaded not guilty and wasted everyone's time by going to trial?"

"You have no reason to believe me," I answered. "The drug war is full of lies and deceit, and it's up to you to sort out what is real and what isn't."

"Was there something in particular that made you testify today?" he asked.

"Well, the fact that the prosecution dragged me here in chains and wore me down definitely played a part. Also, seeing the cop show where I saw Socrates give names up played a role."

He began, "You do realize that Socrates has pleaded not guilty, and is being given no leniency for cooperating, correct? Anything that you saw on that TV show is not a part in his defense. You understand that television is make believe, and can be edited in many ways to manipulate viewers' thoughts and perceptions? You realize that, don't you?" he asked.

"I hadn't really considered that," I replied, honestly.

"Do you understand that if Socrates had given substantial information, he would not be facing a life sentence today?"

"I object under the grounds of speculation," the prosecution blurted out.

"Objection sustained," the judge replied.

"The defense has nothing further," the defense attorney said as he sat down.

I was escorted out of the courtroom, but not without first looking Socrates in the eyes for a good long couple of seconds as I was being led away. He looked broken and defeated, and I felt like 100 pounds of shit stuffed into a ten-pound bag, as I was escorted back up to the unit. Even writing this today, some thirty years later, is incredibly painful, and has my stomach clenched in knots. Some might ask why I chose to include this unfortunate scenario in my memoir, when I could have opted to omit it. The reason is because it's part of my story, which I am trying to tell with integrity.

I collapsed onto my bunk and fell into the deepest sleep that I'd had in a while.

It didn't take long before I made the eight-hour trip in the van with those same two marshals that had transported me there. We stopped at the same McDonald's, and I peed at gunpoint in the same rest area. I processed into El Reno and, thankfully, I processed right out, first thing in the morning, and was back at Springfield before dinner. Once again, I'd lost my corner bunk.

It took many years for me to forgive myself, and to accept the fact that I made the best decision with the information that I had. For the rest of my time inside, and for many years after, I carried this big secret and the shame of it. With everything that had happened to me before my testimony, I had still felt whole somehow. But now I was broken inside and out. The writing of this book is the ultimate release of that secret. I understand now how difficult the situation really was, at the tender age of twenty-four. I was in the deepest trenches of the drug war, and I'd been manipulated by experts into doing something that went against every grain of my moral fiber. There are people that will never forgive me for what happened. Thankfully, Socrates is not one of them.

Cool Colorado Rain

Before I knew it, they transferred me to FCI Englewood Colorado. Sometimes I wonder how much money they spend just moving prisoners around.

A year passed there pretty quickly in a two-man cell, which I shared with an old dope fiend bank robber. I also met an amazing Jewish Buddhist Deadhead acid dealer named Dr. Skillet, who is one of my dear friends to this day. We spent a lot of time walking and talking on the yard, meditating in the Buddhist group and "davening" with the Jews. We listened to the Grateful Dead Hour in the sun, rain, snow and sleet … because there was only one bench on the yard that got the station. With community, a steady flow of herb, my spiritual pursuits and a friend, this period passed pretty smoothly for me.

We had managed to acquire some solid hits of acid. I was unsure about taking it, because with acid, if things go off the rails … they can go WAY off the rails, and that could be a precarious position to be in when you are somewhere as unpredictable as a prison. I thought a lot about it, and felt like I was emotionally ready for the journey. I felt transformation coming and wanted to celebrate that.

I had already undergone one big acid-induced transformation fifteen years earlier. I was in grade ten when I took my first acid trip, and it sent me on a philosophical journey that ended with me swearing off stealing for the rest of my life. I was not happy with the person that I had become. LSD gave me insight into my life as a juvenile thief, and the impetus to change it.

The trip began with two guys from my high school. But they only hung out with me for a couple of hours before sending me off on my own way. I walked back to the trailer I'd been staying in in a buddy's backyard. The distance was about eight miles, but it felt more like eighty. I walked and I walked and I walked and I walked. As I did, I started thinking about everything that had transpired in my life. I delved into my mind like I never had before. I thought about all of the people I'd hurt and betrayed. I thought about my mom, and how deep her love had been for me, and how disappointed she would be with me if she were alive. I thought about what an awful person I felt like most of the time. I cried, and I walked. I thought about morality and my mortality. I thought about what it means to really come into manhood. This was supposed to have happened at my bar mitzvah, but this acid trip did far more to prepare me for manhood than any bar mitzvah. I considered the trauma that I had already experienced in my short life. I thought about the confines of society, and realized that I could choose where I wanted to fall into the mix. It became clear that the daily decisions I made would ultimately place me somewhere, and that the better decisions I made, the better my overall quality of life would be. It also became clear to me that my biggest fuck ups to date had all involved stealing. Stealing from people I loved the most, and stealing from people I didn't know. There was clearly no honor in being a thief, and I knew that I needed to find a way to get by without taking what didn't belong to me.

It was a long and miserable walk — not the first acid trip that I might have hoped for, with butterflies, rainbows and moonbeams — but by the end of it, I had clarity. With the rising of the sun, I had left my thief identity behind. I wasn't sure how I was going to do it, but I made a very conscious choice to make a place in the world for myself. That may have been the most significant lesson I ever learned from psychedelics. That, and the fact that time isn't real, consciousness is an illusion and we probably don't even exist … but those are topics for a different book.

In those teenage years of angst and rebellion, I'd try anything you put in front of me. Cross tops and black beauties (amphetamines), cocaine, and this weird shit called Locker Room Rush, which they sold in the head shops. I'm pretty sure it was amyl nitrate, and you'd get absolutely wasted by inhaling the fumes off this stuff. But at that tender young age, I was only trying to dull the pain of the great loss that I was feeling. When there were no drugs to do, we would do other stupid things. We'd hyperventilated by taking ten deep breaths while crouching down, then standing up while holding our breath and pushing in on our jugular veins. Anything for a buzz. I'm lucky that I lived to tell this tale.

All of these risky behaviors and transformational experiences were on my mind as Dr. Skillet and I were preparing to have our trip in prison. We decided to time our in-house psychedelic excursion to coincide with Jerry Garcia's fifty-second birthday, which was August 1. Jerry was still important to both of us, as was our identity as Deadheads. (Skillet had nineteen pictures of Jerry hanging in his cell, we once counted.) Any Deadhead will tell you that the community plays as big a role as the music. We spent a lot of time talking about people that we had known and telling tales from the road. Jerry's birthday seemed like a perfect day for this "excursion."

We timed it so that the acid would be kicking in just as the yard opened in the morning. We could skip lunch and basically hang on the big yard until the 4:00 p.m. count, where everyone has to be standing up in their cells. (Counts happen five times a day, but only in the 4:00 p.m. count do you have to stand up.)

As we were walking down to the yard, our local radio station played a set of Jerry's music, to honor his birthday, which was a great way to kick things off. Everything got a little more vivid, and a little bit prettier, as we walked the yard. We listened to our radios with headphones around our necks, and talked about everything from how much doing time sucked to the nature of existence. We took joy in the fact that even though we were locked up, our minds were still free enough to enjoy this adventure and each other's company. We talked about our mutual connections to Judaism and Buddhism, and how that related to our legal predicaments. We remembered better times, told road warrior Dead Tour stories and dreamed of amazing futures, while never forgetting to be present in the moment we were in. The one lesson that was reinforced was that life didn't stop in prison. Every moment and every breath still belonged to me; it was just radically altered.

After the count, we left our separate units and met in front of the chow hall. After a halfhearted attempt at a plate of spaghetti, we made a quick exit and sat out on the benches, listening to music and "kicking the bobo" (prison slang for bullshitting) until we had to go in for the night. I know the idea of tripping in a prison probably sounds like an awful experience, but being that it was spent with such a good friend, it was memorable, meaningful and fun ... and fortunately, no bad shit went down that day.

I lay in my bunk and thought about Socrates. I couldn't believe everything that had happened. I've said before that I never thought I was going to do all

151 months … and I had the same feeling about Socrates and his life sentence. I had this intense feeling that he would not die in prison.

That trip reinforced what I already knew about entheogenic drugs. They have the power to open your eyes in a way they've never been opened before, to deepen connections with other people and to connect you with your own sense of spirituality and self-worth. I thought a lot about the information that I'd provided about Socrates. What became abundantly clear to me on that summer day was that there is no instruction manual for this life. We make the best decisions that we can, with the information that we have at the time. While I was sad and uncomfortable with the situation that I'd found myself in, I had to love myself and forgive myself … because if I couldn't love myself, how the hell could anybody else? Happy birthday, Jerry!

Carry That Weight

I was anxious about getting back to court. The carrier weight amendment had passed, and now I had a way out of that mandatory minimum. In early January, I was told to pack my belongings, and I began the journey back to MDCLA, where this whole mess had begun almost three years (156 Mondays) earlier. Surprisingly, there were still three guys on the unit that had been there all that time. I felt for them. MDCLA was a terrible place to be for that long. Seventh floor, no nature, microwaved trays of food.

The prosecutor from Socrates's case said that my testimony had been minimal, and he recommended only a 10 to 15 percent time cut, but my lawyer argued that since I had testified, the judge was now free to abandon the mandatory minimum and revert to the United States Sentencing Guidelines. The prosecution surprisingly did not object, and the judge agreed. I was re-sentenced to thirty-three months (which I'd already served) and five years' probation. Most of me couldn't believe it, but there was (and is) a part of me that remembers I never once believed that I was going to serve the entire 151 months. I always knew that one way or another, the darkness would give.

Much to my chagrin, they didn't let me out on the spot. I was told the process would take a few days, so I was returned to my unit. I was on cloud nine, but I couldn't show too much joy. A lot of guys were not feeling so lucky, and envy can bring out the worst in people. I just played cards and waited. Finally, after three days, the counselor called me to his office and said that I'd be released the following day. I couldn't believe it. I gave all my stuff away to the guys that

I knew. My radio, headphones, sweats, everything, and in return, the boys threw me a nacho feast that night.

The following morning, I went through the entire shuffle of getting up at 4:00 a.m., a bad breakfast, a strip search, facing the back of the elevators … the works. But I didn't care; it was my moment … or so I thought. I spent a few hours in a holding cell, and finally they came to get me. That's when they told me something was wrong. I needed to go back upstairs. I was beside myself. Of course they were going to fuck me on my way out the door. The only mystery was what reason they would give. I went back upstairs, and a few hours later I found out that they'd forgotten to calculate the fourteen days of good time that I had lost in Springfield for the fiasco in the library.

I sat there for the next two weeks noodling on guitar, and honing my scrabble and pinochle skills. I never stopped thinking about Socrates. I felt in my gut that somehow, he would not end up doing life. I didn't know how, but I knew it had to be true. While I was excited to get out, I was also terrified. I had nothing, and I knew I was coming out to a different world than I had left three years prior. Those were, by far, the longest two weeks of the entire three years.

Part 2

...The Courage to Change the Things I Can...

Fifty Bucks and a Pair of Sweats

That's what they gave me on my way out the door. Getting out of prison was amazing, but so many things had changed. Everyone had cell phones now. When I got busted, cell phones were exclusively for lawyers and coke dealers.

Eighteen years after my mother's death, my brother finally bought the rest of us out of the house that our mother had left us. My share was about $23,000. It came at just the right moment.

Those first few weeks were really intense. I had a panic attack trying to choose a toothbrush. For three years, I would just check "toothbrush" on a commissary list, and the next day, I might have one. Now there were hundreds of shapes, sizes and colors to choose from. It was also the first time that I'd stood near women in three years. That'll mess with you. At least I no longer had to face the back of the elevator!

I went to see Cassidy a couple days after I got out. There was literally a moving truck in front of their house. They had bought property near the Rockies and were moving that week. I had made it just in time … to say goodbye again. My heart bled as I stood there realizing he was not going to be a regular part of my daily life, which was something that I'd been yearning for for nearly three years. My early release came as a surprise to everyone. The only good part of Cassidy's exit is that it gave me the freedom to consider leaving LA, which was something that I'd always wanted.

Because my release had come up as unexpectedly as my incarceration had, there was no "reintegration" process. There was no halfway house — you know, that place full of guys who are into way worse shit than you ever were, always in the absolute worst neighborhoods, so there's tons of opportunity for getting up to no good. But I was lucky. I was staying with some friends. Thank G-d for friends. I'd have probably been back inside in a matter of weeks if I didn't have them. It's appalling how we fail to integrate ex-cons back into society.

I appreciated the freedom, and especially the food, but despite a normal mattress and soft pillow and being able to turn the lights off whenever I wanted, I couldn't sleep. I did knock off a bunch of things from my first-things-to-do-when-I-got-out list. I got laid (!!!), ate sushi, drank good coffee and good beer, soaked in a hot spring, swam in a river, and swam in the ocean, all in my first seventy-two hours out. But every night I'd lie down and feel like I'd just had ten espressos. Everyone was sleeping, but I just couldn't. I think I was too young to recognize anxiety and PTSD, but both were omnipresent during this time. These conditions manifested in the form of strained relationships and uncomfortable conversations. I was filled with three years of prison memories, so almost every time I opened my mouth, the words, "When I was doing time …" prefaced whatever I was saying. This can make some people uncomfortable. I just didn't have any other ways to start a conversation.

The anxiety came around the uncertainty of my future. In my time away, a lot of friends had settled down, had kids, bought houses and started businesses or taken "real" jobs. I was back at square one with no direction known. The one thing that I knew for certain was I was not going back to prison.

LA wasn't feeling right for a number of reasons. The city's probation department ran on their own rules, and they were stricter than the actual terms of my probation. I looked into transferring to the Bay Area, but in order for that to happen, I had to have $5,000 in the bank, a place to stay and a job. That money from my mother's house could not have come at a better time.

I got hired at a small vegetarian place called the Smokey Joe's Cafe in Berkeley that had opened a block away from the infamous Chez Panisse the same year, 1971. We used to go to Smokey Joe's after Dead shows and listen to tapes of that night's show while eating amazing breakfasts. Joe's was run by this skinny little older hippie named Ned, a Vietnam vet and really smart guy who loved to read, learn and listen to jazz. I'd known Ned peripherally for many years, and had done a little work for him prior to my arrest, mostly driving him to downtown Oakland to shop, as he normally commuted by bicycle. I'm not sure if he knew how to drive, but I definitely never saw him do that.

This was my very first restaurant job, and my first food service outside of prison. Ned was, and remains, the fastest cook I ever worked with. He ran this twenty-four-seat restaurant by himself, taking orders, making coffee, busing tables, cooking, cutting and squeezing fresh orange and grapefruit juice to order. And he rarely wrote anything down. On a really busy weekend morning, he might rip up some scraps off an envelope for notes, but mostly he remembered everyone's orders while he was doing all this stuff, and adding up checks in his head while working the antique till.

He cut most vegetables right onto the grill with an old knife or a giant box grater, to order. He used to say, "If you can't do five things at once while still doing a math problem in your head, you probably won't make it as a cook." He's the guy who showed me how to work fast and clean in a tight space, lessons that I still use today. The buzz was infectious.

Ned's menu was simple. Below his motto, "Where the elite meet to eat no meat," were whimsical and delicious dishes, like the Holy Moly Frijole, The Urban Cheese Omelet, matzah brei and fresh grits. First thing every morning he would boil a pot of potatoes and make a pot of beans. He'd keep a perpetual pile of crispy home fries on the flattop at all times and would add the right veggies. There was an amazing salsa that didn't have tomatoes in it, served at every table. It was vinegar and carrot-based with chilis, onions, garlic and cilantro, and I can still taste it as I'm writing this.

But I was hungry for more than just good food. I wanted a career, a path. I needed direction, and I figured that cooking was a great one to pursue. Aside from all of the professional options that would be opened up, I would always have to eat, and cooking is a great skill to have. Everyone needs to eat. I really did love the buzz in the prison kitchens as well as at the Smokey Joe's Cafe, and I was intrigued by the travel opportunities that such a career could provide. I was also fascinated by fine dining, something that I'd never really thought about or considered up to this point. I researched culinary schools and found out that the California Culinary Academy, which was just across the bay in San Francisco, was noted as one of the top three schools in America. With a pulse, a checkbook and two professional references, they were happy to sign me up for decades of student loans. I even got a small grant for being an ex-con, proving that crime really does pay.

A few months before school was to start, Campbell called me and told me that he was finally ready to sell his 1982 Harley-Davidson. I had lusted after that bike for years, and he offered me a pretty sweet deal on it. I flew to LA, and he and I spent the weekend at his place up in the high desert. I hadn't seen him since I'd been out, and it was great to reconnect. We made food and played music, while I told him stories of doing time and he told me stories of his travels to Brazil, a country that he had a deep love for.

The thing about our friendship was that we could talk for hours on end, or just sit silently, and it never felt awkward. It was like we could have telepathic conversations, or just enjoy the stillness of the desert. And then he'd pick up his guitar, and the most amazing Spanish rhythms would jump out. He played with such passion.

He gave me his old leather jacket with the bike as well as a basic set of road tools, and I headed out to the coast, driving all the way back up to Berkeley, where I had secured a funky little basement apartment. It was four months after my release, and four months before I was to start culinary school. The June sun was warm on my face as I made my way out of the desert and out to the Pacific Coast Highway. With the ocean on my left side, I made the journey north with a grin so wide it collected bugs. But how could I even contain myself? (Fact: no containment occurred, and thus, I had bugs in my teeth!) I was riding the bike I'd been dreaming about for years. I had chosen a path and committed to it wholeheartedly, and I was about to be trained at what was one of the best culinary schools in the country … and I was fucking free. It was a moment to celebrate … wind in my face, warm salt air coating my body and the roar of the mighty V-twin engine between my legs. It wasn't just freedom … it was ultimate freedom.

I thought a lot about Cassidy on that ride. I was making a difficult choice to not move several states away to the small town that was now his home, but, instead, to get proper training in one of the best food cities in the world. I wasn't sure how I was going to maintain a relationship with him, but I was committed to trying to make it work. I knew that without a career path, I would never be any good to him, or myself. It was difficult, but I needed the direction, and he was living a good life with his family. The distance between us wasn't ideal for relationship building by any means, but then again, neither was having a kid before my eighteenth birthday. Neither was getting busted by the feds. Neither was losing my mother at such a young age. We just play the hand we're dealt, with as much grace and skill as possible, right?

I was doing my best to re-assimilate into society. I was reconnecting with friends, seeing a lot of live music as a volunteer usher at our local venues, and going on lots of dates. I saw a dermatologist and got some slightly better medications for my psoriasis. It wasn't gone, but at this point it was manageable, as was the arthritis. I did all of this while towing the tight line of being on probation. I never missed a meeting, never had a dirty piss test. I wasn't taking any chances … other than motorcycling, which was becoming one of my greatest joys. And as far as my love life went, I don't know what it was, but I never had better luck with women than I did for those first couple of years out of prison. No serious girlfriends, but lots of dates and flings. It was great for my self-esteem … and it was fun.

Grindstone

At twenty-six, I was older than most of the students at the California Culinary Academy (CCA). Being fresh out of prison, and with newly found vigor and direction, I bit into that school with everything I could. I spent my spare time in the library poring over their tremendous collection of books. I had never been a good student, because I had never been that interested in the curriculum, but culinary school was different; I wanted to be there. I was not only spending a lot of money on it, but it was hard work, and it took diligence. It was the first time that I was ever studying something that completely fascinated me. I loved every minute of it. I referred back to the routine and structure that prison had provided me, as well as my spiritual practice, and applied that to my studies. I knew that the time was going to go by quickly, and I didn't want to waste any of it. I did extra credit projects, and if there was something that I wasn't grokking, I stayed after and made sure as hell that I did.

One chef used to give everyone a basket with four to five ingredients, and a set amount of time to make a dish. His standing deal with students was that once you had taken his class, you could sign up to do a mystery basket in your off-hours anytime. I knew that it wouldn't be forever that I could practice with these expensive ingredients in world-class kitchens, followed by honest critique and feedback when I finished, so I did as many as I could. I joined the food and wine pairing club for the opportunity to taste great wines on their dime. I also joined the brewing arts club, and participated in a few beer and food pairing dinners, as well as BBQ and brews parties in Golden Gate Park on the weekends.

I was doing my best to make the money from the house last as long as possible, so I never missed a free meal. There was so much food being produced in this school, I'd be lying if I said I didn't eat (or take home) every extra morsel that wasn't nailed down. The school "hosted" a lot of events. (They charged people big money for events and used student labor to make and serve all the food.) It was a pretty great business model. Not only did they not have to pay their labor … but we were actually paying to be there.

The program was just shy of two years. It was a very French school, steeped in French technique. They accepted California cuisine, but somewhat grudgingly. As a result, we spent a lot of time on classical foods and techniques, and not nearly enough time on modern techniques. Keep in mind, it was right around the time that Modernist cuisine was coming into play. Those were the early years at Spain's famous restaurant, El Bulli, and this cutting-edge cuisine was about to take on global recognition. But the CCA didn't even mention that stuff. I never learned how to even make a foam at school, let alone spherification, food powders or any other molecular gastronomy tricks. But they did teach me the language of the kitchen, and gave me a solid understanding of the fundamental cooking techniques that are universally used in kitchens around the world. In culinary school, as with anything, you get out of it what you put into it, and I gave all my heart, all my soul and all of my rock 'n' roll. I fucking loved every minute of it.

About halfway through my two-year term, I got hired at Stars and the neighboring Stars Cafe, where I had the honor of working with the legendary Jeremiah Tower. Tower had cut his teeth at Chez Panisse and, along with chefs Alice Waters and Wolfgang Puck, helped to put farm-to-table style of dining on the map. Stars was the first really nice restaurant that I worked in, and it kicked my ass. I thought I was hot shit because I was a CCA student and I could filet a salmon … until I saw this young Latino prep cook filet ten salmon in the time that it took me to do two, and his looked 100 times better than mine.

Every night at Stars was like a Saturday night. It was run like a finely oiled machine, and they held high standards, even though we were pumping out 300 to 400 plates per night. The sous chefs were brutal, and it was incredibly cutthroat. Guys would steal your side towels or your mise en place (a generic term in restaurants referring to one's prep work for the night, such as chopped garlic, etc. It literally means "a place for everything, and everything in its place"). There was a lot of pranking going on, but never at the expense of the food. They always made sure that every plate looked and tasted exactly like the chef had envisioned it. It was just enough hazing to fuck with me or the other new guys, to keep us on our toes. After my initiation phase, I proved that I could hold my own on the pantry station, or backing up the grill, or as the sauté guy, so the hazing mostly stopped. Mostly.

I do remember late one particularly rough Saturday night, with a particularly difficult service. Lunch had been so busy, they'd asked me to work a double and help pick up the dinner shift. We had 250 reservations on the books, and the opera was in town that night. Even though I'd put on a fresh chef's coat between shifts, it didn't matter. I was the kind of gritty that only working a double shift in a banging busy restaurant can bring. I'd managed to amass upon me drops of the three different salad dressings that I'd made that afternoon, with an honorable mention going to the Caesar dressing, which left a crusty smear down around the cuff of my pants, and even my sock. And all of that was before we went into dinner service. Once dinner service began, things got really messy. I worked between the grill and sauté station, backing both of them up, and the dirty pots and pans dumping ground was just below my "station," so every time a pan got thrown into that metal bin— with a clang loud enough to make you want to duck for cover — came a few drops of whatever beurre blanc or stock reduction had just happened.

And speaking of stock reductions, we finally made it through service and were breaking down the line. On the back burner was a pot of veal stock that had been bubbling since yesterday. It needed to be strained and cooled in sinks full of ice. I'd gotten help loading the giant pot onto a couple of milk crates on the floor, and now came the task of lining up four to five buckets with a big cone-shaped strainer and a saucepan to use as a ladle, pulling the rich brown liquid and discarding the nasty bits — the mushy, overcooked vegetables, and the pale veal bones, mostly shanks, knuckles, joints and neck bones, if you were lucky, that had been simmering for the past twenty-four hours, having all of the life sucked out of them for the tasty benefits of San Francisco's elite.

The saucepan as a ladle worked well, but it's hard on your wrist and elbow and back and knees, because you have to bend over to get to the bottom of the giant stock pot. With arthritis, these tasks are even harder. And all the while, hot meat steam would be soaking your already sweat-stained head. All of the random bites that I'd taken in the past two shifts were seeping out of my pores. The burnt bits of calamari from the fryer, the little bit of fat at the bottom of a

New York strip that we didn't put on the plates, that little leftover piece of halibut from the fish and chips special we'd been running at lunch. An old chef's secret is that we often get to eat the best bits—the burnt edges that don't make it to the plate become our feeding grounds. But sometimes at the end of the night, you regret them. Especially when the veal stock facial is extracting them through your skin.

Chef Tower had been sitting at the bar for hours in a perfectly pressed and spotless chef coat, drinking champagne and chatting with friends, fans and the bartender. I could feel his gaze as he sat there in the nearly empty restaurant, chatting with the bartender while he put away the bottles for the night. Chef stood up and walked over to where I was straining the veal stock in my grubby uniform, and took the final sip from his champagne glass as he set it down on the edge of the dish pit. "Cooking is a most glamorous profession, isn't it?" he said with a wink and a chuckle as he walked on toward the door.

That moment will never leave me, and for a number of reasons. Aside from stating the obvious that it's really hard work, the fact that he was a celebrity chef and I was one small step below a good dishwasher in the pecking order, wasn't lost on me. In fact, it was the beginning of my realization that I really didn't love restaurant work, where you work a station and cook the same five or six dishes over and over and over again … for months, depending on how often the restaurant changes its menu. It made me consider the many facets of the food industry, be it restaurants, catering, private cheffing, institutional cooking, teaching or consulting. I realized I had options. And after living without much control over my life for three years, to suddenly have choices again was awesome, if not overwhelming at times.

As I was making my way through school, I was seeing my fellow students spend their energies in many different directions. It gave me the clarity to know that no matter what, I would always be able to find a job. In prison, you are assigned a job, and if you find a job in another department that you want, you must submit a request and hope for the best. I was realizing the freedom and opportunities that this education was going to bring me. I'd made a few friends in school, but mostly I kept to myself. With my prison history, and the fact that I was a parent, I found I really didn't have that much in common with the other students, aside from sharing in this culinary journey.

Toward the end of my term, I was required to do a 200-hour unpaid internship at a "reputable food service establishment." This was the make-or-break part of my education. One thing they don't teach you in culinary school is speed. You need to learn that from doing it over and over and over again. You need to know to always have a towel in your hand, because everything on the stove is probably hot. You need to know to move with the caution and precision of a culinary ninja, otherwise you're going to fuck shit up, and potentially hurt yourself or somebody else. But at all costs, the food must go out, and it must go out correctly. Everything else can be taken care of later. Burns can be tended to, spills can be cleaned, friendships can be repaired … but during "go time" the food going out correctly takes priority over everything else. And all of the schooling in the world cannot teach you that. That skillset can only come from the muscle memory of doing it for years.

One day, super chef Paul Prudhomme came to school to do a lecture. At the time, New Orleans food was becoming recognized as a legit American regional cuisine, and I didn't actually know that much about cooking it. As I was getting my cookbook signed at the end of his lecture, I asked him on a whim if he was taking CCA externs, and he jotted down a phone number and a name on a scrap of paper and slid it across to me. "Call Margie, my assistant, and tell her I authorized it myself." And that was all it took to get me signed up to work at K-Paul's. Oh … did I mention that my internship was all January and most of February, during Mardi Gras?

Mardi Gras Mambo

New Orleans is no joke. On my first day of work, I took the trolley down St. Charles Street toward the French Quarter. Just as I was getting off at Magazine Street, I saw this guy running across the street with two other guys chasing him. Before he could make it to the bus, the two guys grabbed him by the shirt, threw him on the ground and began kicking him in the face and torso. They were kicking the crap out of this guy, and I'd swear I saw a couple of teeth fly by. Directly across the street were two cop cars and three cops drinking coffee. They watched this scene unfold for a moment, chuckling, before finishing their coffee, throwing their paper cups on the ground and leisurely strolling over to break it up. The two assailants ran off, and the cops radioed for an ambulance. It said NO PD on the side of their cars, and that is the honest-to-G-d truth.

At this point in his career, Chef Paul spent most of his time at the spice factory, but he still came into the restaurant at least once a week, and he would taste everything. Every sauce, every dressing, every soup, every dessert. He was meticulous, and his palate was so refined, he would always know exactly what adjustment to make to get it just exactly perfect. Once, I went out to the spice factory, where his signature spices are blended into his branded packaging that has been distributed worldwide since the '80s, when no chef knew how to brand themselves. Anyway, this particular day, Chef was tasting all the mixes. He tasted the Meat Magic.

"Margie!" he shouted to his assistant. "Something ain't right with this. I think it's in the salt."

Margie disappeared while Chef and I continued making rounds, tasting seasonings all along the way. Margie came out and said, "Nothing appears to be different, Chef." We tasted the Meat Magic again, and again he said, "It's in the salt, dig a little deeper." I found out a few days later that the purveyors had moved to a different salt mine, about fifty miles away. That's what I mean by a perfect-pitch palate.

K-Paul's was different from any other restaurant I'd ever worked in, in that they didn't hire high-level line cooks. When I was there, every cook, sous chef, the chef de cuisine … every single person had been promoted from within. They hired dishwashers and prep cooks, and every employee worked every station, including the dish pit at some point. That meant that the highest-level employee had stood in the shoes of the lowest-level employee. It also meant that the cooks there may not have had a wide knowledge of many cuisines … but they knew *everything* about *this* cuisine. That was cool with me, because it was Louisiana food that I was there to learn, and I'm proud to say that I learned it from the best.

There were seven stations and I worked each one for a week. Chef Paul's food wasn't difficult, but it was precise, and used a lot of the classical French techniques I'd studied. I wasn't that fast yet, but I had laser focus, which is half the battle. And I think my life experience, in prison and living on the streets, gave me just enough of a hard edge that I could keep up with the kitchen banter, so these guys didn't mess with me too much. Certainly not as much as the other intern, who they once sent to the storage room in the middle of busy dinner service to find the clear food coloring and dehydrated water. I'm not sure if they laughed harder when he left the kitchen, or when he returned a few minutes later, looking sheepish and humiliated. It was a rough-and-tumble crew, and you had to be able to hold your own.

"Hey, intern, you gotta make a five-pound batch of hollandaise," Bundy, the raspy and grumbly sous chef yelled at me on my third day. Everyone snickered. This was clearly a rite of passage. Unbeknownst to them, I had been practicing hollandaise every day at school in anticipation of this very moment. Five pounds is a lot of freaking hollandaise. (They divide it in thirds for sauce Choron, Béarnaise and, my personal favorite, a Tasso/Oyster hollandaise.) I'd been practicing with one-to-two-pound batches, but not five pounds. That was a lot of butter to incorporate into egg yolks without either scrambling the yolks or breaking the emulsification. I mustered up my confidence, gathered the ingredients. They did it old-school, over a bain-marie, whisking yolks and clarified butter at lightning speed. (These days, I use a blender and soft butter.) I wasn't sure I was going to crush it … but I managed to pull it off for the next few nights that I was on that station. This definitely bought me some kitchen cred.

K-Paul's was a legendary New Orleans establishment, and was slamming busy. Every night we'd crank out 300 to 400 plates of food, each sauce made to order. They had an interesting style of plating, where the cooks would bring hot pans to a giant wooden plating table. The protein, starch and veg would either come from different stations or a bain-marie when appropriate. Then the chef de cuisine would build the plates from the components and send them to the dining room from there. That way he could see how every single item was cooked. All night long, he'd taste every sauce and touch every protein to check for doneness. He'd look down and yell, "More parsley on the paillard," knowing just by sight that it was a little light on the green herb.

One of my favorite sauces was called a hot fanny sauce. It's made by deglazing a pan that you've just seared meat in with veal stock. As that reduces, you add garlic, chopped pecans and chopped jalapeños. Once those begin to open up you add a healthy splash of Worcestershire and lemon juice, cook that down and finish with a big knob of butter and fresh parsley. The chef could just look at it and could tell it needed more garlic or fewer jalapeños. It was pretty impressive, and I still make that sauce today.

We'd finish around midnight, and then we'd all go out to a local bar for a few drinks. There was always world-class music for cheap. I have no idea how I had so much fun, worked so hard, partied my ass off and came out with a solid referral, and even a job offer … but I did. I turned down the job offer, though. I still wasn't sure what my path was, but I felt like I'd learned what I came to learn in my time there.

Knocked Down...

Three weeks after my graduation, I'd been promoted to sauté cook at Stars. After a particularly busy shift, I was feeling good and jumped on my bike to head home. I never saw what hit me, but I came to on the ground. I went to pick up the bike, but I could feel my pants sticking to my leg and blood inside of my boot, so I thought better of it and sat down. That accident took me out for eight months, and left me with five pins in my ankle. I also lost my job, which was a real blow. I wound up on food stamps and unemployment, and began the task of learning to stand and then walk again.

I was staying with friends who had a shrine for Jerry Garcia, who had died two years prior, in their living room. Shortly after the accident I was lying in a haze of painkillers, when I noticed a small brown teddy bear staring at me from across the room. I hopped over, scooped him up and named him Darvocet after the pain med that I was on. He's been traveling with me ever since, and makes a decent pillow when there are none. He's always a great icebreaker when I meet children in my travels.

Once I healed, I took a job at a Jewish nursing home. I could have gone back to restaurants and probably could have gone back to Stars, but the nursing home offered me some stability, health insurance and a more grounded lifestyle than restaurant life could provide. It was the responsible path. A steady nine-to-five…. Not as fun or as sexy as a high-end restaurant, but I was cooking in a kosher kitchen again, which brought back memories of my beloved mother.

I went from being a motherless child, to having forty adopted Bubbies (and quite a few Zaides, too!).

My kitchen staff were all older Filipino and Black women, and many of them had been there for more than ten years. They must have seen a lot of young punks like me come and go. My "assistant," Gerry, knew more about that place than I ever could have. She was a hard worker and a wonderful woman, with eighteen years of experience. But I was young, white and male, so I ended up being her boss. Management knew that I had a prison record, but my crew did not. The lead line cook was a woman named Gertrude. Her Filipino accent was so thick, I could barely understand her. Once, I put "soup du jour" on the menu, giving her the creative freedom to use whatever we had around to make soup. But she wasn't familiar with that term, so she came to me and asked, "Eeevan, what is dis soup du whore?" Then there was Pacita. She was all of five feet tall, but she would rock that dish machine like nobody I have ever seen. She wore a giant rubber apron and gloves, and rubber boots that came up above her knees, and would work the machine at lightning speeds. Most dishwashers require one person to load it, and another to unload it. Not Pacita. She ran that thing by herself like a champ. Had dishwashing been an Olympic sport, she'd have taken the gold, no question.

We served a lot of old Eastern European classics like Kasha Varnishkes (bowtie noodles with buckwheat) and tongue with raisin sauce (it's as bad as it sounds). We made chopped liver like it was going out of style, and chicken and matzah ball soup every Friday night. I knew most things about kosher food from my upbringing, and what I didn't know I could call Aunt Marcia to find out. I knew she always felt bad about not being able to help me more after mom died. She did her best by hosting me for all of the Jewish holidays, but my dad kept her at arm's length, and she had her own family of four to raise. But she was incredibly supportive of my culinary education, and I think it made her very happy to see me working in a Jewish organization. I called her my first Chanukah at the home, because my latkes weren't holding together. Add more eggs or more matzah meal to your batter. If that doesn't work … more oil! She was not wrong. Food connects all families, and ours was no exception. I loved being able to reach out to her with these questions, and I could tell that she loved it when I called.

I began dating an employee of mine, which is never a good idea, but seemed like one at the time. We had a lot of fun together, and she was a great addition to my crew. We fell pretty hard, pretty fast for each other, and we jumped quickly into a relationship. Even though we each had our own places, we spent most of our nights together. This was my first girlfriend of significance since Cassidy's mom, and it was great to be in love. We went to tons of shows and festivals together, and ate, drank and partied. Hillinary had been in many relationships, but this was only my second relationship that lasted over a year, and my first one since I'd been out of prison. We had a ball. She was from Pensacola, had a really cute southern drawl, loved music and was just plain fun to be around.

In our off time, we would cater these crazy dinners around the Bay Area and at some local festivals. This was around 1997/98, the earliest of the Medical Cannabis years. I'd become good friends with one of the leading cannabis activists in the Bay Area, and we brainstormed some fundraising dinners together. A few times, we rented a kitchen at a local club, and did what may have been the country's (or the world's) first food and cannabis pairing dinners. They were called the Harvest Feasts. I'd create and execute the menus. In hindsight, they were pretty clumsy, but luckily for me, stoners are a forgiving crowd when it comes to food. I learned a lot about what does — and does not — work at these dinners. I'd spend weeks developing recipes with hemp oils, hemp flour and crushed hemp seeds. Then once the recipes were perfected and we actually did the dinners, I learned how to execute a multi-course dinner for a large group. These dinners taught me about timing, and the dynamics of designing plate-ups that look appealing but are manageable for a small kitchen crew to execute. I learned aspects of recipe development and meal execution that I still use today.

One weekend we were catering at a world music festival up in the Sierras. The morning of the event, Hillinary and I went to the Cannabis Action Network (CAN) office to load the coolers full of cheese and other ingredients into a rented truck. The CAN crew was going to meet us at the festival to work the booth. But a cop who had it in for the people at CAN happened to see us loading the coolers while driving by that morning. He deemed it from his expert experience in law enforcement that coolers are often used to transport cannabis, so these coolers must have been full of cannabis. Meanwhile, we left with the coolers of cheese to go to the festival. (A few hours later, the cops busted the CAN office, and from the seven people there they recovered four grams of cannabis and a collective total of under $100.)

Up in the Sierras, Hillinary and I were setting up the booth and anxiously waiting for the crew to arrive, which they never did because they were all involved in the bust. And this was long before cell phones, too. I forgot to mention, it was about 110 degrees in the shade. We'd rented a propane-powered pizza oven and had two big-ass sixty-five-pound propane tanks. We hired a couple of kids from the lot to help us set up. We fired up the pizza oven, with the spare tank sitting next to it. We managed to get some pies served for our health permit inspection, and we passed with flying colors. But we were not out of the woods yet.

This was the day that I learned that propane expands when it gets hot. Our spare tank was in the sun, not far from the oven, and the heat was so great that it caused the release valve on the spare tank to let go of a steady stream of propane directly into the side of the oven that was cranking at around 700 degrees. Everybody in the booth, including myself, all dove for cover. That's when I realized that actually I was in charge, and I stood up to go muscle the tank shooting out gas.

At that moment, one of the kids we hired came over to help me, but tripped over his shoelaces and into me. I bumped the tank, which was now spewing gas as it rolled toward the next food booth, which is, in that moment, being inspected by the health inspectors. Somehow, we managed to divert the gas-spewing, rolling tank and get it into the shade. With an untrained staff of random parking lot hippies, we plowed through a very difficult weekend, mostly unscathed.

I loved and hated the job at the old folks' home. This was a very stable period in my life, perhaps the most stable ever. I was making decent money for the time, the benefits were good and the job carried a certain amount of respect with it, within my family if nothing else. I loved the residents, and their families too. It was easy and comfortable for me to work in a Jewish environment that was centered around food. I felt very at home and in my element.

But try as I did to lift the levels of the food, it was still institutional food being served to old folks who had nothing better to do than to complain about it. "Good afternoon, ladies, is anything all right today?" I used to say. They'd get a kick out of that, and tell me to cut my hair, sell the motorcycle, find a nice girl and settle down.

Aside from that, there was a mountain of red tape involved in preparing food in that setting. In fact, I rarely cooked in this job. I was mostly managing the others, which was a great skill to learn, but not what I'd been training for. I was even taking nutrition classes at a local junior college, working on a certificate as a food service director. But the home was taken over by a new management company, and a lot of the senior staffers that I had been working with were leaving for greener pastures.

On top of it all, Hillinary dumped me, adding to the confusion, despair and dissatisfaction that I was feeling from the job. I was heartbroken and totally unsure of what to do. I'd been out of prison for five years and had just turned thirty. I'd learned a trade, practiced it in different facets, from fine dining and line cooking to institutional cooking. I was still maintaining some form of spiritual practice, meditating on my own and with a group once a week, but no matter what I did, I was feeling empty. I felt like it was time to try something new and different. To top it all off, my probation was about to end, so I would be free to travel.

Post haste, I gave notice at my job, packed everything I owned into storage, cut my hair for the first time since I was a teenager and set off for Fort Lauderdale. All I really knew about the yachting industry was what a buddy from culinary school always told me: "The chefs make the most money and get all the chicks, bro!" So, with very little money in my pocket, my knives and my backpack, I went for it.

Floating Luxury Prisons

Yachting is an industry like no other. The gigs can last a few days to years, if you find the right match. They promise that you will see the world while getting paid. That is partially true, depending on what position you are working. The chef and the chief steward are constantly having to provision the boat, so if nothing else, we see the markets, which are the heart and soul of most destinations. But if you're the second stew, you might only get off the boat a few times in a season, and the same can be true for the deck crew.

Yachting is a very transient industry. Back then, there were only around 2,000 yachts on Earth that were bigger than 100 feet. It wasn't uncommon to run into yachty friends in crew bars all over the Caribbean, Europe or New England. It was a big party industry. Drugs were on the down-low, but alcohol use was not only accepted but encouraged and was often abused.

Catering to the world's richest comes with its ups and downs. My experience was that the owners and charter guests were usually much easier to deal with than the crew. The guests come and go … but the crew is there to stay, and everyone is working hard and then playing hard. The quarters are small and tensions can run high. And as soon as two crew members hook up, it creates tension for everyone. And that scenario seems to play out more often than not.

Provisioning for a yacht is challenging. You basically have to bring all ingredients for everyone on board for sometimes weeks at a time. I used to think you really needed everything, and I'd pack those fridges, but I learned you can usually get the basics, like milk, eggs and butter in the islands. In the Bahamas it was a pain to find good produce, but fish, lobsters, rice and local pork and chicken were usually plentiful. In the States it's not so bad as there are grocery stores, which tend to be one-stop shops. In Europe, if I needed bread, milk and prosciutto, I was going to three different shops. I'd always do my best to have everything on hand, but sometimes shit happens.

My first yacht gig happened to occur over Thanksgiving. I made a turkey dinner for the crew with all the trimmings. This was the first time that I ever filled up five shopping carts at once, and they were all overflowing. It was also my first time being at sea. I immediately loved the smells, the rocking back and forth, the feeling of the engines engaging. I wasn't making much money, but I didn't care. I was on a multimillion dollar yacht, on my way to the Bahamas and a million miles away from prison.

At that point, my psoriasis was just on my legs and a little bit on my torso, maybe covering 10 percent of my body at most. I'd worn long pants to the interview and to dinner, but I'd decided to wear shorts the following morning. Sun and sea are known to help with psoriasis, so I was feeling pretty good when I walked into the wheelhouse for coffee. The captain, a short stocky guy named Jack, and his wife, who was the chief stewardess, were sitting in the big chairs at the helm holding their steaming cups. The captain gave me a quick nod. I headed right for the coffee pot, so I didn't immediately notice his wife staring.

"What's that? That stuff on your legs?"

I finished pouring my coffee and took a deep breath before I turned toward them. See, here's the thing, yachting is a predominantly "young, white and beautiful" industry. It's the only one that I know where a current photo and your birthday are required on your CV. And even at age thirty, I was an older crew member. And … I wasn't beautiful. So, while the rest of the crew was barefoot in khaki shorts and a polo shirt, my chef pants were an anomaly. I guess I just got too comfortable. And it was clearly a mistake.

"It's psoriasis," I said. "It's mostly just on my legs—" The captain finally dragged his eyes back to my face. "I plan on wearing chef's pants once the guests arrive."

Captain Jack was frowning. "You really should have told us about that before we made our agreement." He took a sip of his coffee. "Just make sure the guests don't see … it."

I nodded, realizing what a huge error I'd just made. I should have told them when I was hired. I should have known that in this industry, there were certain aesthetic standards. But I had already done the provisioning, and it was too late for them to sack me.

We picked up our guests at the famous Atlantis Marina and cruised around the Exumas, which is a lovely chain of islands south of Nassau, the guests in their bikinis, the crew in khaki shorts and polos, and me in my long pants. I was beginning to grok the amount of hard work the job required. Chefs are often the highest-paid crew members behind the captain (and sometimes the engineer), but our job often carries the longest hours and, arguably, the most pressure. Bad food = bad tips, for everyone. It's that simple, and you're really only ever as good as your last meal.

A typical day on a yacht usually begins at 5:30 a.m. I'd hit the galley, and often start with a fruit platter. It became a form of morning meditation. I'd sip a hot beverage, cut fruit, plot and scheme my day, then I'd proceed as follows:

6:00–8:00-ish: Get a jump on any baking breakfast breads, and other baking for later in the day. At this time, I'd also think about my desserts for that afternoon and evening, and get any ice creams or batters out of the way. I'd cook and hold bacon and sausage, and do some prep for omelettes, trying to predict what the guest would order. I'd also throw some breakfast sammies or burritos together for the crew, so they could eat on the go. The most important rule for any yacht chef worth their salt: Always. Feed. The Crew. ALWAYS!!!! Many chefs don't believe in making the crew breakfast. While it wasn't a job requirement, it's not that hard to cook a little extra bacon and eggs, now is it? And I quickly learned, it's always better to have the crew on your good side, and breakfast sammies go a long way.

Once the guests start arriving for breakfast, we'd begin with coffee and cocktail orders. This is a deciding moment on any charter. You know if they start hitting Bloody Mary's before coffee, you're in for a long week. I learned way too much about egg-white omelettes, and no matter how prepared I set out to be, someone always asked for a freaking Belgian waffle, eggs Benedict or something else that I hadn't thought to prepare for, and there I was making batter and whipping cream on the fly. But on a yacht, where people were often paying over $100K a week, the word "no" does not exist.

A universal truth in yachting is that crew lunch is served at noon sharp, and dinner is at six sharp. As I gained more experience, I put out cookies and a round of snacks in the afternoon. Anyway, when breakfast finally ground to a halt, I'd clean the galley and start getting crew lunch together. More often than not, I'd make the crew the same thing I made the guests for lunch, but a simpler version. I found that oftentimes, crew prefer simpler fair. My lunch jam is usually three salads, a grilled protein and a light dessert.

Lunch service is usually quick and easy, until somebody asks for a burger or a pizza, not understanding that you are not a restaurant kitchen. But as I said, "no" isn't an option, and as time went on, in downtime, I'd pre-form patties and freeze them, and try to guess what their future needs might be. If anyone looked at all like a stoner, I'd keep pizza dough on hand 24/7, and this has paid off more than once.

My only break was around 3:00–4:00 p.m., and it didn't happen every day. In fact, I don't think it happened once on that first charter. I'd go downstairs, take a quick rinse and lay on my bunk. I became a master at a short nap, with five minutes on either end to change. One charter, I was so slammed that I left my cabin at 5:30 a.m., and when I went down for a poop at around 4:00 p.m., I realized it was the first time that I had "sat down" since I'd gotten out of bed.

At four, I'd caffeinate, tighten up my lists and spring into action. I had to have crew dinner up by 6:00 p.m., and usually guest happy hour, canapés or some type of snack up by around six thirty, so more often than not, I'd put crew dinner down and just keep working to get the snacks out, and to be ready for dinner by eight-ish. As I got better at the job, I'd make random bits of the dinner, things like salad dressings, some veg prep or stocks, at lulls during the day. Also, when I had downtime in the boat yard, I'd make ice creams, demi-glace, fresh pastas, compound butters and other freezable items. Hell, once I got good at the job, I'd roll out pastas and raviolis in my free time and freeze them. But there was no time for that on this first gig. I was struggling just to keep my head above water on a boat where the chief stew and the captain were bad vibing me about my skin. Fortunately, the guests were quite happy with my food, and there was a freelance second stewardess who was great to work with.

Around 8:00 p.m., if I was lucky, we'd serve dinner. However, more often than not, and especially when I started working in the Mediterranean, dinner was served MUCH later. With any luck, we'd be done serving the three courses by nine thirty, and it would usually take me a couple of hours to clean the galley and pull proteins out of the freezer for the following day. I'd write my proposed menus, shopping and prep lists, and maybe have a beer or a glass of wine if it wasn't a dry ship. Some boats have a strict "no alcohol on charter" rule, though often a blind eye would be turned for the chef — and what might be in his coffee cup.

By now it's usually close to midnight and I'd grab a quick shower and hit the sack, praying that my five thirty alarm would have some mercy on me.

I learned a ton on that first charter, and we got a great tip, which is the telltale sign of a job well done. Nonetheless, this was what the captain told me at the end of it, when we closed out the receipts. "Evan, your food is good, and you're a nice enough guy, but yachting has a certain aesthetic, and you just don't have it. Nobody wants a chef with scales and dry patches all over their legs. We'll give you your pay and tip, but we won't give you a reference. Oh, and you might want to consider killing yourself." Okay, I made up that last part. But that's pretty much what the guy was saying. On one hand, it felt like I'd been kicked in the nuts. I'd given my all, gotten great praise from the guests, but I wasn't leaving with a reference. On the other hand, I'd gotten my first taste of "yachtie cash," and I was determined to succeed. So I decided that from then on I'd wear shorts and just tell the agents and the captains that I had psoriasis. I mean … it's not leprosy.

Back in Fort Lauderdale, I went to one of the crew placement agents and told her everything. She looked at me with empathetic eyes from across her desk, but without wasting a breath, she said, "Yachting is hard enough without having a skin problem. And there isn't a yacht in the water that would hire somebody with your history of drugs." (That first yacht hadn't asked if I had a record, and I didn't volunteer that information.) "I'm sorry, but you don't stand a chance in this industry." While I knew that my criminal history could be a problem, I'd never considered that I might be discriminated against because of my skin. It just hadn't occurred to me.

I walked out nearly in tears and went to grab lunch. Before I was finished eating, I got a call from my favorite crew agent, Beverly. (I'd called her upon my return to tell her what had happened. She encouraged me to not give up.) I shoved the last bits of burger into my mouth, downed my beer and biked over to see her.

She explained that she had a yacht owner who also had psoriasis, and a really cool captain running the boat. Captain Dave had been in yachting long enough to know that many people can do the job, but getting the job done, and being easy to live and work with, was key. The speed of that afternoon transition was yet another indicator of just how quickly a fortune can change, in the course of an afternoon, in yachting, and in life. Within an hour, I went from being told that I was "un-hirable" to having a job interview.

The next morning, I rode my bike to the *T. Lady*, a 120-foot Christianson motor yacht. Two people were at work washing it down. They introduced themselves as Gumby and Michelle, showed me to the wheelhouse and told me that Captain Dave would be there in a minute. I looked around and along with the usual boat shit, such as charts, paperwork, etc. I noticed an inordinate amount of Tigger swag. You know … from *Winnie the Pooh*. The door opens, and in walks this big dude with bright red hair, boxer shorts, a boat shirt (*T. Lady*), a light cotton Tigger robe, with a ginormous Tigger mug full of coffee. I was being interviewed by Tigger! Also, when I say big, I mean *big*. He was 6'4," from Shreveport, Louisiana, with a deep southern drawl.

We shook hands and he sat down across from me and began looking at my resume. "You worked on the *Gargoyle*, eh? What did you think of those Canadian pricks?" Before I could answer, he said, "Bev told me that you've been busted. Mind if I ask what for?"

"Distribution of LSD through the U.S. mail," I replied flatly, yet matter-of-factly.

His eyes lit up like saucers and he said, "Oh, man, me and my friends used to drop acid and go hunt gators back home. Now that was a good ole time!" And like that, the ice was broken. We chatted for nearly two hours, mostly about how he ran the boat, but he also asked me some personal questions. As we were winding up, he asked me where I saw myself in five years. I thought carefully before I slowly responded, "That's a difficult question. I've been round long enough to know that life is full of surprises, and sometimes the only way we get to experience these surprises is to be open and receptive to them. If I were to lock myself into some five-year plan, I might miss out on other opportunities."

The captain smiled, nodded and said, "Can you move on board tomorrow?" as he extended his arm out for a handshake.

We provisioned the boat as heavily as we could, as we were going down island for "a while." It was my first experience provisioning for a whole season. I basically figured that more is better, which it turns out is the mantra in yachting anyway … until it comes time to store it all … then you learn the importance of balance. I did all the final shopping and, upon seeing me in line with five carts, a woman raised her eyebrows and asked, "Y2K?" (Remember that?) It was Christmas, 1999.

I was prepping food like mad. The night before New Year's Eve I made a few chocolate cakes, and was going to frost and decorate them on NYE day. I walked into the galley that morning, and two of the three cakes had been mauled. They literally looked like they had been mauled by a bear, but actually … it was Tigger. Captain Tigger. The family all thought it was hilarious, but I was pretty pissed. With a wink and a nod from the owners, I covered the mauled cakes in ganache and the buffet was a success.

Together we watched what was, at the time, the "most expensive and elaborate fireworks show in the world" at Atlantis Marina from the top deck of the yacht, ringing in the new millennium with champagne that was way out of my pay grade. With the smell of the gunpowder from the fireworks and the gratuitously yeasty bubbles rolling across my gullet, I was taken back to a New Year's Eve just a few years prior. I was in prison in Missouri, drinking jailhouse wine made of fermented orange juice with "dinner roll dough balls" and sugar, watching the icicles hanging down off the razor wire beneath the gun towers covered in freshly fallen snow. The guards used to do target practice just over the fence, so the ominous ring of gunfire was not uncommon. Once again, I relished my freedom.

A few days into the new year, we moved the boat down to Highbourne Cay, an island in the Exumas, tied the boat up and didn't move it for about five weeks. Highbourne Cay is a beautiful island but very remote, with no supplies. As these owners liked to have salads every day, it was difficult to keep the produce alive and well. I learned to roll all of my herbs and greens up in damp paper towels, and change the towels out every couple of days. I could keep a bunch of cilantro for around three weeks like that. Toward the end, I got pretty good at making "jarred salads": artichoke hearts, hearts of palm, pickled asparagus and other preserved vegetables. But the pickings were scarce, and I had to use what I had wisely.

Every day the owners would take off with Captain Dave in the tender and go scuba diving. I was not yet certified, but I made a mental note that this would soon become a part of my life.

We moved down to St. Thomas and then over to Tortola, and stayed tied up there for a couple of months. There's a bar called the Bomba Shack that hosts a full moon mushroom tea party (psychedelic mushrooms were legal there). After dinner service on the night of the full moon, I quickly cleaned up the galley and walked beneath the rising moon to the Bomba Shack. It was still early, and the party took a while to get going, but you could tell this party was going to be different. Everyone and their uncle was arriving at this little beachside bamboo bar. From the prime minister of the island to the Rastafarian fisherman that I'd been buying weed, fish and lobsters from, as well as every tourist on the island. It grew into quite the scene. Some people were dressed to the nines, with suits and ties and ball gowns, which is unheard of in the Caribbean. Some were dressed like clowns or in other Carnival-style outfits. And the rest were in the usual beach attire of board shorts and flip flops.

At around 11:00 p.m., they passed out the mushroom tea. Everyone drank a cup, but it was pretty weak and didn't pack much of a "punch" to the already alcohol-tipsy crowd. The locals, however, walked around with shoeboxes full of the mushrooms and sold them for a reasonable cost. This little Rasta dude walked up to me, looked me in the eye with a curious gaze, carefully chose a mushroom from his stack and gave it to me, saying "Take this one. It's special. I got it from a leprechaun." With an endorsement like that, the only move is to add it to the already growing menagerie of mushrooms and rum punch sloshing around my belly.

Everything peaked a little after midnight, when the music got louder and the "parents" all went home. I'd been dancing with this girl and her friend, and as the music wrapped up, they told me that they were waiting for the first ferry of the morning, which didn't run until six thirty. The one girl and I began to hit it off as we smoked a joint or two in the sand. As it was now getting pretty late, I was faced with a decision. Captain Dave had a strict rule about not bringing guests back to the boat when we had the owners or family on board, which is a pretty standard rule across the industry. (We had just the Mrs. on board, not a full passenger load. But still … the rule was clear.) But this girl and I were beginning to heat up, and her friend didn't seem to mind. In fact, she really just wanted a nap! So I brought them both back to the boat, and snuck them down to my cabin. The tired girl climbed into the top bunk and went to sleep, and her friend and I fooled around in the bottom bunk until daylight, when it was time for me to sneak them back off the boat.

After I cleaned up my cabin and showered, I went upstairs for coffee and to start my day, bleary eyed, but smiling. Dave walked into the galley, poured himself a cup of coffee and said, "Normally I'd fire you for bringing a girl back to the boat when we had the owners on. But since it was TWO girls, I'm gonna let this one slide. Don't do it again, though, Chef." I just let him think that I'd managed a threesome, made a mental note to find the hidden security cameras and went on with my day.

The season ended, the boat went back to the yard to be painted and, with the exception of the Captain and Chief Stew, the rest of the crew, including me, was let go with severance, as the boat would be down for a while.

New Money

My next boat we dubbed the *Fake Tittie II*. (The owner nicknamed it after a mistake was made around his wife's botched boob job.) The boat was a Broward, which is known as the "poor man's yacht," in that it's not built to the highest standards. The running joke is, "Don't be a coward, go to sea on a Broward!" That's not to say that they don't float … it's just like the difference between a two-door Kia sedan and a BMW 7-series.

I met Captain Sean the first day. He told me I'd be sharing a room with the engineer. A crew of four to five, which is common on boats this size (100 to 125 feet), is difficult, because we house as many guests as the big yachts, and try to provide the same level of service with half the crew of the larger yachts. The upside of a smaller crew is fewer personalities in the room. And it's a SMALL room. I had prison cells that were bigger than most of the crew quarters I lived in.

The owners decided to decorate their yacht themselves rather than hire a designer, and each cabin had a different wild animal theme (tiger, giraffe, leopard, lion and zebra) and were named accordingly. It was hands down the ugliest boat I've ever been on. To make things worse, the main salon used *all* those patterns. It was like a cross between a wild animal park and a brothel. In my time on that boat, every broker, contractor and other walking pulse, did a double take upon first entry.

Yachting is a really hard industry, and it's especially hard on young women. To be clearer, it is toxically masculine AF, and this boat was no exception. Most of the jobs for women are for interior stews, which entails detailed cleaning of the heads and beds, and everything else. And I mean every nook and cranny.

On some of the larger yachts, there's usually a person whose sole responsibility is doing laundry. Every day, all day. On other, more prestigious charter yachts, a chief stewardess might act like a concierge in the finest hotels. They make all the arrangements, do all the ordering for interior supplies, inventory everything regularly and clean things to a level that I didn't even know existed.

I once worked on a boat where the captain would turn the porn station on at lunch and would "rate" what was happening on the screen, often comparing our stewardesses' looks to those on the screen. A common derogatory name for the stewardess is the "stewpidess." It was not uncommon for a junior stewardess to end up sleeping with the captain on the promise of a promotion, which sometimes materialized and sometimes didn't. Some captains hire stews based solely upon looks, and some yacht owners request only "hot stews." Not all boats are like this, but misogyny ran deep in yachting when I was in the industry.

I met a lot of people in my yachting days. The worst type was new money with no class. That type loved opulent displays of wealth, even if they were utterly stupid. They wore designer everything, and changed outfits five times a day. The owners of *Fake Tittie II* were into wife-swapping, and some of the swapping ran a little close in the blood lines. I mean, only by marriage, but … there was some weird shit going on "below deck." They also left their sex swing and sex toys out for the crew to find. One guy was a workout freak and he wanted a ten-egg egg-white omelette every day. He was known to eat an unhealthy balance of laxatives and then anti-diarrhea drugs. He was convinced this was the best way to lose weight.

Most of his group were heavy drinkers, and though the owner himself was not, he tried to fake it to be "part of the group." His drink was diet coke and Kahlua, and he brought the absolute worst weed I'd ever seen from Texas. One day he jumped in the water with four joints in his pocket, so he later asked me if we had a microwave on board. I nuked his shitty weed, and handed him three joints back, with a wink and a smile. From that point on, he always brought me a package when he came to the boat. I couldn't tell him that his weed was the worst around. Even the seedy weed that is prevalent all over the Caribbean was better than his. What's the point in being a mega-millionaire if you can't even score some good bud?

One night, while we were preparing the boat for charter, the captain, chief stew and I went out and bought a ton of supplies for charter, including about 150 DVDs, as we were switching the boat from VHS to DVD at the time. The captain was curious about my choices. "Hey, Chef, what's the deal with these

Cheech and Chong movies? Nobody is going to watch them. *Fast Times at Ridgemont High*?!?" But what do you think the first thing the boss and his friends did when they came on board? Stoner movie night, with loaded nachos, chicken wings, popcorn, chili fries and banana splits ... and all the rank seedy Texas weed that they could smoke.

I met a lot of women during those yachting years. Once I met a girl from a very small town in Alaska. The boat was in the marina for the boat show, and I was the only one staying on board, so I invited her back. We were in the crew quarters and beginning to have a good time, but the crew quarters are SMALL. She asked to see the master cabin, and then told me that she'd fool around with me, but only in the master cabin, a.k.a., the boss's bed. She also wanted to use the master bathtub. Now, during the boat show, the boat is all done up for show. Day pillows, towels all folded like swans and other details that there's no way I could replicate. This could be a fireable offense, for sure, but at this point there was no way I was going to say no. So we took a hot bath and drank champagne, and then had an amazing night in the boss's bed and bath. At about 4:00 a.m., I can't remember if I called or texted (did text exist in 2001?) but I let the chief stewardess know that I'd trashed the master cabin, and begged her to come in early and help me get it back in shape. It cost me a sushi dinner and a large amount of sake, but she was a good sport about it.

I dated one woman for a while that I dubbed my "Nazi girlfriend." The first time we made out, and things were heating up, I felt self-conscious about my skin. When I told her about my psoriasis, her response was, "Baby, I am way more freaked out about the fact that you're Jewish than I am about your skin." That is hands down the strangest thing that anyone has ever said to me before sex. I'd like to say that I put my clothes back on and stormed out offended. But that's not quite what happened...

Sometimes it was smooth sailing and other times there were explosions on board that had nothing to do with fireworks. Once we were cruising down the intercoastal, when we hear a tremendous racket from the top deck that sounded something like, "Fuck you, you whore. And you...!" It turned out that the primary guest's best friend and girlfriend had come clean that they'd been having an affair. The primary guest was in a blind rage, and insisted that we charter a helicopter for his escape from the scene. However, the boat was not big enough to land a chopper on, so he went to his room and locked himself in his cabin, presumably doing all of the drugs that he had brought on board. The girlfriend and best friend sat nervously on the top deck, downing copious quantities of expensive champagne until very late. They finally passed out in the main salon on the couches. Sometime in the middle of the night, the girlfriend slipped back into the master cabin with the primary charter guest. The following day, they seemed to have found some resolution, and they disembarked in Key West. They had left behind a few grams of some of the finest pink cocaine that the world has ever seen on the bathroom sink, which we properly disposed of (ahem).

Some of the most challenging jobs involved catering to guests with special diets. I once worked for Russian guests who said that they were Glatt kosher, which is the highest form of Kashrut (Yiddish for kosher, but certification standards are even stricter), and I knew that there was no way I could adhere to those standards in a yacht galley. To put the guests at ease, I explained my kosher upbringing, as well as my experience running a kosher kitchen in the assisted-living facility for two years. I also discussed the challenges of being confined to a yacht's galley, only having one sink for both milk and meat and one oven. I'd be able to get separate cutting boards for milk and meat items, some new pots and pans for keeping meat and dairy separate, dishes, silverware and some basic utensils, but the chances are they would have to be special ordered from the States at a high cost. I'd also be able to order kosher meats on that same shipment. I made it clear that while I would not be able to guarantee them a 100% kosher kitchen, I was well versed in the rules and the obstacles ahead. I would do my best to adhere to their strict diets. They assured me that cost was no issue. They understood that it was not going to be perfect, and they authorized any charges required to get the job done. They also requested cases of fine wines, from France and California, and a kilo of the world's finest caviar. They were into good food … it just had to be kosher.

I set into gear ordering two sets of everything, along with kosher meats and some produce. I felt like I was creating the Noah's Ark of galleys! Everything was all set to be delivered to the plane in Lauderdale, and flown down to St. Thomas, where we had moved the boat to and where the guests were boarding. The plane stopped in Puerto Rico, where it got delayed, as there were high winds for quite a while. I was sweating bullets, as I had tens of thousands of dollars' worth of perishable products on it. Finally, after sundown, the plane was cleared for takeoff and it made its way down to St. Thomas.

We headed to the airfield, which was guarded by two huge men with long dreadlocks, gold chains and machine guns, and we offloaded the goods into our van. It totally felt like a sketchy drug deal scene in a movie, and reminded me of when they would transport me around back on Con Air. I was sure that we were going to get shot for a standing rib roast and some kosher lamb racks, but that didn't happen. We made it back to the boat well after midnight. I worked until dawn getting all the product loaded into my fridges and freezers, creating homes for the new gear and marking it accordingly for meat and dairy cooking. Many appreciations to my mother, my Aunt Marcia and my job at the Home for Jewish Parents in this moment for teaching me these time-honored traditions.

The charter was going as well as a kosher charter could. They had actually chartered two yachts and this was a tandem charter. On Shabbat, I was planning on baking a challah. Mrs. Goldfarb informed me they had a challah recipe they loved, but had forgotten it at home. Before I knew it, I was on the satellite phone speaking with a Mrs. Zukerman in London, who gave me her challah recipe … which turned out to be amazing. (She adds a pinch of saffron to her dough, which I learned is part of the Sephardic tradition. I come from an Ashkenazi background, as did our guests.) Keep in mind that this is in 2001, before cell phones had any sort of range, before the internet was really functional and certainly before it was functional on yachts. This phone call for a challah recipe while at anchor on the coast of Trinidad was a big deal.

I got my dough ready and was working the chicken soup and vegetables. I had planned on serving Cornish game hens. Around four in the afternoon, Mr. Goldfarb asked me if he could invite the other boatload of guests for Shabbat dinner. As I've said, the word "no" does not exist on charter yachts, so I smiled and said, "No problem. That's a great idea!" And this is how I found myself frantically defrosting more game hens in the sink and stretching every other dish to feed sixteen instead of eight. It was an insane effort, but come sunset, the guests asked me to come out and light the Shabbos candles with them … and I did. I then put out a beautiful Shabbat dinner for all sixteen of them, as well as our crew.

Orthodox Jews do not work on Shabbat, and they don't think other Jews should either. The Sabbath meal is usually finished before the sun sets. Knowing this, Mr. Goldfarb asked me if I could have another crew member clean up from supper. I explained that each crew member had their own work to do, and that it wouldn't be ethical (or cool) for me to make this request. He then asked if I could at least have them turn off the oven for me. So in the end, it didn't matter that I was scrubbing the floors on my hands and knees … as long as the goyim turned off the oven. It was a very strange observance of fundamentalism.

When I was finally done with all of my work, the guests asked if I'd like to join them in a cognac and a cigar on the aft deck. While most captains didn't promote fraternizing with the guests, my captain recognized that we had a cultural connection. So that is how I found myself drinking very expensive cognac and smoking a Cuban cigar at one of the most stunning anchorages in the French West Indies late into the night. Adding to this already amazing moment of bobbing at anchor, under a beautiful moon, after a long-ass workday, we began dipping crackers into crème fraiche and caviar, as if it were chips and salsa. By the time I stumbled off to bed, drunk and satiated, the captain just shook his head with a grin, sharing the moment. He said, "Nice work, Chef," as I crawled off to my bunk. Those guests left us the biggest tip I ever got in yachting, or in any other job I ever had — $5,000 each!

But after more than a year cruising the islands, this job was coming to an end. I'd now had decent experience on a busy private yacht and a busy charter yacht. My broken heart from Hillinary had finally healed. I had learned that even though my skin had been problematic at times, I could find ways to work around it. I'd learned that I was capable of working the long and difficult hours that were required of a yacht chef. I had chops. I could think on the fly, and adapt to changes in new and challenging situations, which is paramount to being a decent chef.

My spiritual practice, which had been so rigorous in prison, had taken a spot on the back burner of my consciousness. I still woke up early and meditated out on deck when we didn't have guests on board. And when we did, I found ways of practicing mindfulness in my everyday tasks. For instance, I used to play the Beatles's *Abbey Road* album every morning while I cut my fruit platter. That act in itself became a form of meditation. I took my time, made beautiful platters and cleared my head for the day, listening to a piece of music that I loved (and love) with all of my heart, and know note for note.

I was coming into my own as a yacht chef. The partying was more than I'd anticipated, but the workload kept it all in check. I was committed to the job, and managed a decent balance between work and play. I felt like I was ready to level up. Move to a bigger or more prestigious boat — or at least one that wasn't decorated like a bordello! It was time to move on and see a different part of the world. My culinary and cultural curiosity were piqued. I was ready to taste more flavors, swim in different waters, kiss different women and dance to a different beat.

Mallorca

Less than twenty-four hours later, I found myself in the first city of my European adventure: Barcelona … a city that I loved from the minute I entered. The food, the music, the street art, the buskers … it all felt magical to me. I lost my bank card on one of my first days there, and it took over two weeks to have a new one sent from the bank. I met some street performers in one of the plazas, and they took me under their wing. When they saw that I could play a little guitar, they worked me into their act and we began busking in front of the cafes together. We made just enough to buy hash and beer and maybe bread, cheese and Serrano ham. We would eat simply, smoke plentifully and play music together. These folks were modern gypsies, traveling together, and they knew all of the days that the museums were free, or cheap, so they took me on insider tours of the Picasso Museum, Salvador Dali's house and town, and a few others. We had a great couple of weeks together.

Campbell, my dear friend who'd sold me my Harley and had been there through thick and thin, had also come to Spain to look for a flamenco guitar. His love and understanding of that music was deep. It was the early days of internet and email, and we were able to connect using internet cafes. He had aged quite a bit since I'd last seen him. Coffee and cigarettes were taking a toll on him, though I don't think it bothered him one iota. We walked and talked, ate and drank, and relished the reconnection. Campbell was the type of friend where it didn't matter how much time had passed since we'd seen each other; it felt like no time at all. It was the first familiar face that I'd seen in about a year, and it felt amazing and comforting.

I then headed south through Andalusia, ending in Cádiz where a ferry took me into Morocco. A friend recommended that I head to the Rif Mountains in the far north, to the town of Chefchaouen, where they made the best-quality hash he'd ever seen.

Bon Appétit Meets High Times
Meets National Geographic

This was my first time stepping foot on the African continent, and it was a whole other animal. It's when I learned that it is not uncommon for an old woman to be riding a bus carrying a live chicken that is destined to meet a chopping block before the day is done. It's where I first saw entire families on one motorbike (though SE Asia holds the record for most people and things on one motorbike). I read my guidebook, and tried not to stand out too much, though as a six-foot red-haired white guy with a backpack and a guitar, that is easier said than done.

I walk down the boat ramp and onto the ferry dock. It is bustling with movement, and the smell of diesel and gasoline fumes is oppressive. But as I hit the bottom of the ramp, and enter into the ferry building, it is an entirely different story. My eyes are drawn to a giant skewer of meat over an electric broiler. A skilled cook deftly runs his knife on the sharpening steel before expertly slicing thin pieces of the seasoned lamb meat into his small wooden bowl. He then throws it onto a grill with some seasoned onions and heats a lavash all at the same time. The smell is intoxicating. I consider buying one of these delicacies, but I do not have any of the local currency yet, and I need to see what time my bus is leaving.

I walk a few steps farther and am taken by a small spice stall. There are piles of colored powders that I have never seen before. There were beautiful saffron powders of different grades and slight color variations, dried fruits, nuts, cumin, coriander, different curries and multicolored chili powders. It's a rainbow full of flavor that I cannot wait to dive into. But first … the bus. And some local currency!

Morocco is famous for its carpet salesman, and I promised myself I wouldn't end up in a carpet shop. I wasn't even past the ferry terminal when a guy from the "Ministry of Tourism" approached me. After asking me where I was going, he kindly told me that the bus would be there in about an hour, and they had a luggage room to store my bags … and would I like a cup of tea? Of course I wanted to have a cup of tea with the minister of tourism! That is until I realized that he wanted to drink this tea … in a CARPET SHOP!

We sat down, and were quickly presented with cups of mint tea, which they drink like water; so much so that they call it Berber whiskey. The smell of the tea cut the smell of wool, which tends to have a very gamey odor when carpets are piled into one spot. The smell is not unlike that of raw, grass-fed beef and silk has a rather odiferous taint as well. To demonstrate the quality of the carpets, the guys would hold a lighter to the carpet, to show you that the stitching was so tight that it wouldn't melt. So, on top of it all, there is a mild burning fabric smell. They showed me carpet after carpet. I tried to finish my tea and walk away, but they just kept refilling the cup and showing me more carpets. They were relentless in their tactics, but I somehow made it out of there without buying anything.

Once I was finally on the bus, I sat between a guy named Muhammed and an old lady with a chicken in her lap.

Muhammed, the name of every first-born Muslim man, was from Chefchaouen, which turned out to be a three-hour ride. He told me that he'd show me around. He also told me that his cousin ran the best hostel. I would soon learn that the term "cousin" was used loosely. The Medina (which is what Moroccans call their villages) was small and very tight knit. Once I was settled in, we had an excellent dinner of grilled lamb chops, couscous tajine, curried vegetables and grilled apricots with honey and vanilla ice cream for dessert. We ate, smoked Morocco's finest and drank mint tea, telling stories and asking questions.

The next morning, Muhammed was at the hostel when I awoke. "I'm headed up to my uncle's today, and I was wondering if you felt like making the hike with me? You can see the hash being made."

I quickly dressed, and we hit the trail. We hiked for about four miles, up into the canyon. Along the way, we passed multiple shepherds, and I could hear what sounded like drums beating. The smell of the cool river valley, mixed with woodsmoke and the aroma of food, permeated our nasal passages as we hiked along. Muhammed pointed out different ridgelines and spots of the valley as he explained the rich history of the Rif Mountains and the Berber people.

His uncle lived in a small stone cottage with chickens running around inside and out, and goats roaming a pen constructed just outside of the house. He and his wife looked very old, yet I can't help but wonder if they weren't really that old at all, but were just showing the signs of living a rugged mountain life? The old man took my hand warmly into his withered calloused hands and led me through the stone structure to the back area. One room was filled floor to ceiling with dry cannabis still on the stalk. They grow a very sticky strain of sativa there, but they don't sex their plants (only the male plants produce seeds), which makes for a very seedy, but resinous, product that is all turned into hash. At that time, the small village of 5,000 people produced a large percentage of the hash that made it into Europe and a large percentage of Africa as well.

The old man sat at his spot near the fire, and pulled an old wooden block closer to him. With a sharp rounded knife and a skilled hand, he finely chopped some hash that was on the tray and mixed it with a small amount of local tobacco that was also there. He loaded the sipa sipa, which is a long and skinny pipe, and we shared a pipe and drank mint tea. The piece of wood that he used had a big dip in it that indicated he'd been filing pipes with that thing for decades. Muhammed translated for us as his uncle didn't speak any English, but most of our communication was through "sign language," or unspoken. Some of the best travel moments transcend shared language.

He finally started the process of making the hash. On a tarp, he got a nice pile of the dried cannabis plants. He then pulled out a large plastic wash basin and showed me some very fine silk mesh. He placed two layers over the basin and pulled a bungee cord taut, all the way around the basin. This created a firm surface for the weed. He stripped the drying cannabis off the stalk and onto the tight silk. When he had a good pile of the seedy flower on silkscreen, he gently started agitating it with his hand. He was careful and methodical in the way that he handled the cannabis, being cautious to not press it too hard. Through some translation, and some sign language, he explained that this would bruise the crystals. Once he had worked all the herb with his hands, for maybe ten minutes, he stopped and removed the tarp and the silkscreens. He carefully scraped the resin out of the basin with a playing card, and set it on a piece of newspaper. Then he put the "drum" back together, this time with a tarp over the weed.

He was much rougher with it now, using sticks along with his hands. This was the "drumming" that I heard on the hike in. The entire mountainside had little houses just like this one, making tons of hash. He explained that the first pressing was what they kept for themselves and "special visitors" such as myself. With each round on the drum the quality became lower, as there were fewer cannabis crystals and more particulate matter in the hash product. At that point, he would throw the spent weed on the ground, and the chickens would go nuts for it. The old man pointed to the first batch and indicated that it was for me and him. It was called "00," named for the fine mesh silk material that he used to filter the hash crystals through. He then pointed to the second best, and said it was for the village and tourists in Marrakech, and pointed to the worst of the lot and cackled a big belly laugh as he said, "That's for England" (no offense, England).

This whole process took several hours. In that time, the old lady kept our pot of mint tea full, and the old man kept the sipa sipa full.

All day long, the old lady kept bringing us snacks. Mostly different kinds of flat breads with eggs and different curries with meats, chutneys and pickled vegetables on them. Whenever he was done making a batch of the hashish, he would throw the spent cannabis over to the roaming chickens, and they would hastily gobble it up. Presumably the same chickens that were providing us the eggs and tasty chicken tajines that we'd been snacking on all day. It was a perfect circle of life, culture and food. It was a pretty amazing experience and I felt like I'd been in *National Geographic, Gourmet Magazine* and *High Times* all at the same time. He split the big ball of the finest "00" grade and sold me half, while dropping the other half onto his chopping block. Muhammed and I hiked together back down to the village. Twenty years later, I can't help but wonder if Muhammed is now that old guy on the mountain, beating that drum, in the stony tradition that has been going on in that valley for thousands of years.

The following week was the Muslim holiday Eid al-Adha, when just about every family slaughters a goat or a sheep at the same time on the same day (for Allah) followed by a three-day festival of music and food. It's sort of akin to American Thanksgiving in that it is the busiest travel time of the year. The buses are filled with people and livestock every day for weeks surrounding the holiday. I went to meet the one bus that ran up and down the mountain every day, and every day it was impossible to get a ticket. Finally, I accepted my fate and settled into this quaint village, and decided to try and get invited into a home for the festivities.

That proved to be easier than I expected. Moroccans are very friendly people, and I soon had several offers. People were very excited to share their culture with me. On a Thursday morning at around 10:00 a.m., I walked down to the home of a friend of Muhammed. Every home in the Medina had its front door open, with sheets of plastic strategically placed to catch and divert the blood. At precisely 10:00 a.m., a prayer was uttered by all and the collective blade swiped across the jugulars of many animals in unison. The sound and stench of death were rampant in the air. The release of energy at the same time was palpable. Blood, life, death, prayer, reflection, work, food, community and celebration.

This ritual offering was followed by preparations for the celebrations throughout the community, as the men began to process the animals and the women began to prepare the fires of the local fruit wood for the tajines that would fill the ovens. Bones were roasted on the open fires in the streets, and the young women would shave the burnt fur off the animals' skulls before turning them into rich broths for couscous and stews. Little treats of fire-grilled offal begin to come out, with date chutneys and jams, on flatbreads. In the days to come, we ate every part of the animals that gave their lives, from the organ meats on day one to the loins and chops on day two, and onto the heartier shanks and braising cuts saved on the last day. The entire time, the hashish and mint tea never stopped flowing, and I felt very lucky to be included in this celebration.

Elegant Lady

It was getting closer to the summer yachting season, and I'd only been spending and not earning, so I made my way back to Palma de Mallorca to begin looking for work. I posted up at a great hostel called Hostal Apuntadores that had a lovely rooftop bar. It was here that I regrettably broke my lifelong "no tobacco" practice and started smoking spliffs, a mixture of cannabis and tobacco. I never liked tobacco, but it was *the way they consumed cannabis here*, and so I went with the flow. This began an addiction that would take me many years to break.

In Palma I finally grew to understand the appeal of House Music, and dancing in night clubs. I saw some world-class electronic music there, partied my ass off and boogied many a night away while I continued to "network" in the yachting industry. I was a long way from Grateful Dead land, still dancing, just to a different beat. Many of the clubs would close at 4:00 to 5:00 a.m., and for those nights when we didn't want the party to stop, there was a great after-hours club that opened at 6:00 a.m. and had great ambient house DJ's and sold a bottomless mimosa.

It took me just shy of a month to land a job on a boat called *Elegant Lady*, and she was beautiful. She was a 1927 classic, restored to her original condition (she now ran on diesel not steam, though she did still have some of the original steam controls for show and posterity). I did my first interview with the chief stewardess, a woman named Janis from Oregon, and the first officer, a tall, boisterous musician named Richard. The captain was out of town, so he left the first round of interviews to these two until he got back and could do the second round and make the final decision.

Captain Pat was an older English gentleman who'd been a submarine commander in the British Royal Navy for twenty-plus years before he began his yachting career, which he was twenty years into at this point. When he walked into the room, he had a certain air about him that commanded an immediate and justified respect. He was well-spoken, well-traveled and well-dressed. As we sat down to talk, he asked Janis to bring us both cups of tea. I would learn that tea was a big deal on this boat, and everything stopped at 10:00 a.m. and 3:00 p.m. until tea had been consumed. In another example of yachting misogyny, the stewardesses were expected to bring him a cup of tea every hour, on the hour. In spite of his patriarchal nature he was, by far, the fairest and most professional captain I ever had the pleasure of working for. He had been to New Orleans on a trip to the States, and had fallen in love with the food and the music. The fact that I had interned there was a feather in my cap, and the gumbo with blackened snapper and jambalaya that I made for my tryout helped me in securing the job.

The owners of the boat were British royalty, members of parliament, whom I referred to as Sir and Lady. The boat flew a British Royal flag, which I guess is a pretty big deal in the Med, and it carried a lot of respect.

Elegant Lady proved to be the busiest boat I ever worked on. Janis, the chief stew who had interviewed me, was an empath who may have been the closest thing to a hippie that I met in my entire stint on yachts. She was Rubenesque and had a natural inner beauty that shone through her eyes. She had an international sense of classiness, combined with a down home Eugene vibe. She was the kind of person that you immediately felt close to. Or at least, I did. It felt like she was from my tribe. She was a vegetarian, and I made a mental note that if I got the gig I was going to keep her well-fed. Crew members with special-needs diets can sometimes be the thorn in the side of a chef. I vowed to make that not be the case with her, because I liked her. Phoebe was her second stew, and was from a working-class family in the midlands of England. She had a master's degree in music and was incredibly sharp, if not snarky and eccentric. She would listen to my morning playing of *Abbey Road* and was always willing to discuss the intricacies of the "You Never Give Me Your Money" medley.

Both Phoebe and Janis hated the fact that women were treated poorly on yachts, and did their best to stick up for themselves. In a defiant act of rebellion, Phoebe used to make Captain Pat the worst cups of tea on purpose, so that eventually he began to just make his own. The rest of the crew were English, with the exception of the engineer, who was from Zimbabwe. I moved from the hostel on board, and began provisioning the boat immediately.

Due to the nature and the elegance of the boat, most of our guests were British aristocrats. We had sirs, admirals, lords and ladies, dukes and duchesses, counts and countesses, prime ministers, and celebrities. For a chef, working in Europe was amazing. The produce markets, the fish and meat markets, cheese markets, bakeries, and the cafes could always delight and surprise with their rich and varied offerings. And Captain Pat always insisted that no matter how busy I was in the morning, I should always take just five minutes to enjoy a coffee and a pastry. He especially "got" that I was an American chef in Europe for the first time, and he felt it was important for me to experience the intricate nuances of European culture. I really appreciated that about him.

As elegant as she was, *Elegant Lady* had inadequate crew quarters. The boat was old, and space was tight. Pat had talked the owners into letting the crew take over the bow (the pointy end) of the boat for our meals. This is unheard of in yachting. Usually the crew gets tucked away down below the deck. We had tables and chairs and an awning. We'd eat lunch and dinner together out on deck, weather permitting. In classic European fashion, Pat also believed that wine and beer were part of the meal, and while nobody was allowed to be drunk during the day, it was just fine to have a beer or a glass of wine with lunch. We did a boat show in Genoa, Italy, and the other crews drooled over our unique situation.

Another downside of such an old boat was some of the equipment. My freezer was in a bilge, so when I needed something, I'd have to go down to the former crew area, which involved climbing through a hatch and down a ladder, and lift two big panels up from the floor, which is where the freezer was. I'd then attach a pulley system to a beam in the ceiling, crack any ice that had formed on the edges, and hoist these three big baskets out of the bilge. (I kept a hammer and an ice pick in the top basket for this task.) The more food I had in each basket, the heavier it was. It never failed that after a long, crazy-hard day, I'd have showered and would be in bed when I'd remember that I had forgotten to pull something out of there, and would have to do that whole procedure in my underwear at 2:00 a.m.

I'd been working way too long without a day off. We constantly had back-to-back charters, the owners, friends and family to feed. Not only was this normally a busy boat, but Pat told us all at the beginning of the season that this would be the busiest season that the boat had seen in his twenty years on board.

We were dropping off a charter in Venice in the morning, picking up the bosses' son and his friends, and heading right back to Croatia, where we'd just been. I'd worked with Janis to create a massive order from our provisioner — around $25,000 in food and wine, as well as other items needed for the boat, including linens and some other supplies. The order took several days to put together, and I tossed and turned all night, unsure if I was going to be able to properly store everything that I had ordered. After dropping off the guests, we moved the boat to the dock to refuel and to load our order on board.

As we pulled up to the fuel dock, I went out to help the deck crew throw the lines and fenders. I felt a giant lump forming in my stomach as I looked to the dock. Janis and I looked at each other in shock. There were maybe 100 bags, boxes, coolers and buckets full of our items. Had we ordered too much? Where the hell was I going to put it all? We threw the lines, secured the boat and the boys went to work filling the many fuel tanks. Aside from this being our biggest food and booze order, this was also our biggest fuel intake of the season, and the smell of diesel lined my throat, which only added to my nagging, anxiety-driven headache. It brought me back to the tarmac and Con Air. This was a different kind of anxiety, to be sure ... but it was still extreme anxiety.

I prioritized the tasks at hand. I had to get the fridges emptied out from the last couple weeks of charter, and get all of this new food on board, stowed and secured. And in the process of doing that, I also had to prepare crew dinner and have a late-night dinner ready for the bosses' son, who was arriving with friends sometime after 10:00 p.m. ... and he was purported to be a big partier, which meant late nights. It's incredible how many small bits of leftovers, dressings, sauces, stocks, etc., end up in the fridges after a charter. Phoebe was the worst; she wanted to save every little bit, and hated throwing food away. The joke became, "Hey, Chef, shall I throw this away now or later?"

I hadn't finished emptying the fridges when Janis and Phoebe, with the help of the deckhands, began bringing the supplies on board. It was endless, and it reminded me of the scene from *Fantasia* where the brooms keep on multiplying. There was shit everywhere, and soon there was no room to put anything else down.

I was doing my best to keep up with it all, but truth be told I was buried. Everywhere I looked, there was something that needed to be put away, and so much of it was perishable: clams, mussels, oysters, live lobsters, poultry, cheese, cheese, cheese, produce, cases of Spanish wine, beer, champagne, liquor, mixers, flowers, paper products, pantry items, meats, dairy, sodas, juices ... the list went on and on.

I finally got the fridges to a point where I could begin loading them, but then I saw that somebody had put the box of iced-down clams and mussels on top of a case of heirloom lettuces, so now the lettuces were contaminated. That was the straw that broke this camel's back. I felt my bottom lip begin to quiver, and a tear roll down my cheek. Exhaustion and pent-up stress finally took over, and before I knew it I was sitting on the floor sobbing. It's amazing how a situation like this can make you question every bit of training and experience you've ever had. Suddenly I felt like I was in way over my head, that I'd probably ordered too much food and that I didn't have the skills or the patience to piece this puzzle together. I wept.

Janis walked in and surveyed the situation. She looked me, and said, "Oh, honey..." and came and sat next to me on the floor. She pulled my head to her shoulder and held me as I cried. I had never been this emotionally connected to a job before, and I felt like everything I had was riding on my success.

After a few minutes of this, she asked me to prioritize the tasks at hand. The problem was, it was all important. But the first things were to get this food put away. She went and asked Pat if we could order crew dinner in, which of course he agreed to. We were in Italy, and who doesn't love pizza? Once that was off my plate, I went to work putting things away in the order of their cost to the boat and importance to me. I threw away the contaminated lettuce, called the provisioner and had her bring me another flat. I made a lovely shellfish broth and rendered the fat out of some chorizo, so that when the guests arrived, I could quickly steam off some of the clams and mussels and serve it with one of the fresh, crusty loaves of bread that had just arrived. The culinary goal on a yacht is to burn through your most perishable items first, so it was natural to serve up that shellfish. I made a few nice sauces, and then went to work shucking oysters. I got all of my frozen goods together and went downstairs to fight with the freezer pulley system. I thought that system was so ingenious and cool when I started, but it turned into a royal pain in the ass.

As it happened, these guests were hard partiers, were late arriving to the boat and didn't even want dinner until well after midnight. This was a double-edged sword; I had more time to prep and get my galley in order, but it also meant a shorter night's sleep for me.

We cruised the Dalmatian Coast of Croatia, and back to Venice several times before making our way south to the Greek islands. Once again, I need to commend Captain Pat on his knowledge of that area. We did a lot of "stern to" anchorages. That's when Pat would drop the anchors and the deck crew would tie the stern of the yacht to trees or big rocks, for some of the most serene and private anchorages found anywhere in the Mediterranean. We would sit at these anchorages for a day or two, and wouldn't see another boat, or even another person. It was magical. It was during one of these anchorages that I developed a love for sea urchin, or uni. Two of our Italian charter guests would free-dive off the back of the boat and collect urchins, crack them open and wash them down with cold beer and a squeeze of lime, right there on the back deck. I'd had it before, but never like this, and I have loved uni ever since.

On September 11, 2001, we left Athens with no guests on board and we were heading for Turkey to pick up the owners. It was the early afternoon, and I was doing some work in the galley when Captain Pat called the whole crew to the bridge. We listened on the VHF radio about how America was "under siege." As the only Americans on board, Janis and I were floored by the news. It was such a shocking and helpless feeling to be both at sea and so far from home. Passing sea slips slowly by as we tried to listen through the static of the VHF and figure out what the hell was going on. This was before we had internet on the boat, when you still had to go to cafes and rent time on computers. It would be more than a week before I would see any pictures of the carnage.

As the news continued to unfold, it dawned on Captain Pat that we might want to rethink our next destination. We were a luxury yacht with a British flag, and predominantly British crew, but there were two Americans, and we had no idea what the international feelings were toward Brits and Americans at this moment. There were a lot of unknowns. Pat was able to call the owners of the boat on the satellite phone, and they decided it would probably be prudent to turn the boat around and head toward Rhodes (Southern Greece) to feel things out for a few days at least. The problem was that we had given up our slip, and other boats were returning to Rhodes as well. We could not get a slip. Pat held a crew meeting to report this news to us. "Without a slip," he said, "we have no other choice but to head down to Marmaris, Turkey. I understand if anyone doesn't feel safe and doesn't want to make the trip. As such, if you would like to stay here in Rhodes, the boat will pay for your ticket home." Nobody took him up on it, and it made us feel even closer, as a crew.

Upon arriving in Turkey, we finally saw pictures of 9/11 and caught up on the news. Seeing the devastation that had been done on American soil was shocking. What really took my breath away was the people that jumped from the second tower. Whatever was going on inside must have been truly horrible to justify such a decision. Nobody was sure how the world would change after the attacks, but it was evident that nothing would ever be the same. We grieved, and then went back to the task at hand: preparing for our next charter.

Turkey had new cuisines to explore, new ingredients to play with and a new currency to learn. This was the summer before the Euro kicked in, so seven countries meant seven currencies. I used to enjoy the accounting process with Pat because he was so sharp, and I've always enjoyed math in its practical applications. He referred to all of the coins as "shrapnel." We chartered all around the coastline and small islands. Shop/cook/clean/repeat.

If the illusion of the great money that we were earning hadn't been there, I never would have survived so many eighteen-hour days. What I mean by "illusion" is that the job is so difficult, and the work is so incredibly constant, that if you ever take the time to break it down by the hour, it's actually a pittance. I cannot tell you how many nights I had wicked insomnia, because I was either replaying that night's dinner service in my mind, looking for ways to improve or planning service or menus for the following day. I'd lay there, ruminating on things such as whether I'd pulled all the frozen doughs or proteins that I'd need from the freezer. I kept a pad of paper next to the bed because sometimes I'd wake in a panic from a dead sleep, realizing that I'd used the last of my baking powder and had not yet replaced it. And things like that are not always easy to find in other countries. One time, I tried to find corn starch, but none of the packaging was in English, so I bought every box with a corn husk on the label! I ended up with corn meal, masa harina, semolina flour and corn flakes ... but no corn starch. (I ended up bumming some from a chef on a neighboring yacht.) There is just no way to escape working on a yacht when you are deep in it. If you care about the job, and your food, work will permeate your every moment, asleep or awake.

Most of the charter guests were great people, though occasionally we'd get the odd douchebag. I remember one guy who really wanted to have a pig roasted on the beach over an open fire for his fortieth birthday. A pig roast, in Turkey ... a Muslim country! While we never say no, this was something we just couldn't do. He was pretty upset about it but grudgingly agreed to a lamb roast with fireworks instead. The crew set out to make this the best party ever. The deck crew and the stews went out early to the beach to make a lovely table. They set it up beautifully, with flower arrangements, shells, elaborate napkin folds with rings, finger bowls with lemon and washcloths. They lit tiki torches and brought in champagne buckets with ice. Meanwhile we had hired some locals to roast the lamb on the spit over an open fire, and to provide a fireworks show. I had made some caviar treats and mini lobster rolls as apps, and a couple of salads to accompany the lamb. The smell of meat and fire in the air is nothing short of delectable. Here we are on a small island in Turkey, nobody around, living on board one of the sexiest yachts in the Med, a half-moon hanging in the sky. It seemed like an idyllic setting for a birthday to me.

So the small boat arrives with the guests, and the birthday boy himself comes over, surveys the situation and asks the cooks if they can *move* the fire, and the lamb on the spit, about four feet over so the smoke would change directions. The Turkish cooks looked at us crew with pleading eyes. I nodded to Janis, and she took the guests down to the shoreline while the guys and I moved the table, the torches, and the chairs rather than the fire, giving him appearance that things were moved. He seemed to enjoy himself, though who could really tell?

If the lamb incident didn't tip the scales of douchebaggery to the nth degree, the following morning clinched it. Some fisherman came to the galley side of the yacht with their daily catch, and I bought a whole tuna, among a few other things, straight off their boat. Douche dude asked me if I could coat the fish in caviar. To me, this seemed like a ridiculous waste of one of the world's finest ingredients, but as I have repeatedly said, we try and honor all wishes. I made a court bouillon and poached the fish, and then peeled the skin off it while it was still hot. I then cooled the fish down and coated it in crème fraiche and caviar. It was actually better than I'd expected. He was our most difficult guest, and hands down the worst tipper of the season.

The days moved slowly, but the months flew by. While we were mostly a cohesive crew, we all had moments. Janis ended up hooking up with our deckhand, a sharp cockney boy from West London, who happened to be my roommate. This became problematic on nights that they wanted some private time, because it meant that I slept in the former crew mess or out on deck. I actually didn't mind sleeping on deck once in a while, but I wanted it to be at my leisure, not theirs. Everyone was burning the candle at both ends, and tensions were running high. Pat was sick of Phoebe's crappy cups of tea, and Phoebe was tired of the fact that she was wasting her music degree cleaning heads and making beds. Our deckhand and engineer had gotten into a huge blow-out for unknown reasons and it created for some tense crew meals. On our rare nights off, we no longer spent them together. Nobody wanted to drink with each other anymore. I began a pastime that became a favorite thing in new cities, which I called "Cocktail and Appetizer Tour." It's exactly what it sounds like; I'd go to three or four restaurants and have a couple drinks and a couple of apps at the bar at each one. I'd learn from the bartender where my next stop should be. Mostly, I was just happy to have a little time to myself.

My season had been pretty successful, though there were a few hiccups. Once I pulled some duck breasts out of the freezer and made a Vietnamese duck salad for lunch. The breasts had been frozen too long, and they held a lot of water, so rather than searing, they stewed as they released all the water. It turned out that these particular guests were chefs and restauranteurs, and they hated this lunch. I learned of this after my break, so I went over what I had on board and I set out to make the best meal that I possibly could. I crushed a five-course tasting menu that night.

They ended up being lovely guests, and while they were highly critical of my food, they were (mostly) kind about it and they pushed me to try my absolute hardest. The thing about being a private chef, and cooking for people for days, sometimes weeks, at a time, is that not everyone is going to like every meal. And it feels as if you're only as good as your last meal. But if you try your best to keep it fresh and exciting, and hold true to your vision, you should do all right. And it takes a long, long time to learn this, but it's actually okay if they don't love every meal; it's impossible to please every person every time. Everyone makes mistakes; it's how you bounce back from them that is important.

I also try and cook every meal as if Thomas Keller, Alice Waters or any of my other culinary heroes is at the table. It cranks up the pressure and removes any temptation to take short cuts that will compromise quality. My food philosophy had been consistent since I started in this game: Good ingredients make good food, and great ingredients make great food. This doesn't mean they need to be fancy; they just need to be fresh and in season. I cannot stress this one enough. Mix those great ingredients with solid technique and a sense of situational awareness, and your food should be great. Mine is, most of the time.

Our final charter of the season was in Malta, with the production company of filmmaker Guy Ritchie. The boat had been chartered to film a remake of the old movie *Swept Away*, which was to star Ritchie's then-wife Madonna. Aside from the fact that this was Madonna, this was a big deal, as his movie *Lock, Stock and Two Smoking Barrels* had come out not long before and was predictably a favorite among our predominantly British crew.

I was still making crew food, but now I was also providing snacks for the film crew. I also made all the food that was shown in that film, including a bowl of pasta that gets dumped on Madonna's head. I thought the movie was terrible, but go ahead, watch it and think of me during that scene. At the end of the filming, and the charter, we had a great night with the entire cast and crew drinking and dancing in Malta. Madonna was there for the beginning of the night, but as soon as she got recognized, she retreated back to the hotel. The rest of us partied like it was 1999, dancing and drinking until the wee hours.

Even though the crew was utterly exhausted, and pretty much at wits end, Pat seemed to know how to lighten the mood at just the right time. On the passage between Malta and Spain, on a particularly nice afternoon, he invited the whole crew to jump in the ocean for a random swim while he put the engines in neutral for our safety. We were in about 6,000 feet of water, with no land or other boats for as far as the eye could see. We all jumped from the top deck into the water and blew off a little steam. It came at just the right time and gave us all the slight lift that we needed for this final leg.

Seven months almost to the day from when we departed, we pulled back into Palma Harbor. I had never worked so hard, or been so completely exhausted. But I had done it. I rocked a busy charter season on a highly respected charter boat. I consistently cooked at the highest levels I ever had, and we had mostly great reviews on the food.

When I left *Elegant Lady*, I did what any self-respecting yachty does after a busy season. I partied my ass off. I hung out in Palma, hitting all my old haunts for about a week, and then took off for Ibiza for a massive weekend with a couple of friends. All I can remember of that weekend is it seemed to go from dinner to sunrise in a matter of moments, and every sunrise was a dance party on the beach. It was amazing.

After a week spent with friends in Amsterdam, I made the long journey back to Los Angeles, and spent the holidays with family. It was the first time that I'd seen them all in over a year. Uncle Mickey had passed while I was in Europe, and these were the first holidays without him. He was the patriarch in our family. A leading scientist for NASA's Jet Propulsion Laboratory, he pioneered, created and led their solar energy department. He was this big brilliant, sweet teddy bear of a man who grasped everything life had to offer with both hands. He could explain a complex scientific concept and enjoy a bowl of chocolate ice cream with the same sense of childlike enthusiasm. He made a point of connecting with me when Mom died, as his dad had died when he was a young boy as well. He'd been told that his father was just "away on business," so he spent a large portion of his young life looking for his father in crowds. It was important to him that I was told the truth when Mom died. His absence left a tangible hole in our family. I feel his loss viscerally to this day.

A lot had happened in just a few short years. I felt like I'd accomplished a lot since I left California to go work on yachts, as a professional and as a man. I tried to share some of my adventures with my brothers, but my lifestyle was completely foreign to all three of them. So we did what we do best as brothers, which is to hang out and drink together, listening to classic rock and relishing in the same old stories that we always managed to find some laughs in. I'm not sure if it's the big age gap between us or what, but I've always felt that they're a pod of three, and I was like the pea that fell out of the pod or grew outside it or something. An asterisk on a pre-established paragraph. An afterthought, or a coda (in music). This was, and continues to be, hard on me. It has always been important to me that they be proud of me, yet I've rarely felt that they were. With age and therapy, I have adopted the moniker that what other people think of me is none of my business. It's helped me tremendously.

It had been over a year since I'd seen Cassidy, and so I planned a trip to see him in Colorado. The visits were always a challenge. His mama probably would have preferred if I didn't visit at all. She made our time together very difficult by not letting him come hang out with me until all of his homework and chores were done, and not allowing him to skip any school during my visits. This would leave us very little time in the evenings to spend time together, but these were the rules that she had laid down, and I had to play by them or risk losing my visiting rights. One might think that she did this to instill structure and discipline, and to not "rock the boat" that made up their normal lives. From my point of view, the reason that she did this was to make the visits so challenging that eventually I'd just stop coming. That didn't work. I kept coming back.

I had researched an actual custody battle for him to spend part of his time with me, but I knew that it would get ugly between his mother and me, and neither of us had the money to spend on lawyers. So I followed her rules and did my best to stay connected with phone calls, letters and these awkward visits. We went camping together, visited hot springs and local, state and national parks, went on hikes, and played guitar together. I made it out there once or twice a year. My bust cost us the closeness that we had when he was a kid, but I've always done my best to let him know that I am there, a part of his family forever.

The woman I knew the least and loved the most: my mother.
She went back to college and got her bachelor's degree after the
divorce. She was working on her master's when she was
diagnosed, and she died soon after her diagnosis.

Two short years after my mother's death, and about two short
years before drugs and shenanigans ensued.

Fifth grade, the year I was bussed to the inner city
and I REALLY got my ass kicked.

Campbell, Cassidy and me in the Chatsworth hills shortly after Cass was born.

From the babies raising babies files.

Doing time in Springfield, MO.

Doing time in Colorado.

Free at last. That motorcycle trip up the coast of CA
is something that I will never forget.

Not everything I learned in culinary school was useful.
The fruit basket in this picture is the one and only time
that I have ever pulled sugar.

Elegant Lady, moored somewhere in Croatia.

Buying swordfish from a local fisherman in Malta.

Me and Cassidy once he grew up.

Chef Evan Presents.

Southeast Asia

After seeing family, I was uncertain about what to do. I had a good amount of savings from my marathon season on *Elegant Lady*, but my psoriasis was not doing well. I decided that I was ready for some beach time, and to increase my scuba certification. I also wanted to try a mostly gluten-free and dairy-free lifestyle for my psoriatic arthritis, which is basically a Thai diet, so I left for Southeast Asia.

Your first time in Asia is an experience that one never forgets. Even though I didn't get out of the Bangkok airport until after midnight, it didn't matter. Bangkok is a city that doesn't sleep. When one market is closing, another is opening. The streets are alive with the three-wheeled buggies called tuk-tuks that rule the roads, and the buzz is infectious. The best food in Bangkok is eaten on colored plastic stools in alleyways, with chickens and cats waiting in the wings to munch on your leftovers. The smell of fish sauce and diesel fumes permeate the air, as does garlic, grilling meats, the pungent stench of tamarind and oily noodles jumping out of woks. All this cooked lovingly with recipes and traditions that have been passed down for generations. I had a pad thai noodle plate in an alley on that first trip ... and when I returned seventeen years later, that same woman was tossing noodles exactly where I had left her all those years prior.

Pad thai is different everywhere, yet oddly the same. A hot wok, with a splash of oil. Once the oil is hot, she reaches into a bucket with noodles soaking in water. She throws a handful into the wok, which spits grease as the wet noodles hit the pan. She tosses the noodles a couple of times, and then tosses a small handful of garlic, dried shrimp, a shallot and two to three chilies into the mortar and pestle at her side. She crushes it with a few strokes of the heavy pestle and throws it into the pan, expertly shaking it as she goes. She opens the cooler to her side, takes a small spoonful of chopped chicken thighs and two prawns, and throws them into the wok. Without missing a beat, she shakes the pan to incorporate the proteins. There are several squeeze bottles on her food cart, and I'm pretty sure they are tamarind concentrate, fish sauce and catsup. She gives a squeeze of each and throws in a tablespoon of palm sugar, as she swirls the pan. She then grabs two eggs and cracks them into a small bowl, adds a splash each of fish sauce and soy sauce. She quickly mixes the eggs with a fork, while her other hand makes a "hole" in the noodles with her spatula. She scrambles the eggs into the clear area of pan, and once the proteins coagulate she stirs the eggs into the noodles. To finish she squeezes two lime halves and adds a final squirt of fish sauce. She piles on some bean sprouts, peanuts and a few cilantro leaves and then hands the plate to me, as I hand her the equivalent of a dollar, with a generous tip included. Always steal with your eyes. It is the best way to learn the local tricks. Thailand changed my cooking style forever. It gave me a true understanding of sweet, salty, spicy, sour and bitter, and once you can balance those, the sky is the limit.

Every food cart, every shop, every tuk-tuk, every taxi, has a small shrine honoring the Buddha and the king. Every morning, as the food stalls are setting up, the monks come and collect alms. People take pride and joy in feeding the ones that are doing the deep spiritual work. The belief is that with the intensity of the monks' worship, the society is better off, so it benefits them to feed the monks. I'd learn later that the same practice happens in India, and to an even greater extent. The people who might be considered religious zealots are revered as valuable members of society there. Thai people take stock in the importance of spirituality, and reward those who follow a spiritual path for their efforts. It is so different than our Western ways.

On Koh Tao, a Thai island, I alternated between scuba days and hammock days for several weeks, until I was really beginning to "feel" the Thailand experience. On the islands, there is the omnipresent sensation of garlic and chilis simmering, fish frying, fruit rotting, gasoline burning, mosquito coils and citronella candles, sunscreen, coconut, trash fires, things fermenting, and acrid humid sweat. Once I'd advanced my scuba certification, read a couple of books, played endless hours of guitar on the beach and smoked countless joints of cheap and seedy Thai weed, I went on to explore some of the other islands. I fell in love with a small one on the southwestern coast, where they harvest cashews and there's no electricity, only generators (mostly used for blended drinks and a few internet cafes), and no cars, just motorbikes and bicycles. It's a wonderful little spot that shall remain nameless to preserve its integrity, and I've been back there several times over the years.

I took a two-day train ride to the north country, Chiang Mai, and the moment that I disembarked I could feel the differences from the south. The air was clean and fresh, and it was clear that we'd left the sticky humidity behind. The clothes were woven and embroidered, as opposed to the loose, cotton wraparound garments that were seen farther south. The night markets smelled different, maybe in part because there was no fresh fish there, and there was a huge variety of different spices and ingredients. The one thing that doesn't change anywhere in the country is the famous Thai smile, and the genuine kindness of the people you meet. It truly is the "land of smiles."

I hired a motorbike and went about exploring. It was scallion harvesting season, and everywhere I went there were ox-drawn carts pulling mountains of the green onions. The afternoon air was thick with the rich smells of fresh onions — if you had an allium allergy, you'd have been miserable.

One night in Chiang Mai, walking to the night market from my hostel, I saw a family sitting in front of their home, eating som tam (green papaya salad), chicken curry and sticky rice, drinking whiskey and playing with a beat up old guitar. I smiled and waved as I walked by and they also greeted me and offered me a plastic stool. I politely declined and went on to the market, walked around, but when I walked by a while later, they were still there. They still had a lovely little spread of food, and they insisted I join them. I ran across the street, bought some beers and came back. I should also mention they didn't speak a word of English, and I knew maybe thirty words in Thai. But we ate, drank, played music and laughed together for hours. Communication without words is some of the best.

I took several cooking classes on this trip, though I always felt like the greatest cooking lessons I received in Thai cooking were tricks I could steal with my eyes. At every market, every food stall, every restaurant, my eyes were glued to the cooks, how they set up their stations, how they handled the food, at what point they added ingredients and why they added ingredients when they did. It wasn't always easy, with the language barrier, but it was always fun, and the food was ALWAYS delicious.

On Tour

In autumn 2003, I had never heard of the pop star John Mayer, but I was about to find out about him in a big way. When I finally went back to Lauderdale, I got a call from a company called Deja Catering asking if I wanted to go out on the road cooking for this John Mayer (I thought they meant John Mayall!). Deja specialized in rock 'n' roll tour catering, and they wanted me and three others to cater this tour for the band and road crew, about forty people. Every city on the tour would provide us with a runner that knew the area well, and two helpers who were there mostly to do dishes. Our rolling kitchen came off the same trucks that the equipment for the show traveled in. The tour was in the northeast and Canada, so it would be cold, but it was an exciting new opportunity, and I wanted to get my foot in the door for this rock 'n' roll catering thing, so I took the gig.

I arrived in State College, Pennsylvania, checked into my hotel, and went to the bar to meet my crew. First and foremost I wanted to meet my co-chef, Danielle. She was tall and scrappy and smoked Camel Filters like they were free and good for you. She was a very organized chef, and we seemed to get along well. Like me, she pulled no punches and did not do much to hold her tongue, in praise or in critique. She had been cooking on the rock 'n' roll circuit for several years, and catered for years before that. She was a seasoned veteran of the road. What she lacked in fine-dining skills, she made up in production and organizational skills. She was also great at managing our helpers, assessing their skill level and task loading them accordingly. We assumed the role of co-chefs, splitting responsibilities pretty much down the middle. We each had lots to bring to the table, and neither of our egos got in the way of learning new things as well as sharing older tricks of the trade. We collaborated well together on menus, and would split the tasks accordingly and then help each other out of the weeds when one of us would find ourselves there.

As with yachts, every day was a marathon that began at dawn and ended late night or in the early mornings. We'd wake up in a new city every day. Usually, I would find the two helpers that had been assigned to us and wait for the gear to roll off the trucks, while Danielle did the first shop. Our kitchen included about a dozen rolling cases that took up half a semitruck. The cases popped open to reveal big drawers with anything that a good chef might want, from a microplane to a stand mixer and a convection oven. Our equipment was top notch, and we could be set up and fully functioning in twenty minutes. The tricky part was never knowing where we were going to be setting up. Every venue was different. Sometimes they give you a mop closet somewhere near the dumpsters to cook in, and sometimes you're alongside the stage. There may or may not be running water close by. It's a crapshoot, which added a lot of challenge and mystery to the gig. Aside from cooking for the crew and band, it was our responsibility to order late-night food for the buses from a local joint, usually referred to us by our runner, who was from the area. We traveled between cities during the night, so we'd try and provide brisket in Texas, pizza in Chicago, cheesesteaks in Philly, etc. I called it "farm-to-takeout style" of local eating.

While the food wasn't as fancy as it was on yachts, we were still held to a high standard. Deja is famous for having kickass organic food and a great coffee cart. They knew that coffee is the true fuel of rock 'n' roll, and treated the sacred bean with the respect it deserves. The cart was always stocked with different coffee options, from light to extra-dark roast, all of the alternative milks as well as the traditional ones and real and alternative sugars. We had a top-of-the-line espresso machine as well as a pour-over setup, and every kind of tea that you can dream of. As soon as breakfast was done, we'd get signed off by the fire marshal (on a good day, at least) and move into lunch production.

Every venue has different unions, and different union rules, but timeliness is the one rule that is consistent across the board. You cannot be late with mealtimes for a union crew or you face really steep fines. Even if we're not feeding the union guys, their mealtimes had to coincide with our crew's mealtimes or, again, steep fines.

When they played Madison Square Garden, I got myself into a pickle. We'd planned a big and special menu for these shows, because it was NYC and because Mayer was from that area. We had a huge guest list, including his parents, and these shows were a big deal. We agreed to do pulled pork for lunch, and then a crazy elaborate seafood and prime-rib buffet for dinner.

For some reason, we couldn't get the pork butts until late the night before, so they weren't going to be seared off. They had strict rules about not creating too much smoke backstage at The Garden, so our plan was to oven sear them in a 500-degree oven, cover them in hot BBQ sauce and cook them down to the point of being able to pull it all apart. Danielle was a veteran of this venue, and on her way out for the morning shop she said, "I'll be back asap … whatever you do, don't be late, not even one minute. Also, don't smoke the place up. Technically we are not supposed to be really cooking back here … but we have a good relationship with the local authorities. Don't fuck it up." I got breakfast out a few minutes early, and then got to work on lunch. The priority was getting those pork butts cooking, asap.

The problem came when the electrician was late to hook up my oven (which had to happen every day). I waited and waited, and even asked the stage manager to hunt down the electrician, but he could not be found. I anxiously watched the clock as we put out breakfast. Those pork butts were seasoned and ready to go, but I had no oven. I knew that they needed a solid three hours in the oven, and another thirty minutes (at least) to cool and pull them in sticky BBQ sauce that I'd already made. Weighing the options of being late and pissing off the unions and road crew, or searing the meat off in pans on our butane-burner stovetops instead and potentially pissing off the fire marshal … I lit six burners and got six pans smoking hot. I added the seasoned meat to the hot pans and, sure enough, the backstage area filled up with meat smoke. If you've ever been in a non-ventilated area with lots of meat searing, then you know the visceral reaction that comes with the smoke. It smells good, because meat and heat usually do. But the acrid scent of meat smoke filling the air, the garlic beginning to brown and the sugar from the marinade starting to caramelize was becoming pervasive. The pans sizzled and spattered as the Maillard reaction of meat browning was happening. I knew I was going to be in the shits, but I also knew that the meat had to cook; the show must go on.

"What the hell are you doing?!?" the fire marshal yelled at me. "Your permit clearly calls for 'light cooking' only. This does not look like light cooking to me. I'm pulling the indoor food preparation portion of this permit!"

"Please, it's not my fault," I pleaded. "The electrician was late hooking my ovens up!" It was just at this moment that Danielle walked in, arms heavy with groceries. She surveyed the situation and, with an amused smirk on her face, donned her apron. Once the oven was hooked up, we got the meat in and, incredibly, they did not make us move outside. Our food was out on time.

The next night, however, they made us cook on the loading dock next to the dumpsters under an easy-up off 42nd Street. I had a phone conference with my boss at the main office late that night, and fortunately she backed me up. The food must go out on time, and hot, she agreed. That is the top priority. Every good chef knows that. Everything else comes second, including permits and fire marshals.

Lunch always had three salads, two proteins, a veg option and a selection of sandwich makings. We would get the helpers on cleaning breakfast dishes and then assisting with making the lunch meat platters, etc.

Usually between lunch and dinner, Danielle and I would work on a menu for the following day. The runner would get anything that needed to be processed, or marinated overnight, and we'd get our order in with our production team for breakfast items to be waiting in the next city. Then we'd get our dinner buffet up. The band would sound check at around five, and eat right after that, so our buffet would get hit hard from five thirty to six thirty. No matter how hard we'd try to anticipate and plan for curve balls, an hour to feed forty people in a makeshift kitchen is always going to present challenges. Just getting forty people through a buffet line in sixty minutes can be hard. It allows ninety seconds per person, and leaves little margin for error.

At that point in the night, we'd light a fire under the dishwashers' asses to get everything cleaned so we could get all the equipment back in the road cases and packed out. Fitting all the hotel pans back into their road cases was like a game of Tetris; everything had to be packed in a certain way, or you had to empty the case and begin the loading again. We'd break down the kitchen when the concert was starting and, with a little luck, midway through we'd be done. Then we'd go to the buses to gather up our shower gear and seek out a shower.

Most people don't know this, but there are showers all over the bottom of pretty much every venue such as MSG, Boston Garden, etc. It's a crapshoot whether you can find a good one though. Sometimes, they are in plush backstage dressing rooms, and sometimes they're more like locker rooms; with a little luck, the water is hot. By the time the show was over, we'd be cleaned up and waiting near the buses for the lighting guys, who were always the last ones on the bus (and first ones off, I might add). We'd have a couple of beers, and wind down while processing the events of the day, either bitching about or praising the current helpers. We'd finalize tomorrow's prep and shopping lists as the bus rolled down the road to our next city. It was surreal. Every venue looked the same, yet every one was different.

It's a lifestyle, not unlike yachting. Rock tours run on tight schedules, and setting up and tearing down a kitchen every day is challenging. There's a lack of continuity in the ingredients, and the environment is constantly changing, forcing you to adapt quickly. The cooking world has always been populated by pirates, misfits and miscreants. I think it was easy for this ex-con to get lost in the mix, and then to build a strong enough reputation that my record was overlooked.

Our tour went from early October through mid-December. We worked long hours and lived in tight quarters. The bus had twelve bunks, which eight of us shared. The other four were "junk bunks" for extra bags. There was a lounge in front and one in back, with the bunks in the center section. The unspoken rule was the back lounge was the party lounge, and the front was for snacks and TV. And if you fell asleep anywhere other than your bunk, or with your shoes still on, you became material for drunken Sharpie art.

Even given the tight quarters, rock 'n' roll is a lot more spacious and forgiving than yachting. There are wider margins for error as well as for success. With the exception of my immediate crew, it was much easier to create a little distance and have some autonomy. It was easier to take a walk, though sometimes that walk was into a crowded stadium, which is the last place you want to be when you need a break from work.

On Thanksgiving we had no show, so the management rented out a nice restaurant with an open bar for the band and the crew and we had a great dinner together. A common chef's refrain is, "My favorite food is food that somebody else made for me." They also put us up at the Four Seasons, Chicago. Along with my salary, I was given a nice daily per diem, which I almost never spent as I worked so closely with all the food. I'd save mine up and spend it on room service and delivery food on our days off. I had always grown up with the idea that such things were overpriced and a waste of money. While it is true that they are overpriced, there's something incredibly satisfying about ordering room service and lying in bed all day watching movies, after working forty-five-plus hours in just three days.

Freelance Isn't Really Free

I began taking on freelance gigs. These come about when a boat needs a crew member "on the fly." They are usually lucrative, as they pay on a daily rate, and the great thing about them is that they are finite. There is always an end in sight, which means less opportunity for drama.

Once, I was flying to the Bahamas to meet a boat for a charter. I'd bought a bunch of food and packed it in boxes. But when I got to the airport, the small airline wouldn't let me fly with boxes. After a short and panicked discussion, I learned that duffle bags would be fine. So I ran to the gift shop, bought some duffels, transferred all of the food out of the boxes and into the bags, and ran back to the counter … but now they wouldn't let me check my luggage and board because the plane was taking off in forty-three minutes — and they had a strict forty-five-minute check-in policy. I was furious with the gate agent, who could have told me this while he was denying my boxes, but in a post-9/11 world, being an angry man at the airport is a terrible look. So I took a few deep breaths, arranged for a hotel room, iced down the perishables in the bathtub and flew in the morning.

Another memorable freelance gig was on a boat called *My Sharona*. This is when I learned to never work on a boat named after the owner's spouse. Every chef I knew in the industry had done a stint on this boat, and either quit or got fired. But I needed the work, and I've always had a theory about those notoriously difficult clients that maybe they just haven't had a good fit yet? Maybe my food and vibe is exactly what they are looking for.

They flew me to St. Maarten, where I joined the boat. The captain introduced himself, and he showed me my cabin and the galley. I should have known what a shit show it was going to be when he handed me a stack of medium uniforms, when I'm clearly an XL, and told me that he was sure I could "make it work" for a few days.

I'd heard that the owners liked having a lot of food choices, so I shopped heavily. Then I set out trying to make sense of the galley, which was a wreck. It looked like the last chef had walked out mid-meal, and nobody had bothered to clean up since. There was even a moldy roast still in the oven (veal or pork?)! The fridges were a nightmare, with little bits from previous chefs. There were half-filled squeeze bottles with random, unlabeled sauces. There were rotting vegetables in the veggie drawers, and packages of moldy lunch meats. There were unidentifiable things in Tupperware and I just threw those away without even trying to ascertain what they were. There was a whole lobe of what appeared to be foie gras, but covered in a fuzzy slimy substance. There was a gallon of mayonnaise with little chunks of who knows what on the top (who uses that much mayo on a yacht anyway?!?). The galley looked like it had been abused by chef after freelance chef (read as IDGAF). There were six bottles of cinnamon on one shelf and random things stuffed into cupboards in no order at all. My motto in a situation like this is, when in doubt, throw it out. I worked late into the night to get the galley clean enough to just put my groceries away. I'm sure I wasn't the first chef to have thrown away what amounted to hundreds, if not thousands, of dollars in waste.

The following day, I got to work early. We were on the French side of St. Maarten, so the food shopping was top quality. I didn't have guest breakfast to worry about, as they weren't due on board until noon. I set out preparing every protein I had for a quick fire. I broke down rabbits, carefully removing the tenderloin, fileted fish, tied off steaks, cleaned shellfish and made chicken and shellfish stock. I prepared enough food to run lunch service in a small bistro.

When the owners came on board, they went straight to the top deck and started smoking fat joints of really stinky weed. He was fifty-ish, she was about half his age with lots of plastic surgery and Botox. The stewardess was freelance as well, and didn't know the owners either. She was a bit intimidated to approach them. I wasn't sure if I should approach them myself about lunch. Only the captain was a full-time crew member, and he made it clear that the owners were notoriously difficult, and to just do the best we could.

Finally, I went upstairs and announced, "Hi, I'm Evan, your freelance chef for this trip. Very pleased to meet you both." She glared at me through her Prada glasses. After a long, awkward silence, she said, "What do we have for lunch?" I felt a wave of relief. This was something I could do well, and I had a lot of options. "I have snapper, grouper, lobsters, shrimp and mahi mahi, and I can prepare any of it however you'd like. I've made several salad dressings so you could have any protein over a Caesar, a vinaigrette, or whatever. I've formed some nice burger patties, made pizza dough and fresh pasta. I have caviar, assorted cheese and charcuterie, I could make a nice snack platter. Or a dry-aged rib eye. What are you in the mood for?"

She took a massive toke off the joint. "We'll have the tuna," she coughs, speaking and exhaling at the same time.

Shit. "I'm sorry, that's the one fish the market didn't have. But the mahi mahi is looking really fresh."

"Call Franco's on the other side of the island and get six orders of their tuna tataki. It's simply divine. Tell them it's for us; they adore us there." She put her lips together in a pouty kiss sort of way and walked back to her husband, who was reading a magazine this whole time.

I wandered off the boat to find a taxi and get their tuna. As I've said, dear reader, "no" is never a viable answer, not even for douchebags.

In the next few days, this couple did everything that you can imagine evil people doing to a chef. They had me prepare a big menu for several people, and then ordered twelve pizzas to be delivered ten minutes before service. They put dinner off for several hours, while they picked at the pizza and smoked weed. The next night they told me they were having eight guests for dinner, and then at the last minute, decided to go out instead. Another time they told me they were going out for dinner and later changed their minds, asking for a five-course dinner in "about an hour."

And they smoked dank weed. Constantly. I mean fat joint after fat joint. It was a lot, even by my standards. The only saving grace was they left half joints everywhere, and the captain took pity on my plight. He knew I was miserable, as every other chef had been. He brought me roaches, and I'm sure kept few for himself. But he still busted my balls about not wearing the uniform that didn't fit (I wore my nice chef's coat). Even after I left, my friend Beverly (who had placed me on the boat) asked me why I'd "refused to wear a uniform." She laughed when I explained the situation. The beauty of a freelance gig is that it never lasts long.

The next whacky gig was on a boat I'll call the *Substandard*. The captain was an old Greek guy, and rumor had it that he was actually a ferry boat captain before he got into yachting. Anyway, I joined the boat in West Palm Beach, and shopped for a full day getting the galley ready for a long weekend to the Bahamas. I was getting pretty familiar with that Bahama run and it was always beautiful.

The captain's name was Spiro, and he lived in West Palm Beach with his wife. The plan was the guests were going to come on board in the late afternoon. We'd spend the night at the dock and leave early for the Bahamas.

We lined up on the dock to greet our guests. There were two couples, and they all staggered out of a van with drinks in their hands in a manner befitting either Hunter Thompson or Jeff Spicoli. One of the men was wearing a shirt that said, "You call me a crack whore like it's a bad thing." While they took to the top deck to continue working on their buzz, I went down to the galley, sent out some canapés and continued making dinner, though I wasn't sure they were going to eat it. They looked pretty jacked up, and cocaine is a notorious appetite suppressant.

At some point, the primary charter guest pulled the captain aside and told him, as we weren't leaving the dock until the morning, that he could go home and be with his wife. Captain Spiro insisted that he was happy to stay and keep an eye on things, but the guest was insistent that he leave. So insistent, in fact, that he slapped $1,000 in his hands and told him to take his wife out for dinner. Captain reluctantly agreed to go home for the night, and as soon as he was off the boat and down the dock, the guests gathered us four crew members and told us that the reason they wanted the captain gone was they wanted to party freely, without a "parental figure" on board. They told us that we were welcome and encouraged to party with them, as long as their drink glasses were never empty and the ashtrays were never full. The deckhand wasn't much of a party guy, which was probably a good thing as there really needed to be at least one "adult" in the room. But the two stews and I were keen as could be. We drank champagne and partied with those people till the wee hours. We lived up to our end of the deal, keeping the drinks flowing and the mess at bay, and even managed to feed them a few snacks as the night went on, carefully dancing the fine line between partying and tending to them at the same time. The next morning, Spiro came back and we set sail for the Bahamas. The guests slept the day away, and us crew members that had been up most of the night powered through a pretty rough day at work. We made it to the gate of Atlantis Marina and Resort, when Spiro called the marina, only to find out they had no slips available. He hadn't reserved a slip at one of the most popular marinas in the world!

Nassau Bahamas, where we were, sits right next to New Providence Island, and there's a channel between the two islands that many boats pass through. Now I'm no captain, but when Spiro said he was going to drop the anchor so he could try and figure out a plan, I intuitively knew it was a bad idea. I'd never seen a boat anchored in that channel, and I'd been through there maybe twenty times.

Sure enough, the anchor was barely out when it got tangled in some giant hurricane chains they drape across the channel to catch wayward boats getting blown through in heavy storms. The port authority came out to assess our plight, and the charter guests climbed out of bed to see what all the fuss was about. The port authority sent some divers, who were unable to untangle the mess underwater. The only choice was to drop our anchor and chain completely, which would have rendered the boat inoperable, and the charter would be canceled until a new anchor and chain could be secured.

Then a miraculous thing happened. Spiro had been moving the boat back and forth about ten to twenty feet and somehow the anchor just wiggled loose. He was then able to get us a slip at Hurricane Hole Marina, next door to Atlantis. G-d really does look after the fools and children.

The charter was off to a rough start, and I'm sorry to say that it didn't get any better. We motored down in the Exumas, at a beautiful anchorage, and Spiro was transferring fuel from one tank to another with the help of the deckhand. But the decky didn't have much experience, and a mistake with a shutoff valve caused hundreds of gallons of diesel fuel to spill into the water. The coast guard was on us in no time, and Spiro received a ticket that would ultimately cost the boat $10,000. We just kept on with the charter as if nothing had gone wrong … even though the writing of a "total shit show" was all over the walls.

The following morning we were moving the boat over to the Blue Hole, which is an epic snorkel spot, made famous in the James Bond movie *Thunderball*. I was in the midst of plating up breakfast, and I had everything on the counter for the plate-up, when the boat screeched to a halt and several of my plates slid off the counter and crashed onto the floor.

That fucker of a captain had run us aground on the reef! He was, hands down, the worst captain I ever worked for. We had to wait for the tide to rise before a tugboat could push us off … and the boat received another fat ticket from the Bahamian coast guard for causing harm to the reef. The guests stood on the deck applauding and ridiculing the captain, who was blaming the poor deckhand for both the fuel spill and running us aground.

There was damage to the stabilizers, so we had no other choice than to limp the boat back to Nassau … where we still didn't have a slip at Atlantis. We made it back to the Hurricane Hole Marina. The next morning, the primary charter guest came around to each crew member and gave us each an envelope full of cash. They wanted to make sure the captain didn't see a dime of the tip. Usually, no matter how the guests pass out tips, they're always split evenly, because not every crew member is seen as much as others. (An example of this would be an engineer who is never seen, but stays up all night working on the air conditioner, as opposed to a stewardess that the guests see every day.) But we all agreed to keep these tips, and to keep quiet about them. After the guests disembarked, the captain told us the boat would need to be repaired before he took it back to Florida, so he was going to pay us for our time and buy our flights back home. None of us could get off that sinking ship fast enough.

A few weeks later, I got another freelance gig, this time on Harbour Island. This is a pretty famous movie star island known for having pink, white and black sand beaches. There were no cars, but everyone drove around in golf carts, which would get really fun on a busy night.

I was just getting acquainted with the crew when a strange set of occurrences transpired that almost never happen in yachting. First the owners had to cancel for a family emergency. Since they had a charter booked for the following week, the captain kept me on, so I basically cooked for the crew and then adventured and partied with them. But then, the charter guests had to cancel too! All of a sudden, we had a few more days of crazy stupid fun together. Yachting was really the best, and the worst, of times for me. This was one of the sweet ones. We worked for a few hours each day, and then used all of the toys. We went scuba diving, wakeboarding and a couple of times we just took the tender to a quiet beach for beers and snacks at sunset. And then we'd party in the bars at night.

We had one big night before we left for Lauderdale, which was probably a mistake, especially since the captain was partying as hard as the rest. The crew had asked the captain for his permission to wakeboard off the yacht (which was 130 feet, and created a wake much bigger than our smaller tender did). I wasn't very good at wakeboarding, and I had a crew to feed, so I opted out of this activity and worked in the galley, where I was listening to music, nursing a hangover and cleaning out the fridges. (Come to think of it, is it really called a hangover if you're still a little bit drunk?!?) I headed back to get something out of the freezer, and as I walked to the rear of the boat I discovered that the door of the swim platform was wide open. They had forgotten to close it, and the boat was taking on a lot of water. The washer and dryer, as well as my freezer and all of the scuba gear were floating in about three feet of water. I notified the captain, who quickly put an end to the wakeboarding, turned the boat around and brought it back to the dock, but the damage was done. He had to have the bilge pumped and cleaned of the salt water. All the electronics were toast. The carpets had to be replaced. Three minutes of hungover negligence cost the owner of that yacht well over $100K. The captain made up some cockamamie story about a bilge pump failing at the dock and flew me home. He and the crew stayed behind to clean up the mess. I'm sure that was a fun week (not). Many captains have a rule about not getting hammered the night before a big passage, and this was a great example of why that rule exists.

Not all of the freelance work was nightmarish. I did many more great, uneventful charters than I did bad ones. But they don't make for the good stories, do they?

The Music Never Stopped

I wasn't back in Florida for long when I got a phone call from Deja Catering to see if I was interested in going out on the road as personal chef for the Dead that summer. (The Dead were one of the post–Jerry Garcia incarnations of the Grateful Dead.) Rather than being on a crew and feeding a crew, I would be the sole personal chef for the band and their wives. My favorite band, the band that had provided the soundtrack for my life, had called on me to cook for them. I was beside myself with excitement.

I made it past the first round of telephone interviews and arranged to fly to California for a cooking interview at the home of one of the band members. I flew to SF and drove out to the house to do my trial dinner, a buffet for seven band members, seven wives and a few managers. I had received a list of all of the group's likes and dislikes, and I'd created a menu accordingly. One band member loved mostly vegan food, and wanted it exceptionally spicy, so for him I made a summer gazpacho with avocado chili ice cream (which he loved). Another band member would only eat wild king salmon and organic chicken breasts. One member was on a protein and veg only/no carb diet, which was popular at the time, and he always wanted the meat to be on the bone, so I grilled him a fat cowboy cut rib eye steak, along with some lollipop lamb chops that had been marinated in yogurt, saffron, garlic and lemon zest. There were maybe twenty items going on this buffet, as I had to pander to their individual tastes.

I arrived and met the Mrs. of the house, and she seemed nice enough. She showed me the kitchen in their Marin County mansion. It was an amazing kitchen with a stellar view. What it didn't have was … anything else. Or rather, there was one small sauté pan, one small saucepan and a basket steamer … and that was it. She looked at me, and said, "Is this going to be okay?" I nearly shit myself. There wasn't even salt or pepper or any other food item in that kitchen, nor were there any utensils. Turns out, they'd just moved in.

I stepped outside and called my friend Debby, who I was staying with. She is a huge Deadhead and has more than a full kitchen setup.

"How did it go?" she asked excitedly, knowing where I'd been.

"Well, it went well … except for one thing. They basically have no pots and pans, and I was wondering if I could use yours for tomorrow's dinner?"

"You're gonna use MY pots and pans to cook for the Dead?!? Hell yeah! That's so cool! I may never wash them again! Hey, wait a minute … What are you cooking?!? You know that you cannot cook meat in my pans…" she chortled.

"Yeah, about that…" I sheepishly replied.

"EVAN!!!!!" she shouted, "Are you going to make me trade in my food ethics so you can feed our favorite band?!?"

"That's about the size of it," I said.

It took a bit of persuasion and the bribe of an expensive dinner at Millennium, the Bay Area's best vegetarian restaurant … but in the end, she let me use her pans.

It was a beast of a buffet, as all of their tastes were so different, but I cooked my heart out. I had appropriate garnishes for each dish, and I'd made index cards to put beside the dishes with ingredients. I was hyper focused and the results displayed that. At the end of the night, my favorite musicians were hanging out in the kitchen telling stories, drinking wine and snacking on leftover bits. They offered me a pour from the bottle of wine. While pouring it one member asked me, "So have you ever cooked on the road before?"

I leaned up against the counter and took a sip of wine. "Well," I replied, "I cooked on the road with John Mayer for a few months last year. And I've cooked on yachts for the past several years. But back in my days on Grateful Dead tour, when everyone was selling grilled cheese for $1 made on white bread with plastic cheese and margarine, I sold grilled Buffalo Mozzarella with tomato and basil on wheat bread for $2, which was unheard of back then. But I funded a full summer tour on that menu." They all laughed and raised a glass to me. It was an epic life moment, and I got the call with the offer the next morning.

The tour was broken into two legs, the first starting at Red Rocks in Colorado and ending a month later at The Gorge in Washington. Then there was a three-week break, followed by three weeks of tour up the east coast. Everything started off okay. Cooking at Red Rocks was a dream come true. The whole backstage area is carved into the rocks, and it's right behind the stage and next to their rehearsal room. The rehearsals were my favorite part. I could hear the music coming together, as my kitchen was coming together. I was doing my best to take inspiration from the music and pour it into my food.

But it wasn't easy. I should have known it was going to be difficult because each of the core four members had their own bus, and the rest of the band, crew and management team packed into three more buses, making seven in total.

The thing is that this time I was a crew of one. I had two helpers in every city, but they were really usually only good for dishwashing, etc. I couldn't even have them stock the buses, for security reasons, so, on top of everything else, I had to stock the buses with drinks and snacks myself. I was running ragged every single day.

I invited Cassidy and his family as my guests to that first run of shows, with backstage passes and killer seats. It had been about a year since I'd last seen him. After the arrest, it took a lot of hard work to maintain any relationship. Phone calls with teenagers are tortuously bad. I was excited to get them great seats to the show, and a tour of backstage.

I started off trying to write one menu with four to five items on it, and having them choose, but that never worked; they just ordered whatever they wanted. So I just had to anticipate their needs. The problem for me was with just one band member. No matter what I made him, it was never right. The thing is, he had loved the previous two chefs. As close as the Deadhead culinary community is, I happened to know both of them (one was Danielle, my co-chef from John Mayer tour), so I reached out, and followed their tips and tricks to the letter. It didn't matter. Nothing I did for this guy was ever right. "Oh, here comes our so-called chef, with my so-called dinner," he'd say, as I brought his plate to the stage at soundcheck, which is when he liked to eat. The rest of the band was kind as could be, if not a bit snarky in a playful way. But this one member was un-pleasable. Nothing I did was ever right.

The whole first month was pretty much hell. I had the job of my dreams, working for my favorite band, and it turned out to be one of the worst experiences of my life. The final destination of the first leg of the tour was at an amazing venue, The Gorge in Washington. My kitchen was right behind the stage, and right on the fence of the Columbia Gorge. The wind was whipping through my little easy-up as the sun was going down and I was putting dinner out. The entire sky was pink-orange … one of the most beautiful sunsets, and I was feeding these guys an amazing dinner of king crab and rack of lamb. I should have been on top of the world, but I was beat down.

I was working harder than I ever had before. That wasn't the bad part. The bad part was that no matter how hard I tried, this one guy was still complaining every day. It wasn't ever good enough for him. The Allman Brothers Band were opening for the Dead. Both nights sounded like great shows, but I was too busy and anxious to enjoy the music. Rock 'n' roll is a lot less fun when you're backstage.

I had a bad feeling, and that feeling was not absolved when the production manager told me to get any personal items out of my road cases because they were going back to Tennessee for "re-packing." After the show that night, I flew to D.C. to see one of my friends get married the following day. As a gift, I had asked each band member to sign her wedding invitation, as she was a huge Deadhead. She still has that invitation. The husband … not so much.

The day after the wedding, I went sightseeing in D.C. As we were strolling the plaza area below the Washington monument, my phone rang. I looked at the screen and saw the tour manager's name flashing. My heart dropped to my stomach and there was a lump in my throat as I answered it. I almost let it go to voicemail, but I knew it was best to bite the bullet and not postpone the inevitable. "I'm calling to inform you that your services will no longer be needed by the band, and you will not be returning for the second leg of the tour." I asked about severance, and was given a cold, hard, "It is not this band's policy to provide severance to contract employees." I hung up the phone and had to fight back the tears. It was sticky, hot and humid, as D.C. tends to be in July, and I was dripping with sweat. I sat on the lawn, and the friends I was with did what they could to console me, but to be honest, I was a wreck. I felt as if I'd failed at the greatest job that I'd ever dreamed of. I felt so ashamed. The thing was, the dream and the reality could not have been further apart. Later, I would come to learn that my firing actually had very little to do with me at all. It had more to do with bad band dynamics and interpersonal dramas that had gone on for decades. Even though I knew that the inner dynamics of the band had been screwed up for years and that they had a history of chewing people up and spitting them out when they'd fulfilled their use, I was toast, and it took a quite a while for me to heal from it. One thing about being a private chef, and you've already heard me say this before … you're really only as good as your last meal, and EVERYONE is replaceable (in the workplace).

I didn't go see any act with that band member in it for several years, but on his seventieth birthday there was a show that many of my friends would be at in San Francisco. I decided that the music was important to me, and I mentally buried the hatchet with him. Now I'll go see him every once in a while, and I usually have a good time. That music is still the soundtrack to my life, for which I'm Grateful.

An old friend from Berkeley, who I had just seen at The Gorge, happened to be spending time on a small family-owned island on a lake near Webster, MA. As he tells it, his grandfather had bought that island for a song and a dance just after the Great Depression. There was an old farmhouse on it, but no electricity, just natural gas. It was basically slightly glorified camping in what was probably a haunted old cabin, but it was really beautiful that July to rest and relax on this island for a few weeks and lick my wounds. We fished, smoked pot and drank beer for about three weeks. We did a good old-fashioned New England clam bake, which was a first for me. It was a really great way to get back on my feet.

From there I went to Newport, Rhode Island, to seek yacht work again, but instead got a job at the Clarke Cooke House on Bannister's Wharf. Legendary chef Thomas Keller did a stint there early on in his career and he said that the Cooke House was where he learned how to cook fast. Cooking fast was no joke. Particularly in a place like this with a 200-seat bistro downstairs, and a fine-dining restaurant upstairs with another fifty seats. We'd get the line ready for service upstairs, all the cooks hustling up and down a narrow staircase in the ancient building. It was the first time I had worked on a line in several years, and it was really fun. I totally got in the zone, and by the time the first night was over, I had a grip on maybe three of the six dishes my station put out.

The only downside was that the kitchen was upstairs. And it was so hot. I actually looked at my meat thermometer, and the ambient temperature on the line was 121 degrees. They kept a big tub of ice water at the end of the line, and when cooks had a second they would wet down towels to wrap around their necks to regulate their body temperatures.

After service, I had to go to the top floor with the general manager to fill out some new hire paperwork, and I'd become so overheated during service that I threw up while walking up the stairs. It was a humbling moment that I got teased about until I left that place (in fact, I wouldn't be surprised if some version of that story still gets told to new cooks on exceptionally hot nights up there).

I learned everything that one could possibly know about preparing and cooking lobsters that summer. It was also the year that the Red Sox won the World Series for the first time in nearly a century and New England was buzzing with excitement.

The Cooke House reminded me that I had skills. The job on the road with the Dead beat me down, and I was dead to the core. Being in a restaurant filled with talented cooks and chefs, and being able to hold my own with them, reminded me that I belonged in this game, that I'd made a good career choice coming out of prison. And that just because this one job didn't work out, it did not define me, or my career.

A Fishing Boat
Pretending to Be a Yacht

With my regained culinary confidence, it was time for me to be in charge again. There is something about being the guy responsible for writing the menus, provisioning the ingredients and piecing all of the tasks together so that a "life-changing meal" can be turned out with impeccable timing. Once a few of those are under your belt, you feel unstoppable. I did, at least.

About that time, I was contacted by a boat that I'd worked on about a year prior and was asked to come to Turkey to do their Mediterranean season with them. The yacht was owned by a Saudi prince. Small boat, small crew — it was really a fancy fishing boat impersonating a yacht. The problem with that scenario is that you end up with a boat that's not great for fishing and inadequate as a yacht. They offered to fly me to Turkey, first class, for two months of work, at a good daily rate. The date was June 11.

This job offer put me back on top. I had worked for them once before, and they thought enough of my vibe and my food (on yachts, those things dance a close line) to not only ask me back, but to get me there in style, with hot towel service and a roomy seat. It was an endorsement of my skills and value, and my frail male ego really needed this boost to get over the Dead.

Even in the front of the plane, it was a long flight. I flew to Istanbul where I had a one-day layover. It was pretty late when I got in, jet-lagged, tired and hungry. After settling into my hotel room, I went upstairs to the twenty-four-hour buffet, which looked predictably disgusting, so I decided to venture out for a walk. Even though the city was asleep at this late hour, it still felt incredibly vibrant. The tile work on the buildings were breathtaking works of art. Gardens met architecture, both old and new, in blended harmony. The perfume of sticky jasmine, wet on the vine, blended with the diesel fumes of the late-night delivery trucks.

As a troubled teenager, I had taken to hanging out in a park near my parents' house called Lanark Park (or LA Narc Park, as the local kids called it). It was a hot spot for drugs and petty crime. But there was also a great taco truck there called the Big Burrito, and that truck blossomed into my lifelong love affair with taco trucks, and street food in general. Back then a loaded burrito was $3, and tacos were 50 cents. I'd bet a burrito (which is probably $12 now) that you could score a dime bag somewhere near that taco truck today.

That first night in Istanbul when I was starving, and the crusty, depressing all-night hotel buffet was not going to cut it, I took a walk and found a twenty-four-hour hot dog stand, of all things, that also happened to sell illegal beers out of a cooler. While I was eating, I made conversation with this other guy at the stand. His story was that he was in grad school, but had come to Istanbul to visit his family. He also said he was having insomnia, so we decided to go to a nearby bar and have a drink. "I know a lively place," he said.

He drove us a few blocks to a bar with a sign that said, "Disco Bar." We walked down some stairs and it was immediately apparent that this wasn't a regular bar at all. There were twenty to thirty scantily clad women leaning against the walls and sprawled on couches that ringed the dim room. He'd taken me to a brothel! I immediately took a mental inventory of what I had on me, where my credit card was, etc. "Are you cool with this?" he asked with a coy smile. I responded, "It wasn't what I had in mind, but I'm in."

I'd be lying if I said I never went to any prostitutes in all of my travels. Not a lot … but a few times. I'm not proud of it, nor am I ashamed.

We bellied up to the bar and ordered two beers. Almost immediately, two women approached us. "You would like to buy us a drink?" At this point my "friend" leaned over and whispered to me, "Hey, we're going to split this bar bill, right?" This really should have been a sign that something was amiss but I replied, "Yeah, sure."

We made a little small talk before negotiating €100 blowjobs with the ladies, and asked the bartender for our drink tab. He set it on the bar, and I was shocked when I saw it said €750. Apparently our beers were €25 each, and the girls had each ordered glasses of champagne that the bartender had listed as €350 per glass.

"You guys are nuts, there's no way we're paying that for cheap booze," I blurted. We were instantly surrounded by three really big dudes, one of them asking, "What's problem? You agreed to buy these nice ladies drinks. Now you must pay. We have an ATM if you don't have enough money, and we take credit cards."

"I certainly don't have anything else here," I replied rather indignantly. We're now standing, and these three thugs are backing us into a corner. I pull about €200 out of my wallet, "This is all I have, take it or leave it!" not wanting to arrive at my freelance gig with a busted-up face. My new "friend" had just shy of €300. They took our money, and threw us out on the street.

The dude gave me a ride, apologizing all the way. When we pulled up to the hotel, he looks a little sheepish and says, "So you agreed to split the bar bill with me. I gave them €300, and you only gave them €250. Can you get me the €25 to make it even?" I was so shocked and angry, that I could barely muster up a firm "Go fuck yourself" as I slammed the door and walked away. It was only then that I realized he was in on the scam, and I'd totally been had.

This is the only time in all of my adult travels that I have ever been ripped off. This unnerving experience brought me back to an even more horrible moment in my teenage runaway years, where I also trusted a stranger that I shouldn't have. The consequences of that early mistake were much worse, if only because I was younger and a lot more vulnerable, but both experiences left me feeling raw and questioning some of my decisions on who to trust in this lifetime. I met a guy on a bus on Thanksgiving Day, back when I'd first run away from home. He saw my backpack and decided that I was prey. "Do you have anywhere to eat Thanksgiving dinner?" he asked. "I'm going to a friend's house," I lied.

"Allow me to introduce myself," he said. "My name is David, and I am a teen counselor. I work with troubled youth and runaways." He showed me a business card that said as much, though in hindsight, it was probably a scam that he'd used before. "Please let me buy you dinner," he said. I agreed, and he took me to a Denny's, as not much else was open on Thanksgiving.

Over dinner he started out with small talk, and then asked me how long I'd been on the street. I told him the truth, which was "not long," and then he told me that he found me very attractive, and asked me if I'd consider laying down naked at his house with him. He then showed me a check made out to him for $5,000, and told me that he would pay me that sum if I'd fool around with him. This was around the time that I was using that Locker Room Rush shit … and it did not lead me to a good decision. The drugs, the trauma of this incident and the four decades since have left my memory pretty foggy, but what I think happened is we went back to his house, and he molested and photographed me. His roommate came home and was furious that he'd brought home someone as young as me (I was fourteen). "You need to leave, I'll call you a taxi," he said. "Come back tomorrow and I will cash the check and pay you," he told me as he shoved $10 into my hand and rushed me out the door.

With nowhere to go, I went to my Aunt Marcia's house, which was just a few miles away. I knew they were all away for a Thanksgiving holiday that I should have been a part of … but these were my years of being a train wreck, and I wasn't spending holidays with family. I can't remember if I wasn't invited, or if I was out of touch with the family at that point, but I was undeniably in a bad place.

I broke into their house and stayed the night. The following day I took the keys to a spare car and went out joyriding with a couple of high school buddies. (This was before my first acid trip, when I swore off stealing.) We were drinking beers while racing the car at dangerous speeds through a canyon. I was basically teaching myself to drive a stick shift, and it should come as no surprise that I totaled the car in no time and abandoned it in a ditch. G-d does look after fools and children, of which I was both. It's amazing that we walked out of that canyon that day.

In my recklessness, I had already been caught joyriding my dad's car twice, so it did not take a rocket surgeon to figure out who took their car. Marcia and Mickey pulled me aside at the next family holiday, which was Chanukah, to discuss their car. They had so much love and compassion for me that they did not press any charges. They were worried about my safety, and they had every right to be. They consulted with a probation officer. He told them that once a kid was on the streets for three weeks or more, that kid would be statistically likely to never return to "normalcy."

A day after wrecking the car, I made it back to David's house and, predictably, nobody answered. I came back the next day, and the same thing happened, but this time I was prepared. I set up a tent in his front yard, and made a sign that said, "Owes Me Money!" and parked myself next to my tent.

Well, it didn't take long for the cops to show up, and they immediately figured out what had happened. It turned out that he had a record of molesting young boys. The cops searched his house and found plenty of child pornography. A friend's mom came and picked me up, and I hope that guy ended up doing a lot of time.

Back in Istanbul, I made my flight to Marmaris where I met Captain Patty, a jolly Irish guy with tons of charter experience. Two older guys from the Seychelles were also on deck. Both had fishing boat experience, but neither had worked on a yacht, and it showed. They left buckets out on deck, forgot to coil the hoses or lines and lots of other little things that drove the captain mad. There is a certain level of finesse in yachting that was lost on these guys. Nice guys, and hard workers … but where most yachties are slick and clean cut (not me, mind you) these guys were a little sloppy around the edges.

The owners had brought their steward from their palace in Saudi Arabia. Joseph was a small Filipino man who'd worked for this family since he was a young boy. I quickly discovered that he was being grossly underpaid, and noticed that he seemed to live in terror of being fired. Moreover, this fear was second only to his fear of water. He hated boats.

The crew quarters on this fishing boat that was pretending to be a yacht were practically non-existent. We didn't even have a door that we could close. We had to climb into our bunks, which all faced the table where we ate; we'd pull back curtains when we slept, so the only privacy was a curtain between each bunk and our dining table, which was usually covered in laundry. The boat only had one washer and dryer, and the owners changed in and out of designer clothes so many times a day that Joseph could never keep up with the laundry. Had this been a full-time gig, the living quarters would have been unacceptable, but the money was great and it was only for about six weeks. If doing time gave me anything, it was a high threshold for discomfort and bullshit.

Even so, the laundry thing almost broke us all, me included. Aside from the piles of clothing that were always stacked on the table that we were expected to eat from, there just weren't enough hours in the day to get the laundry done … so Joseph would do it while we slept. The machines were actually situated between our bunks. The spin cycle would rattle the bunks, and don't even get me started on the dryer. But Joseph was so terrified of not keeping up that he'd wake up every few hours to change the laundry out.

The odd thing to me was that he should have just been able to negotiate for better conditions. I still wonder what kind of trouble he really would have gotten into if he'd tried to explain that there was only one washer, and that he couldn't do laundry at night because it kept us all awake. I don't think anything would have happened. The family struck me as very reasonable people. But then again, I was not indentured to them. Quite the opposite. I was freelancing. I imagine that there is a lot more to that story than I know. I wonder if he felt like he was being incarcerated. I wondered, and still wonder, if he was there against his will.

Thankfully, the owners had pretty simple tastes in food, and the crew was even easier to feed. The guys on deck were happy eating fish and rice, pretty much every day. Patty was the classic meat and potato Irishman, and Joseph hardly ate. I can only imagine that he was treated really poorly in their home, because he was so skittish. He was afraid to ask the guests simple questions such as what time they'd like dinner, or how they'd like certain meats cooked. They had asked me to always prepare some white rice for the baby, so I began making it once or twice a day, and always kept some around. I'd ask Joseph to offer the rice as he served dinner, and he told me that he did but they didn't want it. Moments later, they would come into the galley asking for rice for the baby. He lived in such fear, that even something as simple as this question was problematic for him.

He didn't know anything about Western food, so when the guests asked him what I was serving, he had no clue. I began going out on deck before most meals, to explain the menu. Eventually, I developed my own relationship with the owners, and bypassed Joseph as often as I could. The guy was clearly a tortured soul, and I had to wonder what had happened in his life to make him this way.

We cruised the islands around Turkey for a little while, getting the rhythm for how the summer was going to go. I'd now been traveling the yachting circuit for around five years, and I realized that I had bought almost nothing to remember my travels by. It dawned on me that this lifestyle wouldn't go on forever, so I ought to pick up some mementos. It's not like I was consciously deciding to slow down, or go land based … but I was beginning to consider what a home might look like someday, and I knew that I'd love for it to be adorned with treasures from far off lands. And with that, I decided that I really wanted to get a fine Turkish carpet before I left, so I scoped out some of the carpet shops. The sales strategy in these shops was notoriously hardcore, and I really didn't want to get ripped off. I brought €1,000 split between three pockets, which is a standard traveler's negotiating trick. Of course, I am reminded of trying to avoid the carpet shops in Morocco and failing miserably (though I did not buy one at that time).

They began pouring me apple tea and showing me hundreds of carpets. Stack after stack, and from those we'd make a stack of my favorites. After a while they asked me, "Do you like to smoke kif [hashish]?" to which there's only one answer. I could see their strategy. They were going to try and get me baked and dupe me! *Good luck, motherfuckers. I've been training for this moment my whole life!* I start puffing pipe after pipe of hash with these guys, and they kept my teacup full as well. I finally narrowed it down to just a few carpets.

There was one that I really liked. It was rich in oranges and golds and quite intricate, with a really elegant feel to it. They said, "Sir, you have excellent taste. You have chosen a carpet which is worth €2,000. As you have said your budget is half of that, perhaps you can choose a different carpet." I looked at many more, but this one was my favorite, by far. "I want this carpet for not one penny over the €1,000." We negotiated like this for a while, and they kept feeding me more tea and hash. The main guy would hand me pieces of paper with a number on it, and I'd in turn, write down "€1,000," and slide it back to them. It was hot in this shop, and the dusty musty smell of wool, silk and cotton carpets mingled with the rich, earthy smell of Turkish hash and tobacco. They finally handed me a slip of paper with "€1,400" on it, and with sweat on his brow, he said this was the absolute lowest they could go. I laid the ten hundred-euro notes across the carpet, and insisted this was all the money I had.

The man leaned back and took a sip of mint tea. "This came out of your pockets. How much do you have in your wallet?"

I pulled out my wallet and looked, and saw that I had about €110. "I have a little more, but I have a date tonight, and I need this money for the club." (I'd met a German woman on holiday that morning and had asked her out that night.)

"Which club are you going to?"

"Club Pasha" I answered.

He got a big smile on his face. "This club belongs to my brother. Give me the €110, along with your €1,000, and I promise you the best table in the house, with bottle service, all night long."

The guy was true to his word. When we got to the club, we were on the guest list. We had an amazing VIP table with a bottle of vodka and all the mixers. And I was looking pretty suave to my date.

We drank and danced and had a great time, when all a sudden she says, "Oh, shit, give me your things! Put them in this Ziploc!" I'd seen signs around town about a foam party, but I didn't really think much about it. Sure enough, giant foam machines began sloshing and rocking back and forth, and producing a thick, bubble bath–style foam. They filled the dance floor six feet up in bubbles. I'd never seen anything like it. Everyone got all wet and slippery, and the DJ went into overdrive. The bass started pumping, and he built the crescendo up to a massive peak, building, building, musical tension of the highest order … and dropped down a hard beat like no other. It was super fun… for about five minutes, until the bubbles melted, leaving piles of dirty soapy foam everywhere. The house lights came up and the music stopped. Everyone looked around in a daze, gathering their things, and left in a wet, soapy haze. It's actually a pretty great way to clear out a club at the end of the night, and probably doesn't hurt the cleanup efforts.

We left the club cold and slippery, and the boat happened to be docked just 100 meters away. "Wanna go back to the boat with me and get dried off??" I asked, coyly. She was fascinated by my job, and was keen to go and check out the boat. I ended up showing her my new carpet, and telling her the whole story as we fell asleep on the carpet in each other's arms. Many years later, I had that carpet appraised, and it is, indeed, a very high-quality silk carpet, which I still cherish to this day.

After a few stunning days anchored at the isle of Capri, we dropped the owners off for good in Nice. I spent a couple of days getting the galley back in order, and left to fly back to the States. Patty called me a couple of days after I arrived home. "Have you heard anything from Joseph?" he asked. Apparently, the day after I'd left, Joseph packed all his belongings and left in the middle of the night. The thing is, Captain Patty had Joseph's passport in the safe. Patty told me that had Joseph asked for his passport, he would have given it to him. Joseph was not being held against his will, but apparently, he didn't know that. I've always wondered what happened to that guy. I'm so glad he "escaped."

A few years later I was contacted by an assistant of the boat owners and asked if I'd be interested in working full-time for the family. I turned them down.

Part 3

...And the Wisdom to Know the Difference

Save the Man/Burn the Man

A few years before I attended my first Burning Man, I was at a poker game in Fort Lauderdale put on by a chef buddy of mine. Sitting next to me was this sort of eccentric-looking dude with dark hair and oddly shaped, designer eyeglasses, named Soss Boss. He introduced himself as an artist working on a large installation (The Miami Space and Time Project) documenting the construction of the new Miami Performing Arts Center. He was the first person that I ever met who introduced himself as an artist. "What is it that you do?" he asked me in his nasal voice. When I told him I worked as a chef on yachts, his eyes lit up, and he said, "Oh, really? Have you ever been to Burning Man?? Because I run a gourmet BBQ camp out there," he said, rather seductively. I was, indeed, familiar with Burning Man, a seven-day event that began in the mid-'80s, quickly outgrew its home on a beach in San Francisco and moved out to the moon-like Nevada desert in a dry lake bed known as the Playa. I'd been hearing about it since the mid-'90s, and always wanted to go when I was in the Bay Area, but I was on probation then, and it was out of state, so it just never happened.

"Yeah, my camp is called the Playa-Q, and we create gourmet performance barbecue artistry," he said.

"What exactly does *that* mean?" I asked.

"Well, we have a few cheap tricks … such as BBQ napalm … which is Everclear and Worcestershire in a squeeze bottle. Or Everclear and apple cider vinegar … or Everclear and Coke … you get the idea. But what we really aim to do, Chef," he said, as he leaned back in his chair, "is to blow peoples' minds."

He went on to explain that the Black Rock Desert is one of the harshest environments on Earth, and that his group's goal was "to create the best restaurant out there." In fact, he said, "We aim to create one of the best restaurants on the planet … in a gifting economy [meaning no money involved] with no running water. We aim to merge food and art, at the highest levels. And we aim to have an absolute fucking ball, while doing it. Does this pique your interest, Chef?" he asked with a sly smile.

"Keep talking," I replied.

As we were both more interested in the conversation than the poker game, we each lost our twenty-dollar buy-in pretty quickly. We talked and talked as if we were long-lost brothers. The joke was that we'd both lost twenty bucks at poker but won a lifelong friendship. Sadly, that friendship lasted nowhere near as long as it should have, but we did manage to have some great times, and we created some magic together over the years.

Soss lived in a sketchy studio apartment in downtown Miami. He'd built a loft, so his bed was elevated, and he'd also built a giant chess board underneath it. When I say giant, I mean it filled up the room. Soss had a little BBQ chill-out zone up on the roof so he could cook while keeping an eye on the construction across the street at the performance art center. He hosted elaborate BBQ parties, and he would hire some crackhead from the building to do the cleanup. At the time, he rode a ratty old Yamaha 750, and he was always hustling something, most often black market commodities, but also other things, some of them even legal. He was a talented writer, and would write business plans for start-ups as one of his many hustles. He took a lot of freelance writing and editing gigs. He always had his nose in something … literally and figuratively.

His voice was like a cross between Hunter Thompson and Jack Benny, and he always spoke as if he was an expert in whatever topic you were addressing. I've got to hand it to him, he knew a lot about a lot of things, and could usually fake it pretty well when he didn't. "If you can't dazzle 'em with brilliance, you baffle 'em with bullshit," he'd say. "Come and camp with us at Burning Man, I'll make sure you're treated like royalty and you'll have the time of your life!" He went as far as to buy me a ticket in 2004, but that's when I got hired by the Dead and the timing didn't work.

My first year at Burning Man was 2005. Arriving at the site reminded me of rolling into my first Grateful Dead parking lot twenty years prior. It was immediately apparent that this was an alternate universe. The fact that 28,000 people (the attendance in 2005, these days it tops 80,000) were building a temporary city was nothing short of spectacular. The costumes and community, the art cars, the giant structures, the magical colors of the Black Rock Desert, all worked to create a sense of harmonic cacophony. When I say "art cars," I mean like an old city bus, holding up to 120 people, with the accordion split in the center that's been transformed to look like a giant caterpillar with a dance floor and DJ booth on the roof. Or a giant galleon pirate ship called the *Contessa*, that sailed across the flat desert floor. Or ... a simple golf cart that is made to look like a spaceship that holds just two people. Many books and films have been made about Burning Man ... but this is not a book about Burning Man (per se...), so if this piques your interest, I highly suggest you delve deeper.

Once inside the event, the only things to spend money on were ice and coffee. Nothing else is for sale. People build elaborate art projects, bars, restaurants, cafes, bowling alleys, roller rinks, a movie theater ... pretty much anything that exists in most cities also exists here in the very temporary Black Rock City as gifts to the inhabitants.

The event, the city, and the community function on these ten principles:

Radical Inclusion
Gifting
Decommodification
Radical Self-Reliance
Radical Self-Expression
Communal Effort
Civic Responsibility
Leave No Trace
Participation
Immediacy

Soss had already introduced me to his old friend and fellow theater geek, a guy that we called Reverend Smoke, or The Rev. The Rev is a tech geek by day and BBQ champion by night. That guy has more BBQ awards than anyone I've ever met, and knows more about the cookery of meat than any human I have ever known, hands down. When I pulled into camp, he was manning the smokers, as usual, which were on the camp perimeter. As I parked my car and approached The Rev, his face broke out in a huge smile. "Now we can start doing some fucking cooking!" He walked over to me and, reeking of meat smoke and man sweat, gave me a big, dusty hug.

There was some old-school hip hop blasting through the massive speakers, which was a sign that The Rev or The Sheik were running things in this moment. The Sheik was a massive presence of a human, at six-foot-five and maybe 400 pounds. Soss had told me quite a bit about him. He's rather successful, and he exudes a sense of confidence that is admirable, if not a bit intimidating. He wore a gold lamé tracksuit, and his thick blond afro added another four inches of electric hair sizzle to his already massive height and eclectic sense of style. As I approached camp, Soss and The Sheik were plotting and scheming, both things that they excelled at, especially when combining their talents. Soss saw me approach and got a big smile. "Chef!" he said, in his nasally high-pitched voice. "Welcome to the Playa-Q! Why don't you set up your tent, and then come to the dining room. Tonight you are a dinner guest, but don't get too used to it, because you'll be running the kitchen for the rest of the week." I set up my tent, which served as a home for my gear … but I never slept in it once. (I slept in our dining room, or made cuddle buddies to keep warm with as it got very cold at night!)

"Let me show you the kitchen and dining room," Soss said, as The Sheik cranked up the volume on the professional-quality sound system. Biggie Smalls was banging out of our speakers, and there was a small group of scantily clad babes of all genders dancing in front of them.

The kitchen was a giant blue circus-style tent, maybe thirty feet in diameter. That first year, we had one chest freezer and three fridges, all powered by a generator that never stopped humming in the ten days I spent there. And speaking of the generator, as I looked over at it, I saw a suave-looking gentleman with blue hair, wearing a fedora, a tool belt, a pair of work boots … and nothing else. He was adding fuel to the generator. "Kinsky, come meet the chef," Soss yelled over the ever-present hum of the generator. Kinsky walked over and, without saying a word, gave me a sweaty, dusty hug, and said "Welcome home, Chef, let me get you a beer!" He walked over to a cooler, pulled out two ice-cold Coronas, expertly popped the tops off with a lighter, stuffed two dusty wedges of lime that were sitting on a cutting board in the tops and handed me one. This was the first of many beers that he and I shared over the next two decades.

The dust at Burning Man is the main seasoning in everything that you do. Every beer, every bite, every time you brush your teeth … there's a little dust involved. It's just the way it is.

I nosed around the kitchen a little, peeking into the fridges and the totes that held spices, salts, oils and vinegars, foil and saran wrap. I saw stacks of boxes of latex gloves in all sizes on top the fridge, and made a mental note to stash some extra larges away for myself.

At that moment, an older guy who looked as if he'd spent way too many years in the sun, or at the bottom of a vodka bottle, walked up. It actually turned out to be both. He surveyed me, and saw the psoriasis patches on my legs, as I was wearing shorts. "Hey, Psoriasis, get over here and help us with this tent post!" he grunted. That was my introduction to Mayor Joey, a man who had a reputation as the crustiest curmudgeon on the Playa, but who could actually be a bit of a softie. I helped him with the giant pole, which would serve as the center of the bar. As I poked around the kitchen, Soss wrangled a crew of volunteers to help finish setting up the dining-room tent, which was another massive circus tent.

About then, a U-Haul truck pulled up and Soss got a mischievous grin. "Ah, perfect, the furniture for the dining room is right on time. He greeted the driver, and they opened the back of the truck to reveal a stack of mattresses and a flat of lumber. He quickly corralled a crew of volunteers to unload the truck, and in no time the mattresses were spread around the dining room, and the humming of electric saws and hammers filled the air. Soon there were ten low tables, with a mattress on either side of them for your dining pleasure. No sooner were they built and in place, than boxes materialized with LED centerpieces for the tables. In fact, a whole slew of people were decorating the dining room, setting up a dish pit, creating an area for clean pots and building metro racks for the clean pots and pans to live on. This was as legit as any restaurant opening that I'd ever seen.

Around sunset, several of us began to gather in the dining room. I took a seat on one of the mattresses at a table across from a small-framed man who introduced himself as Smooth. He had long braided hair extensions and wore a T-shirt that said, "Thanks Dr. Shulgin," a nod to the chemist best known for creating MDMA. (In an interesting coincidence, the Shulgins were our dinner guests at one of our Rock Star Dinners in a later year.) "Welcome, Chef," Smooth said. "Soss has been talking you up pretty hard. I hope you're ready to throw it down, Playa-Q style."

"I believe that I'm up to the challenge," I replied. (The Rock Star Dinners were a series of dinners that we did on the Playa to honor the people who worked really hard to make Burning Man such a magical event. We invited the founders, the artists and the lower-level volunteers that worked hard to make the event happen.)

At this point a lovely couple appeared and asked if I'd like to have my hands washed. It was an offer I could not refuse. The man pulled a basin and a pitcher of warm water off the tray behind him. The woman, who introduced herself as "Spark," poured the warm water over my hands and rubbed soap into them. As she massaged the soap into my dusty hands, she leaned over and seductively whispered into my ear, "Relax, and welcome to the Playa-Q. The Playa-Q loves you."

Running a camp at Burning Man is no joke, and a food camp is especially challenging. You have to pack in all of your own water and food, and pack out all of your garbage. You also have to do something with your gray water, and as a food camp, we created a lot. We came up with many ways of doing this over the years. Mostly we strained it into a kiddie pool and let it evaporate. A couple of times when we couldn't evaporate it quickly enough, we bribed the porta-potty guys to suck it clean for us. Keep in mind, we had the best brisket and pulled pork on the Playa and, arguably, in the state of Nevada and beyond … in large quantities. Good food at Burning Man is a highly valued commodity. Our camp motto was, "We did not come here to fuck around," and we didn't (except that we did). But in the midst of the fucking around, we created high levels of food-based performance art, and it was magical.

Soss is gone now, so it's a little hard for me to write about him. He was an expert in the drug trade and a firm proponent of ending the drug war. He had friends who were PhDs, scientists, high-level CEOs, some of Miami's top models and politicians. He also had friends who were crackheads and junkies who would do anything for him … and I mean pretty much anything. He fed a lot of them, and hired them to do odd jobs. He commanded a lot of respect in the hood, in the Miami art world, at Burning Man and really anywhere that he applied himself.

Aside from being a talented artist and eclectic and eccentric genius, Soss's greatest superpower was finding out what people were best at, and most passionate about, and creating a space for them to shine their brightest. He would figure out what makes people tick, and would keep them in whatever that thing might be. The Rev, for instance, loves the highest-end cannabis possible, the best coffee available and the occasional Coca-Cola. The cannabis is usually consumed in the form of high-end hashish, vaporized by heating a nail to a certain temperature in a crazy-expensive glass bowl. The coffee must not be ground until the water is boiling and must be weighed to a precise measurement. Nothing with The Rev is ever simple, but it's always the best there is. Soss would make sure The Rev had everything he needed to work countless hours, smoking meat for the Playa-Q. Soss was a master at getting people to work really hard for him, but he always tried to make it feel good for all parties involved.

The camp worked on a dues system. The dues funded all of the ingredients, and Soss then went to Idaho to prepare the food about a month before the event. He marinated skirt steaks and put them in Ziplocs. He stuffed filets with blue cheese, wrapped them in bacon, vacuum sealed and froze them. He made gallons of a Dijon rosemary marinade, and marinated hundreds of pounds of lamb tenderloins and chicken thighs. He'd ordered a few hundred pounds of wild game, different sausages, quail, elk, moose, etc. Once all the meat was portioned, marinated and bagged, he lined a chest freezer with it so that the last day of Burning Man was on the bottom of the freezer, and the first day was on top. This was a pretty genius method, as everyday we'd just pull the meats we'd be cooking the following day out of the freezer, move them to a designated defrosting fridge and then all we had to prepare was vegetables for the grill. If I ever go back to Burning Man, this will be my method. And when he went over budget — which was every year — he always knew who to call to make up the difference. It might cost him a dinner party on the Playa, or some trade that nobody was privy to … but he always managed to get the job done.

Food was served family style on colored cutting boards. Everyone was given a wooden skewer to feed themselves with. Keep in mind, this is a leave-no-trace event. Wooden skewers could easily be burned at the end of the night. Dinner flowed smoothly, and I had a good time learning about the people around me, where they were from, how they found the Q, etc. Soss was a solid BBQ guy … but his plate-ups were crude. He just cut meat and stacked it on these boards. I made a mental note that the next night's food would look much nicer.

The next night I was in charge of dinner. I began by reviewing the marinated proteins pulled from the freezer for me, and the allotted veggies and fruit for that day. I then broke into my own bag of tricks, which included some special ingredients I'd been collecting just for this event. I made a cannabis-infused curry, different purées, the Hot Fanny sauce I'd learned in New Orleans, a demi-glace, a bouillabaisse, a Thai-style chimichurri and more.

I put some ducks on the smoker. Making smoked-duck gumbo is a multi-day event, and it became a Playa-Q tradition. After I pick off all the smoked meat and skin, I'd make a stock out of the bones, a dark roux and then assemble my gumbo. One year we made cannabis-cured bacon. It wasn't strong enough to be psychoactive, but you could taste the cannabis as a pleasant herbaceous note. I have an amazing late-night memory of frying the smoked duck skin up crispy in the cannabis-cured bacon fat, to make the world's best duck chicharrones.

As Soss had marinated and portioned out most of the meat, there wasn't a ton of room for reinterpreting dishes, but it sure did make everything run easily. While Soss made tasty food, he really didn't know how to present it. This is where my skills came into play. The Sheik said my presence in the Q kitchen turned us from a kickass BBQ joint to a Spago-style full-service restaurant. Between you and me, all I really did was bring along some ring molds and squeeze bottles to ramp up our plate presentations, along with a decade of fine-dining experience.

"Hey, Chef," Soss asked, "if I had raw fish delivered, are you capable of making sushi?"

"Well, I'd need rice, seaweed and a few other items ... but yeah, of course," I replied. The words were no sooner out of my mouth than he was off, presumably to find a satellite phone to call in an order to Reno. Moments later, he came back and said that the supplies would arrive Thursday morning at the Black Rock Airport. "Soss, I've always wanted to display sushi on a naked woman," I said. Without missing a beat, a beautiful camper by the name of eLeM shot her hand up into the air ... and that's how collective art comes together. "Kinsky, can you build me a sushi table?" I asked. Kinsky nodded coyly as he lit a cigarette, and said, "For sushi on eLeM, I could build you a house!"

The day of the dinner I still had no sushi table. Kinsky had disappeared for hours, and I was beginning to sweat, but I did my prep work just the same. But he arrived just in time, saying, "Sorry, Chef, I had to rescue a damsel in distress off the Chairway to Heaven." I was too busy cooking to even ask what that meant, and he built me a sturdy little table in about fifteen minutes, still wearing nothing but a tool belt and a pair of boots. Anything can happen at Burning Man.

That night's dinner was a huge success. We had some newlyweds in camp and they loved scallops, so I started the meal with grilled scallops in a cannabis curry sauce (I'd brought a jar of cannabis-infused peanut butter, which I used as a base for my curry). We then did several platters of specialty meats — elk sausage, quail stuffed with cream cheese and chili peppers and wrapped in bacon, ribs, brisket, and game meats. When the tables were all cleared, we carried in the table with eLeM covered in sushi. She'd spent hours bathing, shaving, primping and selecting the most revealing outfit possible. We spent a lot of time arranging the sushi on her body. After some calls for equal gender representation, we added a sushi man into our later menus.

My skin, which had been pretty bad before Burning Man, had cleared up considerably on the Playa, and it did the same in subsequent years there as well. There's something about the alkalinity in the very fine dust that coats everything that seems to work well on psoriasis. There's also something about the Playa that makes everyone shine as their hottest selves. Everyone is sexy. Everyone is a rock star. Everyone has a superpower, whether they know it or not. For me, it was a place where I had the most confidence I've ever had, anywhere. I acquired the Playa name Chef Pimp, as I was pimping the food at the next level. (And for the record, my wife hates that name.)

Perhaps it was because kitchens had become my home, or maybe it's because Burning Man was so similar to what I imagined the legendary Electric Kool-Aid Acid Tests to have been like: An extreme experiment in performance art, lights, music and unbridled creativity held back only by the limitations of the harsh desert, and the imagination. The creative freedoms that take place out there were what I'd been looking for my whole life, and I think I appreciated them even more because all of my own liberties had been stripped so long ago. On some level, I felt as if the magic of Burning Man had been calling to me forever.

The Sheik and Soss taught me that to have a great camp, you need to have a good gender balance, great food, great music and great people. For those first few years on the Playa, we nailed it pretty hard. Also, at an event where people notoriously don't eat very well ... we ate like royalty. In fact, our uncooked leftovers exceeded most camps' original food cache. Who else had whole beef tenderloins and lamb racks leftover in their freezer? As Soss Boss liked to say, "Nothing exceeds like excess."

At the end of the week, Soss sat me down and asked me if I would be the executive chef of the Playa-Q. I didn't quite realize it at the time, but this was a pretty big deal ... AND it meant absolutely nothing at all, except that I was committed to dropping thousands of dollars and man hours per year on this really fun and inspiring project, indefinitely. But Soss was a passionate artist and a masterful salesman, and he always had a way of spinning things as if we were changing the world. I'm not gonna say he was wrong...

Wabbit Season

After having my mind completely blown at Burning Man that first year, it was time to gear up to go and work for my former charter guest at his duck hunting lodge up in Canada. I'd flown up there once to see the place, make an equipment and kitchen assessment, and check out my living quarters. Duck season is September 21 to December 21, and this is the only time in my entire life that I've lived in snow. The property was about thirty-five miles from the Windsor/Detroit border. The wooden lodge was giant, with a big stone-hearth fireplace. It also had a game room with a pool table, foosball table, shuffleboard and a couple of deer hunting video games and pinball machines.

I was to live in one of the small cabins that surrounded the lodge. I had a one-bedroom with a hot plate, microwave and college fridge. The furniture was brand new and high quality and comfortable, and I had a TV with something like 900 channels. They gave me a giant Suburban to drive while I was there. They also had all kinds of ATVs, snowmobiles, cross-country skis, snowshoes … It was clear that these Canadians knew how to do winter.

The American owner, I'll call him the Cool Douche, lived in St. Louis and flew up every weekend during the season with a different group of friends. He was a reasonably nice guy … until he wasn't.

He wasn't much older than I was, in his late thirties, and we liked some of the same music. He was a casual Deadhead, a huge fan of the Allman Brothers and also had a mild case of psoriasis. We'd bonded over these things when we'd met on the yacht.

I didn't know anyone in Canada and, therefore, I didn't have much to do in my free time, so I poured myself into my work. I smoked a ton of meat. I made duck prosciutto, which was a two-month process and really fun. I cooked duck every which way you can imagine — these guys sure shot a lot of ducks! — duck confit, homemade pastas, stocks, glaces and dressings, pies and tarts. I cured and smoked my own bacon. I also baked all my own breads and got way into making ice creams. I definitely put on some weight up there.

These guys hunted all over the world, so they had some strange things in their freezer. Once they gave me some bear steaks, which I braised with root vegetables in Guinness stout. They loved it.

In the time that I was there, it went from kind of cold to really cold TO REALLY FUCKING COLD!!! The place was right on Lake Erie, so sometimes it would be -20 degrees with a -40-degree windchill at 4:00 a.m. when I went to make breakfast #1.

When the guests were gone, and I'd cooked everything there was to cook, I'd get a little bored. I had a lot of long phone conversations with Soss about how we could make Burning Man better. I was also pretty lonely, and when I got word that my dear old friend Campbell had died of emphysema it really hit me hard. This was the first death since my mother that really broke my heart. Losing someone close when you are isolated, with no friends around, is even harder, I think. Campbell had always been a mentor to me, even though there were things about him that I disliked. He could be very pessimistic, and a bit arrogant at times. I've been accused of having some of those same traits, so maybe that's why I disliked seeing them in him. But he also had a generous and a genuine heart. He was a great teacher to me, and I'll never forget the times that we shared.

On top of everything else, my psoriasis didn't appreciate the cold weather, but at least wearing all those layers, I was always able to conceal it. It just meant that at night, I would pick and scratch all by myself, in a cold and isolated cabin (which I called my Unabomber digs).

Sometimes I wasn't lonely, but rather, I was alone, and I liked that. I took a lot of walks in the woods. Snow was new to me, and while it was cold, it was also stark and beautiful. In fact, I'd never been anywhere so remote, and seen so much fresh snow falling. I've kept a journal off and on since I was a teenager, and I wrote a lot up there. The experience was grounding for me. I'd been living out of a backpack, in crew quarters and crew houses, hotels and guesthouses for a good five years, so even though the solitude was constant and sometimes relentless, there were times when I really relished just being in one place. The fact that it was a such a foreign place made it extra special and extra hard.

When the season came to an end, I left with handshakes, an invitation back for the next season and a great reference. I headed back to the Bay Area, with the intention of staying in one place for a while. My psoriasis was a lot worse, and I realized that my vagabond lifestyle was not helping it. I decided that it was time to settle down for a bit, and look for an apartment in the Bay Area. While I loved the lifestyle I was leading, my health and my body did not, and my skin and joints were getting worse and worse. I'd made the difficult decision that my physical and mental health must be a bit more stable for me to continue on as a traveling personal chef.

First, however, I went for a visit to see Cassidy for this eighteenth birthday. He was soon to graduate high school. Over the years telephone calls and visits once or twice a year, I'd given some thought to moving to where he lived, but it seemed too limiting. They had moved to a one-horse town, and I just couldn't see making it as a chef there, or as a single guy. Also, it was such a small town that even when I went for visits, I detected a little stink eye from some of the locals that either knew, or figured out, who I was. Cass's family was ensconced in this small community, and everyone knew everyone. It never felt anywhere close to "home" for me. And while I missed being an active parent in his life, and while I never really got along with his nuclear family, I recognized that they had a good and stable life there. I think that in *their* perfect world, I would have not come for visits, and would have disappeared from their lives entirely. Their lives would have been made easier without me there as a distraction … but I wouldn't let that happen. While the visits were strained, difficult and expensive, I knew they were important, and continued to do them. Choosing the lifestyle that I did may seem selfish on my part, and I had considered moving there … but I never felt as if I'd make it very far.

Back in the Bay Area, I stayed on a friend's very small sailboat in the Sausalito harbor while hunting for a place to rent. It was January, so it was a little cold, but nothing like the cold that I'd experienced in Canada.

Speaking of Canada, Cool Douche still owed me a paycheck for my last month. It was a big check, around $9,000. And all of a sudden, the Douche starts dodging my calls. I had nothing in writing. This whole deal had been done on a handshake. I was in the Bay Area, the lodge was in Canada and the dude that owed me the money was in St. Louis. It seemed insurmountable. Those dark feelings, the loneliness and depression, were creeping back, and I was so angry at myself. Once again, shame and humiliation rose up inside of me. I felt like it was my fault that I wasn't being paid, and I felt ashamed that I was in this position. I know it's not rational, but depression rarely is, and I was clearly in the throngs of a deep one. I wanted to curl up under a blanket in the dark. I wanted to pretend none of it was happening, or just forget about it and move on. But I needed the money, so instead of retreating inward, I called a labor attorney in St. Louis and retained his services.

Cool Douche called me the minute he received contact from my lawyer and threatened me to call the dogs off or he would countersue. They were claiming I'd trashed my cabin, burned holes in the furniture, left cigarette burns on counters (small detail: I wasn't smoking tobacco at that time and if I smoked weed it was outside) and that there was blood all over the brand-new mattress, which was not true. While my psoriasis was bad, in decades of having this disease, I have never bled through to the mattress. And, due to the extreme cold, I was sleeping in long flannel pajamas. At most, there might have been a spot of blood on the sheets, but it couldn't have been much because I didn't see it and I did my own laundry when I was there. My lawyer asked for pictures of the damage, but they couldn't provide any. They claimed they'd already thrown everything away, but they also couldn't provide replacement receipts. They really had no evidence to support their claim of damage. In the end, they settled out of court for a little more than they owed me, plus my legal expenses. Many years later the lawyer emailed me that Cool Douche had gone to prison for securities fraud. Around the same time, I heard that the owner of *Fake Tittie II* was also doing federal time for some kind of scam. I reflected on the time that I had done, and wondered how prison affected these guys. I wondered if they had learned how to play pinochle or make prison nachos. I wondered if they had found a good source of weed, or had managed to avoid fights. I thought about how, inside, we were all reduced to wearing the same clothes and to (mostly) eating the same crap. As demeaning as it was, prison was also a kind of equalizer. I found it odd that I could have been playing cards with these billionaires behind bars a few years prior to cooking on their luxury yachts or in their hunting lodges. It was a full-circle moment. I'd been out of prison long enough that some of my former bosses had managed to catch cases, and were doing time.

I moved into an (almost) two-bedroom apartment (all the rooms were connected by doors). Still, this felt like my first ever grown-up place. It wasn't a cave, and it wasn't a funky basement someone had fixed up … It was a beautiful old building with ornate moldings, built-in glass cabinets and stunning hardwood floors. The stairway, however, smelled like a combination of cat piss and a fresh box of crayons. As I was signing the lease, the manager said, "This is a great apartment, once you get used to the post office down below." "What post office…?" I asked. I looked out the window to see a post office loading dock. I now understood why the rent was so cheap. But really, how loud could it be?

REALLY FUCKING LOUD. Every day from about 4:30 to 8:00 a.m. Giant carts rolling. Trucks revving and idling and beeping as they backed up. I never got used to it. But I wasn't there much for the next two years. I'd barely moved in when I got a call asking if I wanted to go out on the road with Bob Dylan. This was a difficult time for me, so it was actually a hard decision. My skin was still really bad. And even though I'd finally gotten paid for the job in Canada, I felt inexplicably sad. I knew it wasn't a good idea for me to go on the road, but when Bob Dylan calls (not literally), you don't say no. In hindsight, that's exactly what I should have done.

I was to meet my crew in Reno. The tour was all small theaters and clubs, on what has been called the never-ending tour. I think it's been going on since 1987, but I can't be sure. Merle Haggard and his band were the opening act. I loved talking to those guys. They'd been touring together forever, and seemed to enjoy sharing road stories.

I was to be part of a crew of three. The other chef and a woman who handled the backstage hospitality were quite a bit younger than me, and they were good friends. So I felt like the odd man out from day one, and it didn't get better. We just never gelled. While I'd like to blame it on me being shut out by the two of them, that would only be partially true. My depression was so bad at this point, I was struggling just to keep it together. I'm sure it was no picnic to be around me, and in particular to work closely with me in a kitchen for fifteen to eighteen hours a day.

Depression is a beast. To my coworkers on that tour … I take this moment to apologize. Also, to my boss, who had the unpleasant job of calling me at 7:00 a.m. in Memphis, Tennessee, to give me the axe: I'm sorry. She was clear — I wasn't being let go for poor job performance, I was being let go for being difficult to get along with in a tight space. I don't know why that makes me feel a little better … but it does. It's my stupid culinary ego, which feels slight relief in knowing that I got sacked for being an asshole … as long as my food was good.

I do have one great story to tell from that tour though. We were at the Fox Theatre in St. Louis, which is a very small old theater. The only place for us to build our kitchen was below the stage, so they lifted this giant trap door off the stage floor and they loaded our gear down there with a small crane. On the menu that night, I had pork tenderloin stuffed with Granny Smith apples and creamy gorgonzola cheese, with a balsamic reduction. I'm down there below the stage doing my prep work, reducing balsamic vinegar on the stove. If you've ever done that, you know how acrid it can get. They were sound checking on the stage, and that vinegar caught Dylan in the back of the throat and he couldn't make a sound. The stage manager came rushing down. I turned off the stove and was told to never make that dish again. It didn't matter, because soon I would be gone, but it was a funny moment.

Private chef jobs in homes are a bit more difficult to come by in California, though they do exist. At least, that was the story I told myself at the time, when I couldn't find work and didn't want to go back to the yachting industry. It turns out, there are actually plenty of them, if you know how to market yourself, which I would learn in later years. But at that point, I was feeling pretty beat down. I applied for a ton of jobs, and anytime I didn't get one, I sunk lower.

Lucky for me, I got an interview for one job I really wanted — sous chef at an organic catering company called Back to Earth (B2E). I will never forget that interview. My father always said, "A tie is appropriate everywhere, except in the shower, and there it is accepted." Boy was he ever wrong about that! I pulled up in my tie, just as the crew was finishing lunch. They were all tattooed, with many piercings, wearing torn jeans and different Earth activist T-shirts. The two owners were barefoot, sitting cross-legged on the sidewalk, finishing a plate of lunch in front of the kitchen. As we headed inside for the interview, I loosened my tie and wished to hell I'd worn jeans and a "Save the Whales" T-shirt, or something along those lines. We sat around a desk, above which two pictures hung: Malcolm X and His Holiness the Dalai Lama.

These guys were into everything organic. Even their van ran on veggie oil (and always smelled like french fries). It was clear from looking around the kitchen and office space that building community was a priority to them. It seemed like the perfect job for me, but I didn't get the sous chef gig. They did, however, hire me on as an on-call event cook, so at least I would be picking up some work.

This inspired me to sign up with all the big caterers around the Bay Area, and I began keeping pretty busy with gig work. But I really wanted a job with health benefits. My skin and arthritis were brutal, and there were some new meds that I'd been reading about but those drugs were expensive. The worse my health was, the more depressed I would become. The more depressed I would become, the worse my health was. It was a vicious cycle. And on top of that, I wasn't making enough to make ends meet, and I was blowing through my savings.

The work was steady, and the pay was decent for the Bay Area, but it was nowhere near the money that I'd become accustomed to making on yachts, and there were a lot more expenses involved in living on land. I wasn't dating much during this period, and most of my friends were either working on boats or so busy with kids and jobs that we never hung out. When I wasn't working, I was anxious about money, and when I was working, I was resentful at being underpaid, which is the curse of 99 percent of the cooking industry. I just couldn't get comfortable, and no matter what I did, I felt unstable, emotionally and financially, so I decided to seek out therapy. I wanted a therapist who would help me through my depression and wouldn't judge me for what I think is a healthy relationship with drugs. I wanted a therapist who understood my lifestyle. I wanted a therapist from my own community, a tribe member.

Enter, Glinda, the Good Witch of the East Bay. A wise and wonderful redhead with a fiery edge, who had traveled the world, studied with shamans and was well versed in Vipassana, the Hopi way, Judaism and Kabbalah, and many other forms of mysticism and spirituality. We ran in the same circles.

She'd also been to Burning Man, seen Jerry Garcia play, seen a sunrise on LSD. She was exactly what I was looking for. One thing that has always eluded me is the question of how come, when my life is pretty great, I still suffer from depression and anxiety. Through therapy I've learned that we really don't shake the bad things that happen to us in our formative years, and as my youth was so challenging, I learned to understand where the roots of my depression came from. While I had practiced compassion for those around me, the concept of extending compassion to myself was new to me. Over the next twenty months, we did good work together, and I'm so grateful to have had her in my life.

During this time, I applied to be chef de cuisine at a fancy hotel with a restaurant called the Duck Club and a bistro called The Grill. I didn't get the chef de cuisine position but they offered me a job as line cook. For the second time, I applied for management and got a low-level position instead. That does a number on your confidence. The pay was pathetic, but the benefits were decent, and I needed health insurance. For a little while, I got my ass handed to me as I rebuilt the muscle memory of line cooking, making the same dishes hundreds of times over and over in a night, and having it come out just exactly perfect every fucking time.

At a restaurant called "The Grill," you can bet your ass that the grill station was a tricky one to work. Burgers, NY strips, rib eyes, filets, swordfish and tuna all came off my station. And that didn't even include the fryer, which, aside from fries, did jalapeño poppers, crab cakes, and some goat-cheese-and-truffle fritters for the Duck Club menu. For a while, they even ran a special with beer-battered onion rings, but I revolted. The batter would trash my fryer oil for the night, and I'd spend too much time trying to fish out the burning, batter-y bits.

Every night was busy, and Friday and Saturday nights resembled the opening scene from *Saving Private Ryan*. Sometimes I had to sandbag steaks for service. This means searing them off as rare and resting them on a rack, a perfect medium rare if they sold quickly, or we'd pass them off to those ordering medium well or well done if they sat for too long. This practice is frowned upon by seasoned cooks and chefs because you take the risk of not selling them, and once they are seared, that's it. But we were so busy, I never ended up with unsold steaks, and it was the only way I could keep up. Besides, a well-rested steak is a great steak. But the hum of the ticket machine never stopped — the tickets would hang all the way to the floor on a busy night — and that sound would haunt me in my sleep for years to come.

The bummer about working in a restaurant is that most of them are open at least five or six nights a week, and you're always working while other people are partying and having fun. Hotels never close, making the hours even worse. I worked most weekends and holidays. The chef de cuisine was a decent enough guy, and a great chef, but he was a stone-cold junkie with a serious opioid addiction, and his moods swung a lot. He knew I hated being a line cook. He could also see I had skills, so he created a new position for me with the title of saucier/butcher, with the understanding that I'd still have to work the line on busy nights. This meant that all my time was now spent in the back kitchen with the banquet guys who did the weddings and conventions. It was much less stressful and required a bit more finesse and skill. The banquet crew were a bunch of older dudes that had been there for decades. They made all that mediocre wedding food that we've all eaten, and those of us trying to win James Beard Awards sort of looked down on them. In return, they all thought the restaurant crew was nuts because our hours sucked, and we were always getting screamed at by our junkie chef.

At the beginning of the week, I'd get all the stocks going. Chicken, veal and lobster stocks were staples, and sometimes we'd need a specialty stock, like lamb or mushroom. We also ground our own burger meat, which was a big job. The dishwashers would form and freeze our burger patties. I'd break down rib eyes, NY strip loins, and beef tenderloins, as well as whole chickens and lamb racks. We ran salmon and halibut specials when they were in season, and I got good at breaking down both of those fishes, as well. When the chef learned that I'd worked in New England, he started running lobster nights. I've broken down so many live lobsters that I'm fairly certain that if reincarnation exists, I'm coming back as a crustacean, a karmic retribution.

We were famous for our French onion soup because we'd take the bones that had been used for a veal stock, re-roast them and make a second stock (called a remouillage, or a "remy," as it is often referred to in kitchens) and I'd add my highly concentrated demi-glace to the soup. We'd slice fresh Gruyère on top and crisp it up nicely in the salamander (broiler) for service. I can smell that burning cheese as I write this!

My skin was still pretty awful, but I was in the back of the house, where everyone is predictably ugly, so it didn't matter.

Sophomore Syndrome

Burning Man was in my blood. When I wasn't actually on the Playa, I was thinking about it. As we prepared for our next year, we fell victim to a classic case of sophomore syndrome, taking on way more projects than we could handle with any sense of grace. While our camp was four years old, this was only the second year of the restaurant. The first two years were a couple of guys and a grill. We had kicked ass the year before and were ready to take on the world. The Rev, our master of BBQ, didn't like having everything prepared ahead. He felt that made us just line cooks and left very little room to be creative. He came up with an idea to create what he called "The Magic Kitchen." The idea was to have enough equipment and ingredients to create anything that anyone thought up … on a whim, in the desert. Everything would be fresh. Every menu would be brand new. It would be great! He also vetoed pre-marinating and freezing meats. "Raw is religion" was his mantra that year … and man, did it come back to bite us in the ass.

On top of all of those new challenges, we had some internal troubles within the Q. About a month before Burning Man, Soss and The Sheik had a falling out, and The Sheik pulled out. The Sheik had handled the financials, paperwork and a lot of organizational tasks of running our camp. Now it was all going to fall on Soss, who had already bitten off more than he could chew. And … he'd bitten off more than WE could chew, which was just how he rolled. This, combined with The Rev's new Magic Kitchen plan and "Raw is religion" motif, made for an extremely challenging year.

We had lofty goals for our camp, but then Soss went on to do a few things that became problematic. He invited a camp from the Midwest to join us, The

Uber Carnies. All they asked was that we give them space for a bar, and they would help with infrastructure. They camped with us for two years, growing the size of our camp from around fifty to 150 people. This was great for people power, but it meant we had a lot of mouths to feed. And Soss made the Rock Star Dinners slightly larger, and decided there would be three of them.

That year, we created two additional projects for our camp that were really fun but added to our already burgeoning workload. The first was an Iron Chef competition every day at 1:00 p.m., each with a different theme: The Luscious Lobster Battle, The Ceviche Civil War, The Vegan Slaughter, The Gumbo Conspiracy and The Smoked Meats Throw-Down. People would read about us in the guide to Burning Man (known as the *What Where When* book), show up and try and beat us. To say we had home-court advantage is an understatement. We crushed anybody that came along, and mostly we crushed each other. The only thing better than the food for the Iron Chef competitions was the smack talk that came with it.

We also started a project called The Carne Armada. The idea was to pick a camp that works hard for the Burning Man community and is deserving of a gift, and throw them a pop-up surprise party. Our method was to find one "mole" within that camp and get them to gather their troops. Usually they'd spread word that there was a mandatory camp meeting, or a group photo or something. Then, when they were mostly assembled, the Playa-Q would descend upon them, usually on three or four large art cars with around fifty people on each car. We would play *Flight of the Valkyries* at top volume as we pulled up to the camp being "attacked."

Admiral Painjoy, a seasoned burner and camp leader, led the charge of this event. Painjoy is your all-American, blond-haired, blue-eyed, perverted Eagle Scout. He had had a long and illustrious Burning Man career, not missing a year since his first Burn in 1999. He now runs a Kink camp called Spanky's Wine Bar. He and I have had many adventures together, both on the Playa and off. He is also an experienced contractor, who has done loads of work on our house, and he spearheaded a trip to a deserted private island, that you, dear reader, will read about shortly, should you choose to continue on this culinary adventure.

Painjoy, dressed in an admiral's costume, of course, would announce something like, "Campers of Burners Without Borders [one of the camps that we attacked that first year — they formed when Hurricane Katrina hit, with a goal to feed the displaced community, and have been active doing disaster relief work ever since], Playa-Q loves and appreciates the good work that you do. This celebration is our appreciation for your service to communities in need" (or something along those lines).

At that moment, everyone would jump off the art cars carrying platters of smoked meats, lobster rolls, veggies, ceviche in cucumber cups, canapés, Otter Pops injected with vodka and fruit platters. Our resident DJ would be bumping upbeat house music. Keep in mind this was at a week-long event in the desert. Most people are ravenous, dehydrated or exhausted. So we'd also have massage chairs, and party guests would get five-minute sessions, while eating award-worthy brisket and other delicacies. It was a raucous scene, with stilt-walkers, jugglers, fire spinners … and platter upon platter of world-class food. It was kind of like a fine-dining burlesque circus flash mob. About fifty minutes later, Painjoy would give the signal and we'd all pile back on the art cars and disappear into the desert dust, as if it never happened. Ten of our finest always stuck around to pick up any "moop" (matter out of place, is what litter is called on the Playa) that may have fallen to the ground, leaving no trace other than smiling faces and full bellies.

The Carne Armada blew peoples' minds. Over the years we "attacked" the crew that builds The Man, the Media Mecca, Burners Without Borders, the Department of Public Works (DPW), the Flaming Lotus Girls and First Camp, which houses Burning Man's founders.

This would be a lot of work for anyone, anyhow, anywhere … and at Burning Man, it's times ten. We had no running water, we had those evaporation ponds to deal with, plus really smelly garbage and a ton of food. Literally. We had 1,000 pounds of meat, 500 pounds of seafood, 600 pounds of produce, plus all the corn tortillas, dry goods … it was insane. We had so much meat that we ran out of fridge and freezer space, so rotating ice and draining coolers became a full-time job.

Soss Boss was always trying to climb whatever social ladder was in front of him … so some of our events were labeled "too exclusive" and not accessible enough to the public. The Rock Star Dinners were especially vulnerable to that accusation, as seating was limited, and this was where we really tried to showcase our talents. This rubbed some people (or at least the ones without invites) the wrong way, as it was not in accordance with the "radical inclusion" principle of Burning Man. The Rock Star Dinners were actually glaringly exclusive, in total opposition to that principle. To offset this, we created

Reverend Smoke's Pulled Pork Giveaway. Late Saturday night, after they burn the giant effigy of The Man, The Rev would go to the simmering remains of The Man (that had just been burned) with a hotel pan, tongs and gloves, and would collect some embers. He'd then start his smokers and grills with these embers and go into overdrive cooking meat.

The Rev LOVES old-school hip hop, so for four to five hours, on the Sunday, we cranked out music and gave away around 600 pounds of smoked brisket and pulled pork tacos. It took him days and days of prepping, smoking and resting meats. Just trying to store that much meat, and keeping hot foods hot and cold foods cold, was really hard. Then, to get it all hot again in a short window of time, to serve to thousands of strangers, just for the sake of doing it, is nothing short of masterful, beautiful, soulful and one of the many reasons that I love Burning Man (and Reverend Smoke).

One morning, I came out of my tent after a crazy night of fun … because even in the midst of all this work, we still managed to have a hell of a good time. I had met a woman from a neighboring camp the night before. We had hit it off quite nicely, with conversations that flowed like water and intoxicated like wine. We had a ton in common and were both instantly smitten. We arranged for a Playa date that began at about 10:00 p.m., when we both finished with our respective work shifts at our camps.

Once the sun had set, and our shifts were over, we met for a drink. We were going to go for a walk, but it was fucking cold, so we decided to go to my tent and cuddle a little bit to stay warm, and then we'd go exploring. But as things happened, we never left the tent again that night. I think the zipper may have been stuck…

When we woke up a little after sunrise, the desert air was already heating up. It was time to pee and take stock of the tasks at hand for the day ahead. I clambered out of the tent into the blazing sun, thinking about the fact that we had our first Rock Star Dinner that night, and the first thing I saw was a bunch of frozen chicken spread out on tables in the sun. I immediately sprang into action, shaking my head and fists in disbelief at the flagrant health violation that was unfolding before my eyes. A scraggly blond guy who looked to be a few years older than me says, "Yo, I'm Viagra. I run the Fat Elvis Fried Chicken Shack. Soss said I could use the kitchen for a couple of hours until you guys get going today. Don't worry, the chicken will be out of the sun and into the fryer just as soon as I can peel it apart."

My lack of sleep and my sense of culinary ethics kick into overdrive, and I start yelling at the guy with reckless abandon. "What the fuck is wrong with you? What gives you the right to put my health permit and reputation on the line with this kind of bullshit? How fucking dare you compromise people's health and the honor of the Q? Get the fuck out of my kitchen now!"

Soss rushes in to see what all the commotion is about, and starts telling me to chill out. "Viagra is a contributor and a good friend of the Q," he's saying, but I'm still raging. "I don't give a fuck if he's The Man that they are burning, Larry Harvey [founder of Burning Man] or the G-d-damned president," I replied. "He cannot, and will not, defrost chicken in the sun in my kitchen. You made me executive chef for a reason, and this is it! The health permit has my name on it [pointing to our health permit taped to a fridge door] and that's just the fucking way it is." I'm practically frothing at the mouth at this point.

That was around the time Kinsky showed up and tried to calm me down by offering me a cup of coffee and a seat in the shade. I realized then that I still hadn't had a pee. I took a sip of the coffee and looked over at my tent to see my Playa date watching the whole scene with great amusement. We lock eyes, and she motions me back to the tent … but it's too hot, and I have too much work to do. I pee, drink the coffee and manage to calm myself down … But I can see it's going to be a long fucking day. I am fastidious about food safety, and The Rev is even more so, so we always passed our health inspections with flying colors. In fact, once or twice, the health inspectors brought over other camp chefs that were failing their inspections to show them how it was done right. We were on a first-name basis with those guys. We had portable handwashing stations with procedures posted, and gloves a-plenty, three compartment bus tub washing stations with washing instructions posted above each one, including guidelines on water to soap ratio, etc. One thing that we learned from running large camps is that if you give volunteers clear direction, they'll usually do a good job for you, whereas without direction, they can do more harm than good. It's one of the more valuable management tools I've learned, and it has served me well in countless situations, especially with volunteers who mean well but may not have a ton of experience.

At the end of our first year, a furry little dude named Dante had come by, and was amazed at our kitchen, our dining room and at what we'd created. But mostly … he was amazed by The Rev and his expert-level meat-smoking skills. Dante badgered The Rev to let him assist, but The Rev was adamant about not wanting anyone getting in his way. Dante persisted until The Rev finally acquiesced and took on his first (and only) Playa-Q intern. Miraculously, Dante kept up with The Rev on cannabis consumption, which is a feat not many could handle. He was so hungry to learn this culinary magic that he dedicated many hours a day to helping The Rev and learning from him. The difference between them was that Dante needed sleep every once in a while. Dante became our brother, and a valuable and loved member of the Core Q.

One night, I stumbled into camp in the wee hours during a night of psychedelic merriment, and Soss said to me, "Chef, I need you to do me a favor. I need you to bake a cake. It's a birthday cake for a large Playa-Q benefactor, and … and … it doesn't matter, I just need you to bake me a cake." We had acquired a double stacked convection oven that ran on propane and electricity … and it drew so much power that it always fried our generator. Kinsky, our electrical genius, was tripping really hard with me, and warned me that the power might not hold. Somehow or other, I baked the one and only cake that I know how to bake … while tripping my face off in the desert in the middle of the night with a sketchy oven. The cake was a flourless chocolate with bourbon-soaked pecans that one of my yacht captains had dubbed the Anchor Cake. I garnished it with a dark chocolate ganache, and even wrote Happy Birthday in white chocolate. I finished it all before dawn, and managed to nab a little bit of sleep.

A couple days later, as a few of us were waking up and having coffee, Soss arrived, and gathered up the Core Q, the people that really made it all happen. He told us to grab our cameras and to come with him; he had a surprise for us. That surprise was a flight over Black Rock City in a seven-passenger private airplane that was owned by … the guy I'd made the birthday cake for. This was such a classic Soss Boss maneuver.

On our last night, they burned a giant temple that had been there all week. The temple burn is very different from the man burn. All week people had been writing the names of loved ones who have passed, and generally shedding things they wish to leave for the flames of this beautiful structure that has been built in the desert for just this purpose. It is a somber and beautiful catharsis after an incredibly hedonistic week.

As nearly 30,000 people watched in near silence as the temple burned, I reflected upon the work that we had done, the people we had fed, and the community we had built. I found myself crying uncontrollably. It felt like a badly needed cathartic release that had been building up in me all week, or maybe ever for my entire life.

After all that, is it any wonder that I fell asleep at the wheel on my drive home that year? Yup … that happened, and I'm lucky to be alive. I took out a telephone pole and a sign for a Holiday Inn Express, which is where I ended up staying that night after they hauled my totaled car to the junkyard. I was incredibly lucky to not have been hurt. The following morning I had to hitchhike to Reno to rent a car, go to the dump and load all my crap from my totaled car into the rental … and my shit was just dusty enough that I got hit with an extra cleaning fee on the rental car, even though that car never actually went to Burning Man.

Back to Earth

After my accident, and in a post-burn haze of blissful exhaustion, I called in sick to my job at the hotel for a couple of days. Chef was less than understanding. "Look, you can take two more days off, but I'm going to need you in here on Saturday night, so if you can't make it by then, don't bother coming back." I was so shell-shocked, there was no way I was ready for a busy Saturday night. To be perfectly honest, I still hadn't recovered from Burning Man, let alone the accident. Between the dust, extreme heat in the day and near freezing temperatures at night, the elevation, the amount of work that we bit off, the electricity and sheer intensity of sharing in this experience with 30,000 people, I was beyond exhausted.

But I needed the job. So I hauled myself back in. I was on the grill station, and the ticket counter kept a steady hum. I was keeping up all right, but every time the sauce guy finished with a pan, he chucked the dirties in a metal bin between the grill and the stove. *Clang!* Every time, I'd nearly jump out of my skin. And for a moment, I'd be back in the car, banged up, scared shitless and wondering if I was going to die. For a while, I was able to keep up with the ticket machine. I'd methodically load my grill with burgers, steaks and fish that were ordered. I'd sandbag a little by loading my grill heavy, and by the grace of G-d, I was able to keep up the pace. But that fucking sauce guy kept throwing pans harder and harder into the metal bin. This happened over and over until I finally cracked. I just walked off the line. It's the only time I've ever left the line during service. Somewhere behind me I heard Chef yelling that he was going to write me up, but I didn't care. He never did write me up, and things went back to normal shortly after that, except that I've never been able to sleep in a car since. Even as a passenger, as soon as I feel myself beginning to doze, I relive that moment of the crash.

It came as a pleasant surprise when Back to Earth called one day and offered me the sous chef position. I immediately gave notice at the hotel and quietly did my final two weeks. B2E was an amazing place to work. The kitchen was well organized and really clean. In fact, probably the biggest thing I learned from our executive chef, Cheffanie, was catering organization. She was an expert.

It was good to be working at a place that aligned with my values. While yachting had been sexy and fun for a while, it had become soulless and empty to me. Some of the yachts I'd worked on burned 100 gallons of diesel per hour when they were steaming. Now I was working for an organic place where we composted everything. Everybody there, as well as our client base, was committed to preserving the environment, which was a refreshing change, and connected well with the "leave-no-trace" ethos that I admired so much at Burning Man.

We did amazing work, and I managed some parties and weddings that I felt really proud of. Great food, great events, a great team. B2E was, however, also the setting for one of the worst moments of my entire culinary career.

We were catering a three-day conference at UC Berkeley. It was grab-and-go breakfast, snack stations, buffet lunch and dinner … for 1,500 people. It was a monumental task. We set up different service areas, and had a crew to manage the drink and snack stations. In our prep kitchen, we had a full crew doing prep work, and loading and unloading the vans. The gig was so big that we had rented a couple big box trucks.

I was working the dinner shift this particular night. The crew was wiped out, but we were powering though. This was a big and important job for us. I'd been assigned a seasoned catering pro whom I call the Wizard as my assistant. I had catered with him many times before, and I was happy to see that he was on my team. In fact, my whole team was solid.

We were assigned an old cafeteria kitchen to cook in. I assessed the area and made my game plan. We would run three rows of tables off the ovens. The Wizard set up his work space with bakers' racks full of two-inch hotel pans that were being used to marinate chicken. The dish was Marbella, and the pans were lined in olives, dried prunes and a light layer of the sauce, which was made of red wine vinegar, brown sugar and a little butter. It was all small pieces, boneless thighs, which are far more forgiving than breasts. It's pretty hard to dry out a thigh, and as everyone knows it is imperative that chicken is cooked all the way through.

I gathered my crew for a quick meeting. The Wizard was my most experienced cook, so I put him on the ovens, and assigned the rest of the crew their spots. "All right … the plan is for you to fire the chicken four pans at a time. I need you to stagger your timing by as long as it will take you to empty an oven and reload it. This way the pans can keep going out, and we shouldn't have a cluster situation. Meanwhile the other two lines will handle the veggies, potatoes and sauce. The veggies are being sautéed on the flattops and passed down the line. I'll be at the other end of the line, checking the platters and garnishing."

The kitchen was dusty, musty and looked as if it hadn't been used in a long time. I took a moment to take a long pull off my water bottle, and tried my best to stay calm and organized. I was the leader, and I couldn't let my crew know how anxious I was. It was a big moment. This was my first shot at running a big production, and it HAD to come off without a hitch.

About twenty minutes out, I asked each station to fire one round of their assigned dishes so that we could assess the cook time and adjust final seasonings. The chicken took about sixteen minutes to become golden brown on top, the sauce bubbling with goodness. We all gathered around, had a taste and tidied up for service.

"We're ready for hot food, Chef," the front of house manager told me, over the walkie-talkie.

"Copy that," I answered.

"All right, team, let's fire the first round of everything," I told the crew.

"Yes, Chef!" they replied in unison.

We sent the first round of pans out, and were putting the garnishes on the second round when the Wizard came up to me and said the words no chef ever wants to hear. "Hey, Chef, I think the chicken is undercooked."

I reached into the center of the pan in front of me and ripped into a thigh. It was crispy brown on top, and the sauce it was in was bubbling … but sure enough, the center was raw as could be. The ovens were fine with one pan … but loading them up with six pans took too much heat, and compromised the rest of the ovens, which were old and mostly used for pizza. It turned out that the top heating elements were working, but the bottoms had crapped out.

In a near panic, I made my way out to the buffet line and scooped up the chicken as quickly as I could. The diners looked bewildered as I took the main protein source off the buffet line, but I didn't care. As I made my way to the kitchen, I dug my thumb into a piece of the chicken, and sure enough … it was fucking raw in the center.

It was clear to the owners of the company that my kitchen was crashing down, but they gave me the professional courtesy of letting me solve the problem myself. I quickly ordered my cooks to switch the veggies to the ovens, and the chicken to the flattops. We got the sauce cooking on the stovetops, and the Wizard and I went to town on the flattops. "Load this fucker up!" I yelled. Once we could fit no more meat on the flattops, I started yelling to the dishwasher for a stack of sheet pans, and he immediately complied. We covered the chicken with the sheet pans to hold the heat in and shorten the cooking time. I even began to splash water on the flattops to create steam, ensuring that the meat would be cooked through.

It felt like a battle scene in a war movie. People dying left and right, running through blood and guts, pressing on for sheer survival. It wasn't quite that dramatic … but it felt like it. We all had laser focus, trying to make it through service, and eventually the last of the savory food went out and the dessert lines began to spring into action.

We managed to get all the food out, cooked all the way through … and to my knowledge, nobody actually ate any raw chicken. However, in that moment, it didn't matter. In my eyes, I had failed, and I was wrecked. It took all of my strength to finish service, clean up and pack the vans.

By the time I got home, a little after midnight, I had nothing left in me. I sank into my couch and burst into tears. I was broken, dejected and felt like an utter failure. Cheffanie must have picked up my vibes from across town, because she called me … something she had never done that late at night. She could hear in my voice that I'd been crying, and I think that she was surprised to learn that I was so sensitive. My kitchen persona comes off as a bit more macho, I think.

"Look," she said, "shit happens. No matter how hard we try to anticipate it, we get thrown curve balls. In fact, that's exactly what catering is! We don't have the luxury of cooking in the same kitchen for every event. We are always learning and rolling with the punches. While the situation sucked, you handled it with grace. Nobody ate raw meat. I don't think anybody got sick. And you assessed the situation, altered the course and succeeded in getting fifteen hundred people fed in a reasonable amount of time. Rather than feeling bad, you have every reason to be proud of the work that you did tonight." While pride was the last thing that I was feeling in that moment, her words worked to soothe my pain. That is the job of a good team leader, and it was a valuable lesson to me in supporting your crew in the bad moments as well as the good ones.

The following day, we all arrived a little early. "Good morning," Cheffanie said. "We've decided to rent a propane-powered double stack convection oven for you, so you shouldn't have any trouble tonight." It was another great lesson in leadership. The company not only forgave my mistake, and supported the "on the fly" cooking methods I'd adopted, but they took measures to ensure success that next night. But my biggest takeaway was to always keep your cool. Take the time to make sure that your methods are solid, and correct them if they are not. And in a pinch, try your best to maintain your composure.

Seven Deadly Sins

By the time Burning Man 2007 came around, my catering chops were strong. I'd been planning, managing and running large parties for a while now. I had learned to break a menu down into every component, deduce what order the tasks needed to happen in and figured out the most efficient ways to execute them.

Early in the year, I had an idea for a seven-course menu around the seven deadly sins, with each course representing a different sin. I was imagining it as an interactive culinary artistic experience, with music and performance art keyed to the concept. Surprisingly, it took some convincing to get Soss on board. I think that perhaps his frail male ego was challenged by the fact that it was my idea. In the past, all of the brilliant Q ideas had been his. But it didn't matter. He had given me the role of executive chef of the camp, and that meant that this decision was mine. As time went on, I think he saw how committed I was to making this an amazing event, and he warmed up to the idea. Here is the menu I put together:

- Wrath: Scallop ceviche with tequila and habanero (because who hasn't felt the wrath of both of these?)

- Pride: Smoked-duck gumbo with cannabis cornbread croutons (Gumbo is my mantra AND my safe word, and I take great pride in the ancient tradition of making this dish!)

- Sloth: Pork three ways — a smoked pork *tenderloin* wrapped in house-cured *bacon* served over apple purée, chai-cured pork *belly*

- Lust: Sushi served on four naked bodies

- Greed: The money shot — some of the world's most expensive ingredients on a plate: roasted veal tenderloin served with foie gras-truffle-and-goat cheese fritters, sauce bordelaise

- Envy: Mixed greens (with envy)

- Gluttony: Baked Alaska served on fire (Where fire meets ice. The Playa-Q loves you … Fuck you, you gluttonous fucks!)

I wrote the menu in January, which meant I had eight months to work out the details. I figured out what could be prepared in advance and what needed to be done on site. I used the spreadsheet system that I'd learned at work, and even my lists had their own lists. I worked out every detail, from shopping to garnishes and how the cleanup would work. I pored over every task, and the necessary equipment for said tasks, in my head and on paper. I ran my plan through my chef networks, and took advice and pointers where I could.

While I worked on the food, Soss worked on logistics. As I've said, he was masterful at composing a team, and plugging each team member into the role where they would shine the brightest. This spanned from dish pimps to DJs, servers to cooks, performance artists to sushi chefs, and our illustrious team of sushi models. Soss worked on staffing, and the performance art that would accompany the food, while I worked on the menu and execution tactics.

One piece of the puzzle that helped me tremendously was a woman named Dawn. She was the executive sous chef in charge of banquets at the Ritz-Carlton, Chicago, and she happened to be camping with us that year. We invited her to be my sous at Burning Man, with the caveat that she'd work her ass off the day of the event … but not do much else, she accepted the offer.

My prep lists were never better, or more organized. A few weeks before the event, I sent The Rev my smoked meats order. It included what items I'd need, and when I needed them by, for my prep work, as well as defrost dates, etc.

It was a great week leading up to the Rock Star Dinner. Everything was going according to plan.

One afternoon, The Rev was building a fire by the smokers while Dante, our intern, was trimming and seasoning briskets. "Hey, Rev," I said, "let's go out and cause some trouble. Come look at art with me." He set down the logs of pecan wood that he was holding and walked over to me. "It sounds fun, Chef, but you know what really sounds like fun?" From his tone, I knew that he was not going to come adventure with me. "What's that?" I humored him with a response. "Getting these briskets on the smoker, rolling a fat joint and brewing some coffee," he said. "You're lucky," he continued. "You get to cook every single day. I spend most of my time in front of a screen. I wish I had more time to cook. This is what I want to do when I come out here. I want to smoke weed, smoke meat, cook the best food that I know how to, with people I love. I want to feed people, and blow their minds with the best fucking BBQ for hundreds of miles. That's where my joy comes from." How could I argue with that?

The day before the dinner, production ramped up. I had a full crew of volunteers. Kinsky and Smooth were on deck to ensure that our kitchen was functioning, which was good, because the convection oven would trip the generator every time we turned it on. We had seven fridges and three freezers running 24/7. A generator failure was just not an option.

All of the components for the ceviche were prepped; all it needed was the lime juice to start working its acidic magic for the heatless cooking process. I made the dark roux that thickened the rich duck stock, harmoniously emulsifying into a viscous, tasty broth. The roux has to be the color of dark chocolate, without ever tasting burnt or bitter. One trick that I'd learned in NOLA was to have your holy trinity (onions, celery and bell pepper) prepped before you start the roux. Once it hits the color you want, which takes about forty minutes, you turn the heat off and add your trinity while continuing to stir. This both cools the roux down and adds the flavor of these veggies, which are hitting a 700-degree cauldron of fat and flour. It's fun to see the transition from broth to gravy.

We made the apple purée that worked as the "glue" to wrap the pork tenderloins with bacon, carefully hiding a few sage leaves inside, in the tradition of the classic Italian dish, Saltimbocca. The pork bellies had been curing in a dried chai solution for about two weeks, and on this day they would be smoked, and then broken down into two-inch squares. For service, they'd be seared on the outsides, and then brought up to temperature and slowly braised in a rich chai broth. Our seafood order was coming in the morning, for the sushi, so there wasn't much that we could do for the Lust course until then.

We made the salad dressing for our mixed greens and went into production for the Baked Alaska. This was the most challenging aspect of the entire menu, as we wanted to serve it on fire. I made about 100 cookie disks in our incredibly inefficient propane-powered double stacked convection oven and separated about 150 eggs so I'd be ready to make my meringue the following day. The plan was that each cookie crust would get a hefty scoop of ice cream, then my team of culinary gangsters and badasses would pipe the meringue around the ice cream. We had Everclear in squeeze bottles, and the idea was we would douse the whole thing in booze and light them on fire as they were being walked out to the diners in the dark circus tent.

This was the plan … and it was an ambitious plan. It might have worked, had all gone perfectly, but at Burning Man, nothing ever goes perfectly.

Our head count for the dinner was seventy-five guests and almost the same number of cooks, servers, dishwashers, performers, musicians, fire spinners, etc. It had all the makings of any great theatrical production … that offers fine dining in the desert … with no running water.

It was game day. I woke up feeling charged. This dinner I'd been planning for months was finally here. I made coffee and pulled out my ubiquitous clipboard. I made a few notes and scratched a few items off yesterday's list. I put the gumbo on the stove to begin heating slowly through and set up an expediting station. We had always served food family style, but on this night we were doing seven courses plated. Precision in organization was the key to the success of this ambitious project.

As I poured my second cup of coffee, Soss pulled up on the magic carpet art car, a golf cart made to look like a flying purple carpet, adorned with LED lights, a kickass sound system … and a stripper pole. They were coming from the air strip where our fish order had landed. Soss threw the fish in one of the fridges, and poured himself a cup from the pot. "Morning, Chef," he said in his most nasally voice. He was wearing a pink and black kimono and a pair of Doc Martens boots. Soss had made a tradition of wearing only bathrobes at Burning Man, and he had a notable collection.

We began to go over the timing and some of the details of the evening event and, as we did, my ragtag team of cooks began to appear. It was pretty clear that some of them were still going from the night before, but they appeared to be up to the challenges ahead.

I was happy to see Dawn, my sous chef. She and I went over the prep list and she jumped into leading production. As we were getting going, we could see a dust storm approaching. The Black Rock Desert is famous for blinding whiteouts. The wind blows the dust in such a way that you cannot see your hand in front of your face, and you never know how long it's going to last. Before we knew it, we were in the middle of just such a storm. "Cover everything!" I yelled to the crew. I threw a lid on the gumbo, and everyone sprang into action, covering what they were working on with hotel pans. We secured everything as much as we could, and climbed into the back of the box truck, trying to avoid the dust and the wind. "I hope this passes quickly," I muttered, to nobody in particular.

The bad news was … it did not pass quickly. We were stuck with whiteout conditions for the next four hours. But the good news was that we were so far ahead, and in such good shape, that I wasn't too worried about it affecting service. We hunkered down in the box truck and did side work, making silverware rolls, folding napkins and such. After a couple hours, the storm subsided, and while it was still dusty as could be, it was no longer a whiteout.

We sprang back into action. I broke down all of the fish for the sushi. Speaking of the sushi, this year we had an actual sushi chef on our crew. We had become known for serving sushi on naked women, and this year we'd had a request for a naked man as well. Soss had procured four military-style gurneys. We had set up a separate tent for the sushi team to get cleaned up, both before and after service. A team of concubines (and concubones) helped our three women and one man get cleaned up for the event, bathing them with warm soapy water, and then keeping the dust off with baby wipes. We even had robes for them to lounge in as they waited.

About an hour before service, I counted our martini glasses, which the ceviche would be served in. We only had sixty-four and needed seventy-five. "Smooth!" I yelled.

"Yes, Chef," he responded, with a slightly drunken slur.

"I need eleven martini glasses as quickly as you can round them up."

He looked at me with a cockeyed grin and said, "Do they need to be full, or can I drink them?" He was off before I could answer.

Painjoy would be the emcee, describing the courses to our diners. Soss would be the general manager, production director and liaison between the dining room and the kitchen.

Another camp from San Diego built a blacklight art gallery that led the way into the dining-room tent. In the blacklight gallery, we had chairs for people to remove their shoes, and we had hand- and foot-washing stations and a team of volunteers to run that area.

The kitchen was buzzing with energy as the diners began to arrive. People were gathering in the dining room with freshly washed hands and feet, being served signature cocktails from our bar.

Soss sent the message to Painjoy to get the diners in their seats. At this point the dining room filled up with fire dancers and fire spinners. The smokers were filling the air with pleasant meat smells, a nice distraction from the scent of burning white gas that the fire spinners were dousing on their tools. Once everybody was seated, Soss welcomed the diners and passed the emcee responsibilities to Painjoy. PJ can be a bit long-winded when given a microphone, and we had to keep him on a short leash … which is his preference anyway, as his name might suggest.

In the kitchen, I had already put the finishing touches on the ceviche, and we were pulling the martini glasses out of the freezer. (It had taken Smooth about forty minutes to come back with nine martini glasses in a box, ready to go for service … and two full ones in his hands, one of which he handed to me, with extra olives.)

Sous Chef Dawn expertly led the plate-up of that course, while I went to collect my pork from The Rev at the smokers. Meanwhile in the dining room fire performers danced their interpretation of the wrath course, paired with the DJ's music, and the concubines and concubones made sure that everyone had what they needed to enjoy their meal … even if that meant massages at the table.

Myself and one cook sliced the tenderloins into quarter-inch medallions. The apple/sage purée was warm on the stove, and the chai-cured pork belly was hot, sitting in covered hotel pans. As the servers began clearing the first course, we pulled the plates, which had been wrapped in foil and were in the hot boxes, staying as dust free as they could in the Black Rock Desert. Playa dust is the seasoning for all things, and as soon as you accept that fact, the event becomes much more fun. A drag of apple purée on the plate with a sauce spoon, two slices of the tenderloin with a tablespoon of apple and chive with lemon zest salad on top, and a square of the pork belly on the opposite side of the plate with a drizzle of chai reduction underneath. This was a sexy course. I'm not sure how it related to sloth … but it's what I came up with.

As soon as course two went out, I made sure course three was set and ready. This was gumbo in a bowl with a few cannabis cornbread croutons on top. It was a simple plate-up, leaving me time and space to assist with the sushi course. The gumbo was served while a New Orleans brass band played a little Dixieland in the dining tent. The entire spectacle inside was a sight to be seen … and heard. Food, music, community and art, all at high levels, in a circus tent in the desert. It was insanity, and I loved every minute of it.

The three sushi women and one sushi man, freshly cleaned by our sushi team, were lying on the gurneys, and our sushi chef, Dr. O-top, was working his magic. I had prepped all of the fish into perfect slabs for slicing, removing any blood lines and unwanted fat. Fresh wasabi had been grated, and ginger was on deck. One of our sushi platters was a young woman whom we called Nineteen (even though she was twenty-six). It was she who informed me that the wasabi was burning her nipples. We remedied that situation by placing a Shiso leaf between the wasabi and the nipple. You can go ahead and file that piece of information under the "things I never thought I'd need to know" category.

As soon as the gumbo course cleared, a team of belly dancers and Bedouin musicians entered the tent, and the dancers performed a version of the Dance of the Seven Veils. The four gurneys of sushi people were carried into the tent and placed on four tables in the center of the room. Diners were then encouraged to gather at the tables. People began feeding each other. It was sensual, sexual and delicious, with belly dancers and the sounds of an oud, a tabla and a violin wafting through the dining area. This course was meant to be akin to a seventh inning stretch. It was nice for people to get up, interact and move about.

Once the sushi shenanigans subsided, people returned to their seats. Greed was the next course, with veal tenderloin being the star of the show. This was in the early days of sous vide, and we cooked the veal slowly with that method, before searing the outsides on the wood-fired grill just before service. The accompanying fritters were equal parts mashed potato and foie gras that had been run through a potato ricer for a smooth and uniform texture. A little bit of goat's cheese and a can of truffle shavings were then added to the mix, with just enough flour to bind them together. They were deep-fried, served with the tenderloin and a smear of bordelaise sauce on the bottom of the plate. Those fritters may have been my favorite component of the night. So decadent and unexpected.

This was the last complex course of the evening, apart from the desert. Baked Alaska can be tricky, but I was pumped. Things were going perfectly … until they weren't.

I made sure that course six was going out smoothly, which was mixed greens (with envy). Dawn could have done this one herself, but she had a team of helpers. On my side of the kitchen, I put all of the egg whites in the mixer and began making the meringue. I then laid all of the cookie crusts out. "Grab me the ice cream!" I yelled over to Dawn.

She replied with a hearty "Yes, Chef!" But then she came out of the truck, looking mortified.

"What's wrong?" I said with a pit in my stomach.

"We have a problem. The deep freezer got unplugged … and all of the ice cream has melted."

"All of it?!?" I bounded up into the truck with the freezer before she could reply. My fears were confirmed. The ice cream was all soft and mostly melted. It was still cold … but no way could I scoop it onto cookie crusts and cover it in meringue.

My mind went into overdrive. Could I get away without serving dessert? This meal had been over the top already … but there weren't six deadly sins; there were seven, and every diner had a printed menu in front of them confirming that.

Out of the corner of my eye, I saw the dish pit and our crew of volunteers happily cranking out dishes in our three-tub system. That's when I got the idea. "I need those martini glasses washed, NOW," I shouted. I then grabbed a bowl and began breaking up those cookie crusts that had taken many painstaking hours to make the day prior. I grabbed a few glasses off the clean rack and dusted the rims with cookie crumbs. Dawn got a big grin as she realized what I was up to, and began lining up the glasses as fast as they came out of the dishwashers' water-logged hands. Without a word, she went to work dusting all the rims, while I poured cold melted ice cream into the glasses. I grabbed the meringue off the mixer stand and scooped a dollop onto each martini glass milkshake. The real test came as I threw a splash of Everclear on the meringue and set it on fire. It worked beautifully. Soss had been watching quietly from the dining-room entrance, shaking his head in disbelief. We served as fast as we could, and when Painjoy killed the lights in the dining room and all the makeshift deserts made it out at the same time — on fire — nobody was the wiser.

I was covered in food, sweat and dust … but I had done it. In just over two and a half hours, we had served seven elegant courses to seventy-five diners in the most hostile kitchen conditions imaginable on Earth … and we had done it in style. This dinner remains my favorite that I have ever made in my career … and it happened on a dusty night at Burning Man!

A Graduation of Sorts

Not long after this, my feet began to get itchy. But not from my psoriasis. In fact, I was feeling better than ever on that front. I had decent health insurance, a dermatologist working with a rheumatologist and there was a new style of biological drugs on the market for my condition. The downside was that I had to inject into my stomach once a week, and the drug left me with an elevated risk of infection. But it worked better than anything else I'd tried, so I was feeling better, working full time with B2E and doing weekly therapy with Glinda.

This was a different kind of itch. The traveling itch. It's a powerful one, and it needed to be scratched. I decided I would give yachting another try. This would mean ending my therapy, at least for the time being. Glinda was supportive. But she also asked if I would be interested in doing a medicine session with her before I left. She worked with plant-based medicine — psilocybin mushrooms — and what Terence McKenna called a "heroic dose" of five grams (one-to-three grams is an average dose). The journey would be eight hours and cost $400, which was an awful lot of money for me at the time. We had to prepare before the journey began, setting an intention for my journey, discussing what it meant to me and working with it. The basis was that I was finally coming into manhood, no longer a boy (at thirty-eight years old), and I wanted to continue to evolve in ways that would be healthy for me, spiritually, mentally, psychically, emotionally and financially.

She told me to bring a nest, or rather a cozy blanket, my favorite pillow, Darvocet (the bear that has been traveling with me since my motorcycle accident) and cozy pajamas. She also asked me to bring a few photos and a mixed CD with six or seven songs that were special to me.

Song List:

"Take a Giant Step" (Taj Mahal)

"I Am the Light of This World" (Jorma Kaukonen)

"Across the Universe" (The Beatles)

"Don't Think Twice, It's All Right" (Bob Dylan)

"Ripple" (Grateful Dead)

"Castles Made of Sand" (Jimi Hendrix)

"Fearless" (Pink Floyd)

As per Glinda's instruction, I hadn't eaten anything since the night before. I had taken a long walk after eating dinner, spending the time thinking about what I was preparing to embark on, and in the morning I packed my stuff for the day. When I arrived, she greeted me warmly and took me into the ceremony room. I built my cozy nest and changed into my jammies. We talked for a bit about my intention, about the work we'd done and about how the day would go. She had portioned my dose with a quarter of a banana and some water, and she had a bucket nearby in case I needed to purge (puke). I agreed to wear an eye mask, so that I could only go internally, and not get lost in the many interesting artifacts she had around the room. We also agreed that I would spend the day in silence. We could talk about the journey after it happened, but for the journey itself, I was to be with myself, with blackness over my eyes, and not getting lost in words, only being in the experience. If I had to go to the bathroom, I was to tell her and she would guide me there. And under no circumstances were either of us to open the front door. I would be there all day.

I ate the medicine with the banana, put on the eye mask, laid back and waited for it to take effect. It didn't take long for things to get weird. She played music from around the world. I heard Native American chants, Kirtan from India and Gregorian monks chanting. The medicine gripped me with a light tingle at first, but then went deeper and deeper. I smelled sage, sweetgrass, palo santo and tobacco being burned around me. I could feel Glinda near me, praying, healing, being with me. I began to feel consumed with a heaviness and a lightness at the same time. I thought about all the people I'd met over the years, and that web was infinite. I was beginning to surrender my sense of self to the medicine, and to truly take a giant step outside of my mind (and being). It was beautiful, terrifying, unbearably sad and ecstatically joyful, all at the same time.

It felt like time didn't exist at all, but space … space was flying by me faster than I could see.

I reached my hand out and felt Glinda quickly take it. Her touch calmed me. I felt a connectedness to every being I'd ever encountered, from my mother and my many mentors to homeless people and buskers who I'd given change to on the street. I thought about a random cab driver from many years ago, and about my best friends. I felt the intrinsic presence of every single sentient being I'd ever come into contact with. It became clear to me that all meetings have relevance, whether we know it at the time or not.

I felt nurtured by the spirit of my mother. I felt forgiven and loved by her. I felt Campbell in the room with me, and a sense of relief as I realized that he respected me. I never even knew that was important to me. I even felt the spirit of Jerry Garcia, who was laughing at the fact that I was losing my shit. I'm pretty sure he was laughing with me, and not at me, but who knows; you can never really trust a prankster.

Everything was getting really intense. I felt the death of my mother and of Campbell (and even Garcia). All of these spirits flying though the room, like I was being exorcised. I reached for the bucket, and felt my body wretch and heave. With each convulsion I went deeper and deeper into the spirit world. While I would not call the experience fun or pleasant, I was fascinated by it all, and yet I couldn't wait for it to end. I felt like it couldn't end, because to end would be to acknowledge the existence of time, and all that was real was this moment.

My stomach settled, and I drank a bunch of water. Glinda guided me to the bathroom, and I sat down to pee. Even with the mask on, the lighting in the bathroom was different than the lighting in the ceremony room, as was the smell. The window was open, and I could feel the fresh air coming in from outside. I sat there in respite for a moment before standing up to make my way back to the sanctuary. Once inside, I was immediately back in the spirit world.

I was exhausted. But more than that, I was awash in emotions. I had so much guilt and shame all my life. Much of it was around my son, Cassidy, and how I'd failed him as a father by getting busted. And around Socrates, and the deal I made with the feds. Even my own brothers had always treated me like I was never good enough or smart enough to garner their respect.

I laid back in my nest, curled up and began to weep. I cried for the pain I'd caused, as well as the pain I'd suffered and held onto. I forgave myself for decisions I'd made; I forgave my mother for dying; I forgave G-d for scarring me with this awful disease. I forgave my family for not taking an interest in me. I forgave my father for being incapable.

And eventually I felt awash in love and light. I not only felt okay, but I felt as if I'd be okay … and that was the first time I'd felt like that since my mother died. I felt secure. Glinda seemed to sense it. She played "Don't Think Twice, It's All Right," and "Across the Universe" back to back, and I sobbed some more.

As the medicine began to wear off I sat up and tried to remove my mask, but Glinda encouraged me to keep it on and keep the silence a bit longer. I was nowhere near "down," but I was no longer in the peak of it. I laid back with the mask on, embracing the bear, who happily absorbed my tears, as he had done so many times before and has done since. In that short moment when I'd taken my mask off, I'd seen the pictures on my alter, of my mother, Campbell, Cassidy and Jerry Garcia, among a few others. I thought of these people and the roles they had played in my life, and I acknowledged each of them with gratitude.

After quite a while in silence, Glinda invited me to sit up and take my mask off. She presented me with a beautiful fruit platter and a cup of tea. As the chef who has made hundreds of fruit platters, her attention to detail in the presentation warmed my heart, and I cried some more, only this time in gratitude. I think I cried more that day than I have in my entire life. I was surprised to see that seven hours had passed since I arrived.

For a while after the experience, I felt a sense of "closure" around the deaths in my life, but as more time has passed, I realized that it's (what I like to call) a sense of "openure," as I feel very open and at peace with these losses now. While I still have some pain and struggle around some of these losses and lessons, the shame, resentment and self-loathing have never been close to what they were before this journey.

Snow at the Beach

I got a call about a rather large yacht, 240 feet, that had three chefs on board. The owners also owned an estate in Santa Barbara, a wealthy California beach town. Once I passed the phone interviews, they flew me to the estate to cook for the family. I had heard that this family had gone through twenty chefs in just two years, but I always took these stories with a grain of salt, and went into the situation with a clean head.

It was December and I was meant to cook at the estate over the Christmas holidays. They were trying out another chef at the same time, and they liked us both, so we were told that we were both being hired. I should have seen the red flags, with the rules of the estate, but I needed the work and this was a particularly well-paying gig. Some of those rules were: We were not allowed to speak directly with the family. All communications had to go through the minions. All leftovers had to be thrown away, and we were not allowed to feed the house staff. Latex gloves had to be worn at all times, and for all tasks. Knives had to be placed with the blades under the cutting boards, when not in use. There were a few more that I can't remember. There were cameras all over the kitchen, and we were under constant surveillance.

We had done several dinners leading up to Christmas. On Christmas Eve, we got a request for Christmas goose on the following day. As it was too late to order any, we began calling every fine-dining restaurant all the way down the coast, until we finally found one that had goose on the menu. "May I please speak to the chef?" I asked. "I am a fellow chef in a bind," I explained.

A moment later a gruff voice picked up the phone. "Kitchen," he grumbled.

"Hi, my name is Evan and I'm a private chef in Santa Barbara [about ninety miles away from where the restaurant was]. Any chance you have some goose that you'd sell me? I'll pay you full menu price for all that you have."

"So you want all of my goose? Do you want the sides?" he asked.

"Nope, just the raw product."

"Hang on a minute," he said, and put the phone down. After a long couple of minutes, he picks up the phone and says, "I have seven orders left and we are closed tomorrow. I'll let you have them for twenty percent over cost. Come down and get 'em."

"Great!" I say. "The only thing is … I'm in Santa Barbara. Do me a favor, and ask your dishwasher if he'll drive them up to me. I'll pay him $300."

He must think I'm nuts at this point, but he puts the phone down, returns a moment later and says, "He wants $500. It's Christmas Eve." Admiring his shrewd skills, I agree to his terms, and we serve Christmas goose the following day.

And speaking of the following day, early the next morning, while we are preparing the goose, among many other things, we see a giant truck deliver some big, odd-looking machinery, that we learn are snow-making machines. What follows is a series of flatbed trucks all filled with blocks of ice. Truckload after truckload — there must have been at least twenty of them. The machines start humming away, and by 1:00 p.m. the entire back yard of this seventy-degree California Coastal house is covered in one foot of fresh powdered snow. I must say, it made for a dramatic presentation of the antique model Ford that was the Christmas present that year, but the sheer waste and disregard of the environmental impact of such a charade sickened me to my core. I was a long way from "leave no trace" and the environmental ethos of Burning Man and B2E.

As we approached the year's end, we got word that the bosses wanted us to put together a New Year's Eve party menu. They wanted twenty passed appetizers for thirty people over four hours. We began writing menus and sending them back through the minions to the Mrs. for approval. We went back and forth quite a bit. She wanted WeightWatchers points assigned to each appetizer. The problem came with the foie gras. At that time, WeightWatchers did not include it in their points system, most likely because it is 100 percent fat.

It was December 30 in the evening, and we had just sent another revised menu to the Mrs. via her assistant. She walked out of the kitchen and returned moments later, stating, "Mrs. is now having her spa treatment and will not be reviewing any more menus until tomorrow." We clean the kitchen, feeling uncertain about how the following day will go down. My colleagues and I agree to shop in the morning, and hope for the best.

Sometime mid-morning, we receive word that the Mrs. has decided that she wants to change the entire menu and theme of the party. We explain that we've already shopped and are working on the menu that we had discussed. The minions disappear. Moments later, the estate manager arrives with three giant security staff. "Gentleman, will you please pack your knives and grab your personal belongings. Your services will no longer be needed here."

"Wait, what? We have all of this ..."

"Don't worry about that. We will take care of it. No need to turn anything off. Really, let's just leave the property, now. We will have checks drawn up for your time here." And like that, we're whisked off the property. We weren't fired, and we didn't quit ... but we were definitely escorted off the property by security! I imagined the maids throwing away all of the expensive ingredients that we had been prepping for that night.

Something about the experience left me feeling sullied. I decided it was time for me to make the pilgrimage where all dedicated travelers need to go at some point ... I headed to India.

Nah, Must Stay

Arriving in India is the assault on the senses that you've always heard about. It began before the plane even landed, when after serving a very smelly vegetable curry, the flight attendants walked down the aisles spraying Lysol, I assume in an effort to kill the smell of the dish. What actually happens is that the airplane, which already smelled like locker room socks, now smells like curry, perfume, disinfectant … and locker room socks.

The smells in India go from the very best scents imaginable to the absolute worst. Gas, diesel, cow dung, rotting garbage, marigolds, roses, so many roses, fried food, cloves, curry, cardamom, durian, livestock, cigarettes, bidis, hashish, coffee, chai, bakeries, cinnamon, rotting fruit, something fermenting, life, death, soap, dirt, detergent, frying dough, human excrement, all the other excrement … it never stops. Not in the big cities, at least. I ended up doing my best to avoid the big cities, but there's something intoxicating about the energy that comes from being in them. Also, in a country as densely populated as India, even some of the smallish cities are still millions of people deep.

I had planned on buying a motorcycle upon arrival, but as soon as I got there I scrapped that idea. Clearly the traffic patterns were … unique, and some time would have to be spent studying them before I would be confident enough to take to the roads. I tripped around the south for a few weeks, until I found what I'd come searching for, which was a clinic that specialized in Ayurvedic medicine. The psoriasis meds were losing their efficacy, and my psoriatic arthritis was rearing its ugly head. I decided to do a cleanse, and this clinic came highly recommended.

It was in a coastal town called Kumta, near the holy city of Gokarna. They treated as many as twelve people at a time, and we shared meals in a common dining area. Most of the others were European. One older woman from Israel had come to die, with her daughter and granddaughters as escorts to the other side. It was a very serene and sweet environment. There was a French musician with a liver problem. When I was there, I kept to myself a lot.

I'd been on the road for ten solid years. I'd had a lot of highs and lows, and seen a lot. I had succeeded as a yacht chef, when I was told there was no way that I would, but it was not without a lot of strife. Was it worth it all? Here I was in India, hoping to finally find some relief from my fucked up skin disease. I was tens of thousands of miles from any semblance of home. I was alone, and I felt it, though I also felt a part of the Panchakarma community that surrounded me. The thing was, we were all going through this intense experience, all of us alone and all of us together. It felt communal and desolate, all at the same time.

I had various treatments every morning, from warm cups of ghee to massage and steam baths. I loved it when the therapists would heat up buttermilk with some medicinal herbs in it. One would massage this mixture into my scalp while the other would collect the runoff in a basin, heat it again, and begin the process over. It felt amazing.

The doctor who ran the place was a peculiar little dude, and highly revered in the Ayurvedic communities. He stressed that if we committed to the diet and to the lifestyle, all our ailments would eventually be cured. Ayurveda is a 3,000-year-old practice, that literally translates to "life science." He emphasized rest and relaxation when we were not in treatment … but not to sleep during the day because it was "disrespectful to the sun." Westerners in India all want to do yoga … but for this treatment (known as Panchakarma), he requested that we kept our yoga to a minimum so that our bodies could focus on resting.

The food was all grown on the premises, or nearby. The meals were usually served on a scoop of a local red rice, which was very nutty and rich in flavor. There was usually some form of mushy squash, or pumpkin, and a pile of incredibly bitter greens. The doctor once told me the more bitter the vegetable, the better it is for your liver. Probably the most difficult transition for me was the lack of caffeine and sugar. I went from drinking the traditional endless cups of chai every day, to drinking none. In India, chai is served everywhere, and all the time. All day, all night, very sweet, very strong. The withdrawal headaches were fierce, and I was exhausted … but it didn't matter because I had nothing to do anyway, as long as I didn't fall asleep during the day.

I loved the experience and I often think back to it, but in the end, my skin and joints were still a mess. While my growing reputation as a decent charter chef had kept me in work, my aches and pains were making the actual job more difficult all the time. Cooking professionally is a physically demanding job, and if your body isn't 100 percent, it's that much harder. Had I seen results in the month I was there, I might have been more willing to commit to this lifestyle. Ayurveda is probably better suited to people with cases that are milder than mine, and for other ailments.

I bummed around Rajasthan for a bit, took a couple of cooking classes, and learned about the differences between Northern and Southern Indian food. I discovered a love for dosas and idli sambar (steamed rice dumplings with chili sambar sauce, usually served at breakfast) from the south, and the spices of the north, which are intriguing in their delicate balances. Lassis are prevalent all over this northern area as well as the ubiquitous bhang lassi, which is made from a cannabis and oil base, sweetened with mango and yogurt. Rajasthan was inspiring and delightful.

One particularly hot afternoon, I was enjoying a lassi (a virgin one, not a bhang lassi) in the shade. An old woman and her two granddaughters came up to me and tried to sell me a henna tattoo, which is common there. The hawkers are aggressive, and will grab your hand and begin drawing on it before you know it's even happening. Anyway, I didn't want the tattoo, but I looked to the lassi vendor and said, "I'd like to order three small lassis for this family," and he went to work peeling mangos. A well-dressed man, clearly a Brahmin, the highest caste in India, had witnessed this and said to me, "Good sir, you should not patronize the beggars. It only encourages them." I smiled and said, "It's a very hot day, and kindness is always a good thing."

He shrugged and looked down his nose at me. In that moment, the vendor handed the two kids and the old lady their lassis. They all lit up in big smiles. The old woman, with tears in her eyes, bent down, touched my feet and kissed her hands. Without missing a beat, I bent down, touched her feet and kissed my hands. I knew from my medicine session that this interaction was relevant in the whole scheme of things.

The man standing there began to laugh uproariously, and said, "These people are gypsies, the lowest caste. Don't waste your time on them." Leaning back, taking a sip of my lassi, I didn't say a word; I just watched as the two little girls gulped down the beverage, and the old lady savored hers, watching the serene desert sky.

I toodled around Northern India by bus, train, camel, rickshaw and the odd rented motorcycle or scooter. I was becoming a bit more fearless as I began to understand the chaotic roads. Also, as my understanding of the buses and trains improved, my travels became easier. I learned that the second-class sleeper cars were the best value on the trains, and that your odds of actually having a bed increased greatly. First class and passenger class were always packed full. I figured out which type of station had the longest stops, and would depart the train for hot food. I tried to avoid buying prepared foods if I could not see them being cooked, and this saved me a lot of tummy aches. If I couldn't see the food being cooked, or if it wasn't piping hot, I'd buy packaged chips and cookies to tide me over.

I opted to spend my fortieth birthday at the Taj Mahal, and was so glad I did. It was majestic, magnificent and every bit as breathtaking as I'd hoped it would be. It struck me that I'd seen many incredible structures built for faith and religion, but that the Taj was different in that it had been built for love.

In India, people call elders *Baba*, as a sign of respect. Men often call other men *Ji*, in sort of the same way that men call other men *dude* in the states, or *mate* in England. *Babaji* is a sign of respect for an elder man and for reasons that have NEVER become clear to me, people began to call me Babaji on my fortieth birthday. I have no idea of how they knew ... they just knew. It made sense, as I was really feeling as if I was coming into my own as a man. I felt like the intention that I'd set going into my medicine session with Glinda was coming to fruition.

I made my way to a very small village called Kasar Devi. I'd been moving around for several months and was getting tired. I needed a little continuity before the planned arrival of one of my Burning Man crew, Lady PJ. As I walked up the road into a village, an old man with a cane asked me if I needed a guesthouse, which I did. He walked me up a path that had giant wild cannabis plants growing on either side. At the top of the ridge stood a small one-room cottage with a window on each wall and a 360-degree view that revealed miles and miles of Himalayan ridges. It had no running water, but there was an old well outside with a bucket on a rope. There was a firepit in the corner, a thin mat for a bed and a small table. The cost for any more than a week was just fifty rupees a day, which was about $1.50. I shook his hand, paid him for a couple of weeks and sat down by myself to take in the view. Thin air, billowy gray clouds, rain in the distance, but sun shining clearly above me, and the sweet smell of sage, wild weed and unidentifiable herbs. I'd sweat a little bit when the wind stopped, and would wish for a hoodie when it picked up. On the shelf was some tea and sugar, so I stoked the small firepit and put on a pot of water. Bhopal, the owner, ran a small store just at the bottom of the stairs, so I went down and bought some fresh milk, a couple of eggs and bananas, and a loaf of bread, and made my way back up to my new abode to make a cup of chai. While I had probably been averaging ten cups of chai per day, this was the first time that I had actually made it myself. I was shocked to realize just how much sugar went into a cup when made the way the locals did it. I'd have to keep an eye on that.

There are places on the backpackers' trail that just seem to entice people to stay for extended periods. Kasar Devi was one of them. It dawned on me that this might be a good place to settle for a while and work on my memoir. But who the fuck writes a memoir anyway? So pretentious.

After a couple of weeks, Lady PJ arrived and we hung out in the mountains for a week or so before heading to an orphanage/ashram where we'd agreed to do some volunteering. As a flight attendant, she could jump on a plane and meet friends anywhere in the world, and her adventurous spirit made this a common occurrence. This orphanage was different than most, in that it didn't adopt out the kids but, rather, raised them in the ways of their chosen guru, Baba Hari Dass, who also had a temple in the Santa Cruz Mountains (California). This sense of stability was really evident in the kids that lived there. They had a feeling of radical acceptance and they appeared to be content and happy at Shree Ram. I marveled at how readily the kids did their lessons and chores, and how they even seemed to be excited for evening puja, the prayer and chanting ceremonies that took place every night after dinner. These group activities reminded me of the singalongs we used to do at summer camp, but this was next level. There was a spiritual devotion that one doesn't normally see in young kids from the West. I noticed the same spiritual devotion across the spectrum of society in India, but it was especially prevalent among the young ones at the orphanage. The community was strong, and these kids, who stayed at Shree Ram until they were "of age," obviously felt like family.

The campus itself looked like a college, hospital or even a prison, with four buildings that surrounded a courtyard. It had a functional feel, like any big institution, which made sense. The kids lived in dorms upstairs, and the downstairs housed a dining room, kitchen, learning rooms and a worship room. There were benches in the courtyard, a sandbox, swings and a slide.

Lady PJ had brought a giant bag of colored pencils and erasers from the States, and she had a trail of kids following her at all times, as her reputation as the bearer of gifts got out. She gravitated to the little ones, and I played with some of the older kids. I even organized a game of ultimate Frisbee, a game that no one there had ever heard of, but took to quickly. Then I found my way to the kitchen…

The kitchen produced three meals a day for 150 people, pumping out traditional Indian fare of dahl, rice, chili sambar, chapati, chana masala, etc. It's always weird volunteering in a place that already has systems set up. They didn't know what to make of me because most people volunteered with the kids, not the kitchen, but they quickly ascertained that I knew my way around a kitchen. I love cooking in other people's kitchens, especially when there's a cultural and a language barrier. The language of food transcends. Again, I stole with my eyes. It always amazes me just how many ways there are to cut an onion, yet most people learn only one and stick to it their entire life.

The orphanage touched my heart in a special way. Losing my mother at the tender age of eight had always had a profound impact on me and my sense of self. Even though I had a father and a stepmother, I always felt that they only took me into their home out of a sense of obligation, not because they actually wanted me to be there. And since my brothers were all so much older than me, I always felt like some kind of mixture of orphan/motherless child/redheaded stepchild … whatever you want to call it. Losing everything at once when Mom died had messed me up more than I'd realized. I'd felt like an outcast for most of my life. The fact that these kids weren't up for adoption, that they were *wanted* by this community, touched me deeply. It was an eye opener, as well as a heart opener.

From the orphanage, we went to the holy city of Rishikesh, made famous by the Beatles's visit in 1967. The city hugs the two sides of the Ganges and features guesthouses, yoga centers and everything that you could ever want to buy on either side of the holy river. I decided that I was ready to rent a motorcycle, which was great because Lady PJ had found someone that she wanted to study yoga and meditation with, and we agreed to meet up in a month. I set out to rent a motorcycle, but I couldn't find one I could rent for a month, so I ended up buying an Enfield from a guy named Lucky, who owned a bike shop. He told me that if I brought the bike back in good condition, he would "probably buy it back" from me.

For a couple of days, I prepared for the journey, while trying to decide between going to Gangotri, the source of the Ganges, or to Dharamsala, the home of the Dalai Lama. After beating my head against the wall trying to decide which would be "more rewarding," I came to the conclusion that there were no wrong paths. That either path would be new and exciting for me. So I flipped a coin and began my journey by going to Gangotri, the source of the holiest river on Earth.

India is very different on a bike. I was traveling at my own pace. Some of the places I stopped at were not used to seeing a six-foot white guy with red hair. At times, there were no restaurants, or even markets, but rather little chai shops that "happened" to sell a "plate of the day." There were also "thali" restaurants, which sell inexpensive daily plates of rice, veg and lentils with chapati. And I was able to taste some local flavors that I never would have otherwise been able to try. I was mostly vegetarian in India, but I did make a point of eating goat or lamb when I was in areas where I'd see shepherds grazing flocks.

I'd considered taking another cooking class or two, but cooking classes are for tourists, and I was far off the tourist path at this point. So, instead, I stole with my eyes. This was before smart phones with cameras existed, at least in this part of the world, so after ordering food, I would sit and stare intently at how the cooks prepared everything. A meal often began with a run down the street for a couple of eggs or some fry oil.

Mama Ganges

The ride to Gangotri took about three days. I gained a lot of altitude as I climbed the mountain that housed the source of India's holiest river. I got used to the roar of the mighty Enfield, with my backpacks delicately balanced in the rear luggage racks and secured with a bungee cord. There is something special about riding a single-cylinder motorcycle. They call them "thumpers." Thump, thump, thump up the mountains. It took some getting used to as the bike is set up very differently than Western bikes are. The shifter is on the right foot peg rather than the left. And in the U.S., the shifting pattern is one click down, three (or four, depending on the bike) up. In India, it is one up and four down. The good news is that since it's on the side where the rear brake would normally be on a Western bike, should you hit it thinking it's the brake, it will downshift, which is the first step toward slowing down.

Visually, this place was unlike anywhere I'd ever seen — lots of switchback trails and small farming villages, farmers tending their fields with ox-drawn carriages, little old women at the reins, women and children walking for miles to unknown destinations with water on their heads for the day's cooking and washing. The climate was getting cooler as I ascended in elevation. I bought a wool sweater, hat and gloves from a roadside vendor, and I was glad that I did.

The glacier that feeds the River Ganges is eighteen kilometers outside of the village. There's an ashram that people hike to about fourteen kilometers in, where they have some food and spend the night before going to see the glacier in the morning and then hiking back. This was my plan, so I hiked quickly to make it before dark, which I just barely did.

The ashram was small and quaint. It was run on donations only, and pilgrims of all kinds came to stay here. It is considered a very holy act to bathe in the Ganges. Travelers from all over the planet stop here as well as Indian people. Once I set up my bed in a communal sleeping area, I walked to the dining room, where I had a simple and delicious meal with some Japanese tourists who were excited to take pictures at sunrise. There was a feeling of serenity crossed with excitement in the air.

The following morning, I decided to take a half hit of LSD with my morning chai, and headed off just as dawn was breaking. Lady PJ had brought four hits with her. We were going to take them in Rishikesh, but the energy there was just too intense; it was too crowded, and it never felt right. So she sent them with me on my journey. I'd not taken any psychedelics since my medicine journey with Glinda, and this seemed like a perfect time and place.

The air was sharp and fresh as the sun broke through the cool Himalayan sky. It was clearly going to be a stunning day. By the time I made it up to the glacier I was feeling pretty good … the acid was very clean, and on the mild side, so I ate the other half hit. Everything had a crisp, clear glow. While India has garbage everywhere, there was no garbage on the ground here at all. The respect and reverence for this holy spot was palpable.

When I reached the glacier, I sat there in the morning sunshine and looked out upon the Himalayas before stripping down to my skivvies and a sarong, and found a spot in the river where the water wasn't rushing too quickly. This water was freshly melted ice, and it was cold. But I didn't travel this far to NOT get wet.

I took a moment to psyche myself up for this — I thought about the many people I love, how lucky I was to have such a wonderful family and so many friends. And I thought about how much effort and courage it had taken me to get to this spot — a Jewish kid from the San Fernando Valley, an ex-con, chef, father, lover, human. I had made it all the way to this incredibly holy place. I blew a kiss to All My Relations and plunged myself into this sacred water. It was biting cold, and I began to sob. The cold took my breath away, but my heart being filled with love was what caused the tears to flow.

I got out and sat on the rocks to warm up in the sun. One of the Babas (Sadhus, holy men) walked over and smiled at me.

"I am proud of you for getting into our holy water," he said.

"I knew it would be powerful. But I didn't expect myself to become so emotional," I said.

"Mama Ganges touches us all differently. Be sure and listen to the message that she leaves you." He smiled and walked back to where he'd been sitting.

I watched the power of the river rushing by me. I thought about how far this water would travel, and how much it meant to the masses that worshipped it in its path.

I began my journey down the mountain, stopping for a chai and a snack at the ashram, then I continued on my path. Sitting on a rock by the river was an older Westerner who had stopped for a smoke. He was wearing the traditional orange robes that the Babas wore, and had a small bag with him. I stopped and made pleasantries, and we began chatting. I asked how long he'd been in India, and he said, "Well, I came here in the late eighties after some rough times in the UK. I was a musician on tour, and I just got sick of the business, so I came here with an acoustic guitar and very little money. I managed to get some great LSD in Goa, though, and I came here and took it. I ended up having quite the experience. I smashed my guitar in the Ganges, and threw her my passport and the last of my money. I've been here ever since … about twenty-two years. As long as I don't leave, I never need my passport!" he laughed. "I do love it here, though. I managed to get myself another guitar, and I still play music. I never have much money, but I really don't need much. I help out at the ashrams for food and a place to sleep. I pray with the other Babas, and G-d makes sure we have food, a little tobacco and a little charas to smoke. The only thing is, I wish I could take acid just one more time. I feel like I learned so much from that last trip, but I still have more to learn. I reckon I could make another trip to Goa … but I'm pretty rooted here by Mama Ganges. She really has a hold on my heart."

"It's funny that you mention it," I replied. "I took a small dose of acid today. It was beautiful." I reflected on just how fresh and magical everything had been on this day. I realized that I probably wouldn't be taking any more, so I said, "Here, man, I have a little left over," and handed him the three hits of blotter that were left. Without missing a beat, he popped all three of them into his mouth. Then he jumped up and grabbed his small bag. "Gotta make it to the glacier before sunset. Thanks, man. Namaste!" And like that, he was gone, up the mountain.

A Tow at the Right Time Is
a Great Deal at Any Price

I left for the other side of the Himalayas. Gangotri to the Parvati Valley is not a route that is followed by many. But since I was curious about the Hindu faith, interested in the hash-making process and content with my clear understanding that the "journey was the goal," I went for it. I knew before I started that the road trip might be more memorable than the destinations, and I was not really wrong about that...

It took me about four days of riding down mountainsides, and up others, through farmlands, rural areas and military zones. I'd stop for fuel and food, and once I even paid a guy to throw a cot in a mop closet and let me crash the night there. He also cooked me a beautiful fish dinner with a fish he'd just caught.

The mountains turned to valleys, the valleys into canyons, the canyons into hillsides, which turned back into mountains. One after another, small villages dotted the highway, with the odd farm stand and the ever-present chai stalls and tobacco stands.

It was on this part of the journey that I had my one and only problem on the bike. I was climbing in elevation rapidly, to the point where I had to don my new woolies in order to keep from freezing. I saw a military checkpoint ahead of me, and was flagged down by an officer with a big gun slung on his back.

"Where are you going?" he asked. I pulled out my map and showed him the Parvati Valley.

"You cannot go this way," he said. "This is a military road, and the public is not allowed on it. I will need to see your passport."

"Sir, I am coming from Gangotri. I've been riding for two days. There is no other choice; it will take me days to go an alternate route," I said, as I handed him my passport.

"You have been to Gangotri? Did you bathe in the holy waters of the Ganges?" he asked.

"I certainly did," I answered politely.

At that moment, I noticed his name tag. "Your name is Tenzin," I said. "Same name as His Holiness, Dalai Lama! How lucky!!" I exclaimed.

He smiled widely, and said, "Do you know the Dalai Lama?!?"

"Well, I don't know him personally," I replied, "but I certainly know who he is, and I follow his teachings."

He closed my passport and handed it back to me. "Okay, you can pass," he said. "There is a fifty rupee fee, and you must promise to not take any photos."

I handed over the obvious baksheesh (bribe), promised not to take any pictures and headed up the mountain.

Not ten minutes later, another checkpoint appeared and, miraculously, the guard's name was also Tenzin. I had the identical conversation, only he required a 100 rupee "toll" and I was on my way.

The road was desolate from this point on. Not even a chai stall. Nothing. No cars, trucks or other vehicles. I drove in the desolation for maybe thirty minutes, when I felt the rear end wobble in what was unmistakably … a flat tire.

Fuck.

I pulled over and assessed the situation. Then I found a nice log to sit on and rolled a smoke. As I sat there, pondering my predicament, I heard the unmistakable bleating of a herd of goats. Around the corner walks a twelve-year-old shepherd with his flock. He sees me and walks over. I say hello, but he clearly speaks no English. I point to my flat tire, and he shakes his head. Then he points down the road, the direction that he came from, and says, "My village, one kilometer." I thank him and push the heavy bike the short distance down the road.

Sure enough, there was a village. Or should I say, a chai stall, six shacks and a tobacco/lottery stall. As I approached, everyone poked their heads out of their doors. Word got out quickly that I was at the chai stall, and as I stood there sipping the hot sweet drink, about a dozen people of all ages came to check me out. They looked at the tire, and the one guy that spoke a little English said, "Tire shop, fifty kilometers." As I finished my tea, they seemed to get bored of watching me, and went back to their shacks and about their business. I sat down and pulled out the novel I was reading. I figured that, eventually, a bus or truck would come by, and I could hitch a ride.

About three hours later, I heard a loud vehicle blaring Hindi pop music. A big jeep holding no fewer than seventeen people comes around the corner, sees me and stops. In his native tongue, the oldest guy in the village quickly tells the oldest guy in the jeep what's going on. They both nod, understandingly.

The old guy in the jeep looks at my bike and back at the jeep, and says, "How much you pay for me to drive you to the tire shop?" The jeep was so full of grain sacks, boxes and people that I had no idea that this was even an option. "Five hundred rupees?" He smiles, and says, "A thousand rupees" (about $33 at that time). I couldn't help but wonder if he would have doubled anything I said, recognizing the desperation of my predicament. "Deal," I say, and we shake on it.

The jeep was mostly filled with boys around fifteen to twenty years old. They quickly set to work emptying the jeep, lifting my bike into the back and securing it with ropes, and then carefully stacking the large burlap sacks of rice, lentils and other grains around the bike. Then old man motioned for me to climb in the cab with him, but the front looked really crowded and the back looked like more fun. So I jumped right onto the seat of my secured motorcycle, and the boys all shouted with joy and excitement as they clamored into the back of the jeep, hanging onto the roll bars, laughing and shouting at me in Hindi.

The next hour was spent on a narrow, terrifying road, with 1,000-foot drops on either side. We stopped in a couple of small villages and dropped off some sacks of grain, before ending up in their village of about seventy-five people. Everyone came out to greet the jeep, and to stare at me. The vehicle was emptied, and my bike was re-secured to make up for the loss of grain sacks that were helping to hold it in place. The old man and I shared a chai and a chillum of hash and tobacco before the two-hour ride to the "big town" with the tire shop. Upon arrival, I found a place to eat dinner and my tire was repaired before I finished my meal.

I began to see signs in Hebrew(!), and advertisements for falafel and shakshouka (traditional Israeli breakfasts), so I knew that I must be getting closer to the charas (hashish). There are so many young Israelis fresh out of the army here that this area is known by locals as the Hummus Trail. This is where most of the charas is grown and made and, after my time in Morocco, I felt curious to check it out. It wasn't harvest season, so there was no production to see, but the hash was the best, and the cheapest, that I had found in the entire country, at about $1 per gram. It was a nice place to rest for a couple of days and eat Western food, and I managed to have a short fling with an Israeli traveler, which lasted all of the three days that I stayed there.

India is so big, and so dense, that even if something doesn't appear to be that far, it can be worlds apart. Amritsar, a Sikh city, was deep in the desert. But it's the home of the golden temple, which feeds 100,000 visitors (for free) per day, all run by volunteers. Let me repeat that: 100,000 free meals every day. I just had to see this kitchen.

The ride to get there was long and dirty. It's hard to stay hydrated on a motorcycle, because your hands are on the handlebars, and it was a couple hundred miles of long, straight, dusty highway, with giant trucks and buses flying by. It was so hot I could feel the heat off the black tar reflecting upward. When I'd stop to rest, my sneakers would stick to the hot asphalt.

Finally, I arrived in Amritsar, dirty, disheveled and sick as a dog with dehydration and Delhi Belly. Roadside food can get sketchy, though a small series of "rules" that I follow has helped me avoid getting sick very often in my travels. I watch street vendors closely, and I only eat from busy vendors that seem to be using good practices. I make sure they are not chopping raw proteins on the same board as cooked proteins. I ensure that risky proteins are properly iced down and, most importantly, I make sure that hot food is served hot and cold food is served cold. Ambient temperature is not an option, and I generally won't eat food where I cannot see its preparation. Too often, on the trains, guys would walk around selling dosas wrapped in newspaper, but without seeing where they were cooked, I have no idea how old they are or whether they were properly handled. I will sometimes try and touch one, and if it's still warm I might take the chance.

But with limited options on the bike for food and the challenge of drinking enough water while driving a motorcycle (it takes both hands), I was a wreck upon arrival. I rented the nicest hotel room I could afford, with air conditioning, which always costs extra, and passed out cold for a day and a half. The hotelier noticed that I hadn't emerged, and kindly brought me some chicken broth, plain rice and chapati. It took me a couple of days to bounce back.

The Golden Temple was nothing short of stunning. I walked around for a day, and then I volunteered in the massive kitchen for two days. They had pots bigger than I am for cooking rice and dhal. Giant griddles handled hundreds of chapati at a time, two guys flattening the balls of dough and throwing them on the griddle, and two guys flipping and removing them. It was an amazing operation, and it made me think back to busting my ass on a Saturday night to put out a mere 400 plates.

After I cooked for a while, they sent me out to the courtyard. A few thousand people had been queuing up. One thing I've learned in India is that if people line up for something, there's probably a reason, so I got in the line. Suddenly two giant wooden doors opened up and everybody filed into a giant courtyard. It felt like the grounds of a school. People sat on either side of the many concrete walkways lined with grass. I followed their lead. There were times and places in India where many people spoke English, and there were times and places where not one person did. This place was the latter, but it didn't matter. I could feel an amazing feast was about to happen.

People were kind and curious about me, as is often the nature of Indian people. The few that knew a couple words of English would ask me the same questions over and over.

Hello. What's your name? Where are you from? Then they would fall over laughing, and tell their friends and family whatever they could glean from my answers.

I sat there for maybe ten minutes when all of a sudden two guys began walking down the rows, giving each person a banana leaf, which everybody laid in front of them. Then another pair carried a giant pot of rice and two more guys spooned a scoop of rice onto each person's banana leaf. Then two more guys came by with a giant pot of dhal (curried lentils) and dropped a scoop of that on each pile of rice. This was followed by two guys carrying a giant pot of roast cauliflower and potato (aloo gobi), and two servers serving it. Each team had two runners following them with smaller pots that they would run back to the kitchen to refill, so the big pots never ran dry. Then came the guys throwing a chapati to each person. At the end of the procession, two final guys came with pitchers of chili sambar, and poured a small amount over the top. In about thirty minutes, they had fed 5,000 people a hot and healthy meal on a banana leaf. My catering culinary heart melted at the sheer efficiency of this operation.

My time in India was coming to an end. I made it back to Rishikesh, and sold my bike back to Lucky for about $100 less than I'd paid for it a month earlier. Sadly, I haven't made it back yet, but I hope to. I spent six months in that country and I saw more of it than most Indian people ever see … yet I still feel as if I barely scratched the surface.

We Put the Fun in Katafanga

I made it back to the Bay Area with no idea of what I was going to do next. As if on cue, I got a call from Admiral Painjoy. He was negotiating a contract to build a house on a small private island in Fiji. Having built Burning Man camps for years, Painjoy knew that without a good kitchen his project would never fly, so he wrote a chef into the budget, and asked me if I wanted to come. The gig had come from another guy we knew from Burning Man, who had seen Painjoy run massive theme camps in the Black Rock Desert, managing and organizing hundreds of people and moving parts. (His camps are legendary on the Playa. If you ever make it to Burning Man, be sure and visit Spanky's Wine Bar and tell them Chef Pimp sent you. That endorsement may hurt more than help, but I'd say give it a shot anyway.)

Shortly before our departure, my left ankle began to get swollen and sore. Years earlier, when I had my ankle injury, the doctor told me that with my arthritis, I'd probably have about ten years before it started to hurt me. But he encouraged me to wait as long as I could, as medical technology would only get better. Now, twelve years later, the old injury was giving me trouble. I told Painjoy I wasn't 100 percent, and he offered to get me a local assistant, which was kind of him. He said he didn't know any other chefs with my skillset, being able to cook pretty much anywhere, and he really wanted to have me there with him.

This was not my first private island. When I was freelancing a few years prior, I'd worked on a small island in the Bahamas called Little Whale Cay. The island was owned by a prominent British family, and was small, about 100 acres. I'd fly in and out on a chartered seaplane, with most of the produce that I'd need. The job was okay, though I got very lonely there. I was kept busy, so that made the time go by, and when I wasn't cooking I'd found a beautiful little beach on the windward side that nobody ever went to that I claimed as my own. I did three to four gigs there over a couple of years, all of them about two weeks in length.

For Katafanga, we spent the first two weeks at a hotel in Suva, a larger port city where we were able to find a giant building and supply/hardware store. It was pretty wild, setting up shop in what amounted to a Fijian Home Depot. Painjoy introduced me to his assistant, Mr. Dean, who was also a tattoo artist. This guy had a lot of tattoos, mostly jailhouse style. The dude had never done a day's time in his life, but you'd never know it looking at him. We needed a lot of materials and would only have one shot at getting them because the port city was hundreds of miles away from the island of Katafanga. So Mr. Dean and I went off to find some nonperishables and equipment. I'm used to jumping into taxis in foreign countries with a pocket full of cash and odd requests, but Dean had grown up in the central valley of California and had hardly ever left, let alone embarked on an international mission like this. It was all brand new to him.

From my end of the project, the biggest challenge was refrigeration. There would be none when we got to the island, as there was no power. We'd be bringing a few fridges, a generator the size of a VW van and hundreds of gallons of diesel, but the barge ride was going to take two days, and then it would take a couple more to unload everything. And nobody really knew how we were going to offload this massive generator. What this all meant to me was that I could bring almost no perishables. No meat, minimal dairy and only as much produce as I might be able to keep alive for two to three weeks, the first week or so being without refrigeration. Everything had to be dry or canned. It was agreed that the Fijian crew would help us with fishing and lobstering, and they also had their own camp and cooked their own food. I was only feeding the Westerners, though all of us did break bread together on several occasions.

On a whim, while shopping with Mr. Dean one day, I asked a taxi driver if he knew where to buy some chickens and goats. He smiled broadly and said, "My cousin has a farm on the outskirts of town. I can take you to him."

We drove for a little bit and arrived at a small compound. Our taxi driver ran in and spoke with a guy. They both came back to the taxi, and the guy introduced himself as the mayor of the small village. I've done a lot of sketchy shit in a lot of counties, bought fish on the docks and meat from people that slaughtered the animal in their backyards. Mr. Dean was out of his element though, and wasn't 100 percent sure that these guys weren't going to rob us … or worse. We drove onto the compound and met with the cabbie's cousin. He showed us a massive henhouse with hundreds of chickens and asked how many we wanted. I told him twenty egg fowl, twenty meat fowl and four goats. He said he would throw in four ducks for a good price. I couldn't believe my luck! Mr. Dean couldn't believe we'd just met a local mayor and bought a bunch of livestock. I paid half up front, and they agreed to deliver the goods at the dock in a few days, when we were loading the barge. We made it back, and I was feeling rather accomplished.

Over the next few days, I bought a gas BBQ, pots and pans, serving spoons, several charcoal water purifiers, refrigerators and freezers, cutting boards, knives, teapots, coffee pots, a meat grinder … the list goes on and on. I even bought a couple easy-up tents. I knew there was an old farmhouse with a small kitchen I'd be using as the base until I built what amounted to an outdoor kitchen, but I really didn't know how much I could count on that, so digging into the Burning Man principle of "radical self-reliance," if I thought I needed it, I bought it.

Once I was done, I managed to sneak in a couple of days of excellent scuba diving before Mr. Dean and I prepared to ride on the barge with all the materials, food and livestock.

We were instructed to "supervise" the loading of the barge. This was absurd because we knew nothing about loading barges. It was a very hot day, at a very busy port, with ferry boats coming in and out and hundreds of people milling about, carrying chickens in small cages, loading and unloading cars and motorbikes, with gas fumes, diesel fumes. There were families with blankets and food, sitting in any shade they could find, eating food that they had prepared. Tons of motorbikes were moving from here to there, there to here. Not unlike India, the smells went from fried dough, spices and flowers to rotting fruit and sewage, and then back again, in mere moments. And always always always, an old lady with a chicken!

And speaking of chickens, as soon as the taxi driver arrived with our livestock, I knew we were in trouble. The chickens were all pretty sickly looking, as were the goats. The ducks looked all right, but they were really aggressive when we got near the cage. As for the cages, the one for the forty chickens was much smaller than it should have been. I felt awful about the conditions these birds were being transported in. I filled up a small tub of water and tried to put it in the cage, but they were packed in so tightly that they kept knocking it over. I was sitting with all the stuff being loaded on the barge, including an ice chest full of cabbage, so I got a head of cabbage out and tore it up for them to eat and stay hydrated, which was a decent short-term solution.

The loading took most of the day. By the time the chickens were on board, three had died, so we gave them to the cook, who immediately went to work cleaning and de-feathering them. We had the crew load the animals onto the boat, rather than the barge we were towing, so we could tend to them. A crew member rigged up a tarp so they were all shaded, and we rigged up a giant crate with some holes, so we were able to move the birds around and they weren't so packed in. They seemed to relax once we were at sea.

Not only had Mr. Dean never been to many places, but he had most definitely never spent two days at sea, and this was no luxury yacht. It was a greasy, grubby old tugboat towing a grubby old barge, run by grubby old sailors who spoke in a different language, and whose customs and culture were totally foreign. Mr. Dean didn't want to go. He began to ask if we could just charter a plane or a helicopter to get to the island. He even offered to pay for it. I loved being at sea, and wasn't the least bit worried, but Mr. Dean was 100 percent certain that the boat men were pirates, and were going to kidnap us, dismember us, perhaps even harvest and sell our organs. He chain-smoked menthol cigarettes and paced the dock anxiously.

A little before sunset, the captain gave us the word that they were ready to set sail. Mr. Dean made one more desperate attempt at not boarding, but he knew he had to do it. We pulled out of Suva Harbour with everything we'd need to build a house and a remote kitchen, and survive for a couple of months, or so we hoped. I pulled a few beers from our cache and sipped on them as the sun set. The gentle rocking of the boat was rather soothing on my arthritic joints, and I appreciated the relief from the omnipresent pain that I lived in.

The sweet smells of the chicken curry, the salty sea air and the slowness of the boat set the pace as we settled into this new situation. Mr. Dean was almost convinced that the crew wasn't going to kill us, though I know he slept with one eye open that night, if he got any sleep at all.

After a delicious dinner of the freshest chicken curry possible(!), the crew came out with a big pot filled with a murky brown liquid. This turned out to be kava kava, which I had heard of but never tried. Kava kava is a root that is common in the South Pacific islands, and a few other places in the world. It's brewed into a tea, has mild sedative effects and is sometimes used in health food store sleep-aids. The captain explained to me that this was the common way for them to relax at the end of a long day. He also said that either he or the first officer would not drink kava if the other one was, so there was always a clear head on board. We still had a thirty-five-hour passage ahead of us, but he seemed to have a good grip on things.

Mr. Dean and I were offered some kava, to which I readily accepted, and Mr. Dean reluctantly agreed to. With a customary toast of "bula vinaka" we slugged down our first cup. It tasted a bit like dirt … but it wasn't terrible dirt, with an earthy and herbal sort of finish. I felt nothing after the first cup. One of the crew explained that it took six to seven cups to feel the effects. We sat up there trading stories and sipping on this brew for a few hours, watching the sunset turn into moonlight. I probably had about ten cups altogether, and in the end, my lips were tingly and it felt like I'd had maybe half a valium and a cup of Sleepy Time tea. Mellowed out, relaxed and ready for bed. I had strung up a hammock on deck, and I was loving being back on the water. I slept wonderfully that night as the sea gently rocked me. Mr. Dean was still pretty stressed out, though he did calm down on the second day, and I'm sure it's a story he'll tell his grandkids.

After a couple of calm days, we made it to the island unscathed. The 225-acre island of Katafanga was very remote, and there wasn't much on it. Once, many years earlier, a previous owner had begun to build twenty bures (the name for a small Fijian home, usually a wood-and-straw hut), a restaurant and a night club area. He'd built a warehouse on the island and it was like a giant hardware store, with plumbing and electrical parts, construction equipment, etc. They'd gotten as far as laying the foundations and throwing some basic steel frames together, and then it appeared that everyone just up and left, and the island took over. The jungle swallowed entire bulldozers and excavators whole. Most of the stuff in the warehouse had rusted or was eaten up by mold. The steel frames of the buildings rusted and were taken over by vines and bushes. It was as if someone had dumped fifty million dollars into this island, and then, when they needed the fifty-first million, it just wasn't there, so they packed up and left.

At one point, the island was a coconut plantation, and there were coconut trees everywhere. As a result, there were several coconut-fed delicacies running around the island. One of them was the coconut crab. These land crabs are about three feet across, and a beautiful shade of blue. Their shells are thick, and they have pincers that routinely break coconut shells open and could tear through your fingers like a warm knife through butter. As a result of their coconut diet, they produce the most amazingly sweet crab meat you have ever tasted in your life. And speaking of butter, there's a "yucky brown part" in the back of the shell, which locals call the crab butter, and it's basically coconut-fed crab fat. It is one of the best things I've ever tasted.

The item the island was famous for, though, was its pigs. Jack, the island caretaker, was Australian, and had an advanced degree in animal husbandry. He'd managed to keep the pigs from inbreeding (not sure how one does that), and as a result, these were purebred, coconut-fed pigs of greatness. Even when we were loading the barge before we left Suva, when the port cop found out where we were going, he licked his lips as he talked about these legendary Katafanga pigs. While I was concerned about going to the island without bringing enough proteins with me, I was confident we would not starve. As a chef, it was perhaps my greatest challenge, forcing me to think out of the box. I had to bring enough grains, oils, spices and cooking implements to be able to cook whatever proteins we managed to get our hands on.

Katafanga's beaches are white sand and pristine, and the surrounding waters are some of the most beautiful in the world. The middle of the island is dense, lush jungle, which of course comes with heat, humidity and its share of bugs, making it also a jungle from hell. The mosquitos were like Hitler's henchmen on meth, and they seemed to eat Deet (heavy duty mosquito repellent) for breakfast. It was not uncommon for us to be in mid-conversation, randomly smacking our foreheads (or sometimes someone else's) while screaming expletives. We called this Katafanga Tourette's.

The vegetation was lush with fruit trees, including breadfruit, mango and papaya, as well as an avocado tree. Only the breadfruit was in season while we were there, though. An old plantation-style house sat close to the beach with some funky bungalows on the side. We all chose our rooms, mine being just off the kitchen. The kitchen was basic, but functional ... except there was no electricity. There was running water, though it was not potable, a gas stove and an old fridge that once ran on propane, but no longer worked. For reasons that we never figured out, there was also a giant hole in the kitchen floor with a three-foot drop to a crawl space underneath the house. We called it the hole of death, and Painjoy got the guys fixing that right away. He also introduced me to an older woman with very dark skin and impeccable teeth (which I later learned were dentures) named Sura, who would be my assistant. I was hobbling pretty heavily with a cane at this point, anticipating my ankle surgery after this trip, and she was a great help to me.

The Fijian laborers were already on the island, and they had created a makeshift village in the jungle, leaving the main beach for us. By this time, another member of our crew had flown in, a Burner named Kenny, who reminded me of Steve Buscemi. He talked so much, he drove me nuts those first couple of days. He told me, "I know you hate me right now, but you're gonna grow to love me. Everybody does." That's exactly what happened. I wanted to kill him during the first week, and by the end I'd have counted on him to bust me out of a foreign jail if it came to that. And had I continued to hang out with him, it certainly could have.

The guys went to work unloading the barge, beginning with the chickens and ducks. We tied the goats up in a big field, and they seemed pretty content to graze away. All of my stuff was packed together, and as it came off, Sura and I began to organize the kitchen. We popped up the easy-up behind the house, and set up some charcoal water-filtration systems, as well as putting the BBQ together alongside a three-burner camp stove and a prep table. I set up a pantry, put together the metro racks and began unpacking dry goods.

We laid cardboard all over the floor of our storeroom, and separated the carrots, onions, cabbage and potatoes. Every day, we'd go in and cut away any mold that began to grow, increasing the life of the produce. By now the dry ice had melted. Working on yachts had taught me how to stretch out the life of fruits and veggies for a long time. I was about to find out how long they'd keep out of refrigeration.

Speaking of refrigeration, the units had been offloaded from the barge, and were in place. The elephant in the room was the generator. It weighed about 1,800 pounds and was the size of a VW van. The barge, with all of the gear, was anchored close to shore, and the boat was anchored farther out. The barge had ramps that dropped to about ten feet offshore, where the guys would enter and exit to grab loads of stuff. Once we figured out how to get the generator off the boat, there was still about 150 feet of soft beach sand before a light dirt incline of about eighteen inches, and then another thirty-five feet of dirt to move this beast through to its new home. Everyone stared at that thing as they worked, nobody knowing how it was going to come off the barge.

We worked into the night, and I made a simple dinner for everyone before we all collapsed in exhaustion. The next morning, over coffee, Kenny had an idea to make a sled out of coconut tree logs, secure a big link of chain to it and then, with the power of twelve men (literally), pull it up the beach to its new home. It was a daunting plan, but as nobody had any better ideas, the Fijian team went to work. The sled was finished by sunset, but by then the tide was high, and we needed a low tide for the best chance of success.

The following morning at sunrise, I made a big pot of coffee and breakfast. I had filled one cooler with some frozen bacon, eggs, stuff for sandwiches and a few other things so we'd have easy meals to eat for those first days of setup. Mr. Dean was used to eating fast food several days a week. He hated fish, and he hated curry. He also disliked vegetables, which were not in abundance anyway. In fact … he disliked a lot of food that wasn't fried, wrapped in plastic and served by pimply-faced teenagers. This was going to be a challenge.

The guys were able to slide the generator from the pallet onto the sled. It went pretty smoothly and we were all feeling pretty good … until it hit the sand. That's when the weight of the machine met with the "gravity" of the situation. It took Herculean efforts, and the entire day, but inch by inch, they pulled this thing to its spot and got it running, which for me meant I now had refrigeration.

I had brought some bread to the island, but bread molds quickly in the tropics. When it ran out, I busted out some of my grilled bread tricks, such as naan, chapati and skillet cornbread. I also made BBQ pizza by grilling one side of the dough for a minute or two, before flipping and topping it with sauce and cheese, and quickly closing the grill to melt it. I was even successful at baking some muffins on the BBQ with indirect heat.

The Fijians began catching us some fish, mostly snapper, which was nice. I'd sometimes get up early and go fishing with them. If I breaded and fried it up to look like chicken fingers, and made a couple of dipping sauces, Mr. Dean would eat it, mostly because he literally had no choice. As time went on, he tried more things. Hunger breeds an adventurous palate.

I'd hike up to the "village" every day to check for eggs, but most of the time, there were none. The other guys were convinced that the Fijians were stealing them from us, but truth be told, these were some pretty tired looking old hens. One day, Sura asked me, "Why you buy grandmother chickens, Chef? They no lay eggs." That's when I learned you should never buy livestock from your taxi driver's cousin. And I had been so smug about being able to pull off the scoring of livestock out of nowhere. I think we got twelve eggs the entire time we were there. We began slaughtering the chickens, one every few days. They didn't have a ton of meat on them, but the bones made for good broths. My menus had to stay flexible, as our daily protein sources were always a mystery.

Jack, the caretaker, showed up one morning with a freshly slaughtered pig. He wanted most of the organ meat for himself and the village, but he said that we could have all the carcass meat. He and I spent the afternoon breaking it down. I had a vacuum-seal machine, and was sealing up the better cuts. I ground a lot of the tougher cuts for sausages and burgers. I was excited to make ribs, but wild pigs are a lot smaller than conventional pigs and the racks are small, so I ended up making them as an appetizer once the smoker was finished.

Wait, did he say smoker? Yep, we built a smoker out of a fifty-five-gallon drum. It worked "good enough," and I used the hell out of that thing while I was there, brining and smoking my own bacon, pulled pork, pork brisket and smoked fish.

When the barge was unloaded, the boat left and we were truly on our own. I think as we all stood on the beach watching it sail away, we truly got a sense of how alone we were. We set about our individual tasks at hand, which were endless. The pig was a game changer and, soon enough, we were getting lobsters and giant clams, too. The clams were amazing, and I made a few ceviches out of the clam lip muscles that were out of this world. Mr. Dean would have no part of those, but the rest of us loved them. He broke down and ate some when I would bread and fry them, Boston style. Once I fried things, he became a lot more amenable to trying them.

Christmas was coming up, though it didn't feel like it in the heat of the tropics. I decided to harvest two of the ducks and make a pot of smoked duck and sausage gumbo. It turned out the ducks were a lot tougher to harvest than the chickens. They were wily little fuckers. Plus the ducks were named Gumbo, Christmas, Paul and Ringo, and it's always harder to slaughter animals once they have names. Harder … but not impossible. In an ironic turn of events, Gumbo and Christmas were faster than Paul and Ringo, so they lived through the New Year, while Paul and Ringo were not so lucky. We did the dirty work a couple of days before Christmas so I had time to brine them, making them more tender and palatable. Then I smoked them, removed the meat from the carcass and made a stock out of the bones. Gumbo and Christmas were a little bit weirded out, and they kept their distance from us for a few days, which was understandable.

On Christmas Eve, we took a joy ride around the island on an old front loader that Kenny had managed to get running — and he'd painted it and glued a bunch of coconut shells all over it. It was his own personal art car project.

On Christmas morning Jack and two of the guys showed up with another pig. This one the Fijians were going to cook on a bamboo spit over an open fire called a lovo. They cooked it low and slow, all day long, using coconut palm fronds to baste it with coconut oil and rotated it by hand. My smoked-duck stock was bubbling away, and Jack said he'd take us up to a hidden cave. It ended up being quite a hike, and so worth the effort. We entered through a crevice in the rocks at the top of the island, which opened into a cave with another crevice. It went down the mountain for several hundred meters, ending at a fresh stream. We washed our dirty faces in the stream and reveled in being there. I was walking with a cane full-time at this point, and was anticipating the installation of a titanium ankle … so I was happy and proud to have made the hike.

We made it back in the mid-afternoon, and I went to work assembling my gumbo. I strained the stock and made a dark roux, as I had learned so many years ago at K-Paul's. I added the roux to my strained stock, thickening it from a broth into more of a gravy. I then browned the sausage (made by hand from our local pigs) and added it, along with the duck and whatever onions and celery I had left. I like to finish it with garlic, a small splash of apple cider vinegar and a little Worcestershire sauce.

Mr. Dean and Kenny talked APJ into hooking up a forty-two-inch LED flat-screen TV that was brand-new technology at the time. We all shared an island Christmas dinner of spit-roasted pig, smoked-duck gumbo, rice and grilled lobster tails. Sura made a steamed coconut pudding with mangos that weren't quite ripe, so she macerated them in sugar and lemon juice. Delicious. After dinner, we made big bowls of popcorn, and the Fijians brewed up a batch of the ever-present kava kava. We watched *Avatar*, which had only recently been released, and made the best out of a holiday spent a very long way from family.

In the end, we completed our mission, and left the island with one finished bure. To Painjoy's credit, he'd brought every single nail, screw and tool needed to build that place. To Kenny's credit, he got the front loader running, created a few tools on the fly out of what we had and made some lifelong friendships with the Fijians. To Mr. Dean's credit, he worked hard every day and stepped WAY out of his comfort zone for the experience of a lifetime. And to my credit … nobody starved!

I later heard through the grapevine that the owner used that bure once, and then put the island up for sale. I'm not sure if anyone ever bought it, but at the time of writing this book, it was for sale, either still or again, for seventeen million dollars.

One strange thing about traveling is coming home. In some ways, nothing has changed other than you. In other ways, nothing is the same, except for you. I stayed with a group of poet and activist friends for the few weeks before the surgery, one of whom was conceiving an international movement called "The Body Is Not an Apology," which teaches Radical Self-Love. This really resonated with me, since I'd been apologizing for my body for decades. Life has a way of throwing people and lessons at you in the moments when you need them the most.

Better, Stronger, Faster

It had been twelve years since my motorcycle accident, and Dr. Schuberth, the guy who originally screwed me back together, had told me I'd be lucky to get a decade out of my ankle. Just before leaving for my island adventure, the good doctor, who was still the head of podiatry, showed me two pieces of titanium called the Scandinavian Total Ankle Replacement (STAR). I would have tried anything then — my pain level was at an all-time high. I checked into the hospital for surgery.

I must have been pretty heavily medicated because I don't remember much, except my body warmed by the morning sunlight and my mind warmed by some spacey Grateful Dead music.

After the surgery, I spent a couple of weeks at my brother's house in Marin, before moving down to my cousin's tomato farm in the Santa Cruz Mountains.

On the tomato farm was a small cabin, called the Love Shack, that my cousin lived in for many years while he built his family house. It was a little A-frame cabin and was just as cute as could be, with a world-class view of the redwoods and the Pacific Ocean off in the distance. The farm was off the grid, and they lived on solar power and generators. While the Love Shack did have a sink, the toilet was a self-composting model about thirty feet from the cabin, and just beyond that was a stunning outdoor clawfoot bathtub with an on-demand propane heater. When my doctor told me that I could begin to put weight on my ankle for short tips to the bathroom, I had to laugh. He had no idea what that meant for me … hobbling along a trail in the mountains.

The place was beautiful, with tons of flowers, plants and succulents. There was an eclectic array of yard art everywhere you looked. Mardi Gras beads in the trees, sculptures, even the string and hammer portion of a piano hanging from a tree. There was an old Underwood typewriter with flowers growing out of it, and a pair of hiking boots (that my cousin had hiked the Pacific Crest Trail in) that had long since been turned into planters. With the view, the natural beauty, an odd array of art and being surrounded by family, it wasn't a bad place to be laid up.

But I was still feeling pretty low. Depression doesn't care how nice your surroundings are. I was lonely, I was faded on pain meds for my ankle and since my skin meds increased the risk of infection, I was off them. So my psoriasis was raging.

I spent a lot of time just watching the plants grow and making simple meals on my camp stove. A few friends brought me food, and I did have some dinners with the cousins, though they were deep in their work seasons.

I would wrap my ankle in plastic and take long hot baths in the outdoor tub, with cups of tea, looking over the redwoods and out to the Pacific. Even in this idyllic environment, this was a tough time for me.

Once I could manage to drive down the three-and-a-half-mile dirt road and open and close the giant steel gate whilst hopping on one foot, I began to go to the strawberry farm next door to use their Wi-Fi. They had a jam tasting room with an honor store that sold coffee, cocoa and baked goods. (An honor store, as the name implies, is a store with no clerk. You just leave your money in the till and take your change, writing down what you took.) They also had couches, games and books, and they created a lovely little community space where locals would congregate. It was a wonderful resource, and the epitome of Northern California — cute, quaint and eclectic.

I'd sit there for hours, looking at personal chef jobs online, hoping to find a position in a local estate. I also toyed with the idea of starting a food truck, either in Santa Cruz, the Bay Area or Miami. I had a potential partner and financial backer in Miami, but I didn't love the idea of all my time being spent in a food truck in a hot and humid city.

Then I learned of a start-up called Kitchit.com, where chefs could post menus with pricing for intimate dinner parties. I spent some time writing new menus, assembling my references and building a profile. They even offered to hire a professional photographer for food styling on the site, and I took advantage of that. I was beginning to market myself, but to be honest, I was still unable to work. (I wasn't able to put weight on the ankle for about ninety days after the surgery.)

A woman I know asked me to help her circulate a petition for the release of Socrates. We were able to collect almost 200,000 signatures and, after twenty-three years, Socrates was granted clemency and released. He and I spoke several times, and I helped him out with enough money to buy a car and get settled. Once that happened, he created some distance between us. When I asked him about it, he told me that while he forgave me for what had happened all of those years ago, he had no interest in remaining friends. He said that to forgive was usually a gift to the person being forgiven. He was happy to give me that gift, but it ended there. He had no interest in anything related to the Grateful Dead or to his life before prison. The last time we spoke, he was living a quiet life, working a quiet job and enjoying his freedom. Fare thee well, Socrates ... fare thee well.

Nearly thirty years after my arrest, not a day goes by that I don't think of my experiences in prison.

Bruce Wayne and True Love

Pretty much as soon as I could hobble with weight on my ankle, I started booking gigs on the new private chef website. One day, I was contacted by the personal assistant of one of my clients. She told me that her boss had loved my meal and that I was being included on their preferred-staffing roster. I'd made a spicy Thai dinner, and it turned out that he loved spice and was a very adventurous eater. I'll call him Bruce Wayne, because, like Batman, he has pulled off some monumentally heroic things that have changed the world as we know it today. Due to my NDA, as well as a general respect for Bruce Wayne, I can't say much more than that. But I will say that he is a handsome, brilliant, suave, self-made zillionaire, who was never short of being a perfect gentleman to me.

From the time Jerry Garcia died in '95, I saw all the incarnations of the members formerly known as the Grateful Dead. Some were good — others, not so much. In fall 2011, the incarnation called Furthur was playing two shows at the Monterey County Fairgrounds. My former roommate and friend, Lost Sailor, was meeting up with his friend Marsea, who had an RV and said Lost Sailor and I could stay in the RV that night. But I was planning on going home after the show as it was only an hour away, so I declined the offer … and then I met Marsea.

I knew right away she was not like others when I saw her RV. It was painted to look like a weeping willow tree and covered in the dust that can only be found at Burning Man. She was just over five feet tall, and was, and is, a human ball of compassion. There is no situation that I have seen her in that she doesn't attack with kindness. I was still limping pretty heavily from the surgery, but she remembers it as me "swaggering on up" and introducing myself. She'd loaded up on refreshments, so we sat around and ate and drank and watched all the people arriving for the show. I learned she was Jewish, and a therapist, and had been seeing Dead shows and going to Burning Man for many years. We discovered we had spent time in many of the same places and had been to many of the same events. We even realized that she'd eaten my food, at a catered event in the Bay Area.

As the afternoon turned into evening, we made our way into the show. We had a great time dancing, and I could see that she knew and loved this music at least as much as I did, if not more. After the show, the three of us walked around the camping area and enjoyed the after-show glow for a while, then Lost Sailor finally "got lost" while Marsea and I sat by her RV and talked about everything and anything. It wasn't difficult to persuade me to stay the night, and she, Lost Sailor and I all drifted off to sleep in the bunks of the RV.

Chef Evan Presents

I was getting more and more work locally, and it was time to start a legitimate business. Stealing a line from one of my heroes, rock impresario Bill Graham, I named my business Chef Evan Presents. Bruce Wayne was keeping me very busy. He entertained a lot, and had many high-ranking dinner guests. It was not uncommon for the secret service or bodyguards to be stationed outside. Once again, I found myself cooking for senators, members of congress, past and present prime ministers, and even a presidential candidate. And now I could add the tech elite of the Silicon Valley to that list.

But perhaps the biggest honor was when I was asked to cook a Passover Seder for Bruce's entire family, including his Bubby, who was nearly 100 years old. I need to take a quick moment to discuss matzah balls, or knaidlech (Yiddish for matzah balls) as I'd known them my whole life. Most people know matzah balls to be light and fluffy, not unlike a dumpling. My family knaidlech are different. First of all, after you make the batter, you remove one third of it, add some extra egg yolks, a little cinnamon sugar and some extra schmaltz (chicken fat). This is called the "neshama," which translates to "the soul." As the saying goes, "The neshama in the knaidlech is what the soul is to the person." They are formed by making the ball, and then poking a hole and adding the neshama into the center. They are then boiled until they float, at which point they are removed from the water, rubbed in schmaltz and baked for forty-five minutes. This makes for a dense ball, with a dark sweet center and a crispy outer skin. It's all I knew for my whole life, so it was the "right way" to make them.

I made the typical, classic light and fluffy knaidlech the first night, but the second night's seder, I made my Lithuanian family version. After the Seder, I went over to the Bubby and I asked her what she thought of the knaidlech. "They tasted just like my mother's knaidlech," she said in her thick Yiddish accent. "Yeah?" I replied excitedly. And then with a total deadpan look, and without missing a beat, she said, "Yeah ... I always *hated* my mother's knaidlech." It was a dig that only a Bubby could drop, and I took the fact that I'd invoked a childhood memory through food as the highest praise I could possibly have hoped for.

I also began working with my friend, Sassy, who specialized in retreat catering held in beautiful places, out in nature. The first gig was a two-week Brazilian music and dance camp in the Sonoma redwoods. Two hundred and fifty musicians and dancers came from all over the globe to study their instruments and dance moves all day, and party and dance all night long. Sassy runs a really fun kitchen, and draws an eclectic group of amazing chefs, artists, dancers, musicians and weirdos to produce food with her. As one of the chief Weirdos, I cooked at Brazil Camp for ten summers in a row.

It's always fun to fire up the giant flattop and make Sassy's lemon ricotta pancakes with blueberry syrup ... at one camp we served these to 400 people. We started before dawn, cracking and separating about 375 eggs, using a giant Hobart mixer to whip the egg whites to stiff peaks (fluffy and firm), then folded them all in using sauté pans as spatulas.

We also cook meat at Brazil Camp. A lot of it ... and I'm the meat guy. It's usually 140 pounds at lunch, and 140 pounds at dinner. For late night, the Brazilians will fire the grill and cook off another twenty or thirty pounds of tri-tip and sausage, while drinking and dancing the night away. It's always insane numbers, and it's a very different style of cooking than I usually do. I love it and look forward to gigging with her every summer.

Love and Heartbreak

After those Monterey shows, Marsea and I began hanging out regularly. It started out as meeting regularly for lunch, taking long walks and having deeply getting-to-know-each-other conversations. She saw clients in the late afternoons and evenings, so she was free in the mornings, and my gigs were also at night.

It was not long before we became inseparable. It had been thirteen years since Hillinary and I had split up, and in that time, while I had many flings, nothing had been that serious, or that satisfying. This was different. I felt as if I had landed home. She nurtured me in a way that nobody ever had. She loved me for who I am, and embraced my quirks, even the ones that she didn't necessarily care for. Regarding my psoriasis, she said it was like the "dust at Burning Man, just part of the experience."

I've always had this sneaking suspicion that my long-lost and much-loved mother had something to do with me meeting Marsea. Like on the cosmic chess board that makes up our lives, Mom moved the piece that led me to this amazing woman. She nurtures me in a way that feels maternal at times … just pure, unconditional love. The kind that happens in books and movies … but stronger because it's real.

And so, not long after, we decided to get a place of our own. She'd actually been house-hunting for a few years, but our needs were now different than her needs prior to me. We found an amazing house that we turned into a home pretty quickly. It wasn't long before it was dubbed the WOW house. There's an expansive treetop view of about ten miles, and not one other house is visible. Somehow, I'd gone from living out of a backpack for ten years to owning a tractor, two chainsaws, four bedrooms and land. I sure didn't see that one coming.

We received the keys on June 11, 2012 … twenty years to the day after I was arrested. In twenty "short" years, I had learned a skill, built a career, traveled the world, had more adventures than many ever have. I also have not added to the ever-growing prison recidivism rate in this country. I'm proud of my accomplishments, and I own the failures with equal regard.

With Marsea in my life, I became happier than ever before, and as a result, my confidence increased and my business began to flourish. Bruce Wayne was booking me a few nights a week, and as my reputation made it around, I was getting plenty of other gigs as well. This was a good thing, because all Marsea and I wanted to do for a while was have epic fun together, and that was often expensive. (I keep thinking this fun period may end at some point, but it hasn't as of yet.)

Bruce Wayne acquired an additional home in San Francisco for entertaining, so about half of my dinners were moved to his incredible downtown penthouse apartment. It was at one of these events that I got the word that Soss Boss had died of heart failure.

One of the closest friends I had ever known (and loved) was gone. I just stood there for a moment, paralyzed in shock. And then I had to get out of the kitchen. I made it to the bathroom, where I locked myself in and cried for a while. When I came out, Bruce Wayne must have seen that I was shaken, and he asked me what was going on.

"I just lost one of my closest friends. My friend Soss. He's gone." It sounded so weird. And I must have looked a wreck because Bruce Wayne took a step toward me and gave me the first hug he had ever given me (but not the last). He asked if I needed to leave. He said they could just order food somewhere. It was a sweet offer, but it was Easter Sunday, and it would have been difficult to order food. Besides, I had nowhere to go, and I'd already bought all the ingredients, so I went back in the kitchen, tucked my head down and focused on my craft. It was probably the best thing for me.

I've lost friends over the years, but losing Soss really hurt. He brought out the best and the worst in me. I could talk to him about anything. And I mean anything. We talked politics, art and culture, and music, as well as deeply personal topics like emotions, interpersonal relationships, sex and drugs. He was a talented artist and author, and was well versed in negotiations of all sorts, so he was always one to bounce ideas off. Soss treated everybody with the amount of respect, or disrespect, they deserved.

He'd been recognized by the city of Miami as an important artist, yet he chose to live in the ghetto so he could document the building of the performing arts center, but also because he liked it. Sadly, he suffered from addiction, and living in the ghetto didn't help with that. It's hard to have friends who are addicts, especially if you knew them before their addiction really got out of hand. But for me, his addiction didn't diminish the friendship, or decrease the love I had for him.

In 2017, a year and a bit after Soss checked out, we "got the band back together" and honored him by having "Final-Q" at Burning Man. We built a camp in his name, and it was one that would have made him proud. I called on a dear friend of mine who is a catering ninja, as well as a seasoned Burner, to manage the front of the house, and she showed up in spades for me, and for all of us. We did our final Rock Star Dinner and our last Carne Armada, which was at the camp of the founders of Burning Man. Soss would have loved that choice.

The "Last Supper" was one of our best, with three of the five courses prepared tableside. The table itself was in an airplane hangar of a tent, that was maybe 100 feet long by 30 feet wide. Members of camp had built a long table to seat around seventy people, with five indentions strategically cut out for our tableside courses. For the first course, my sous chef prepared five sheet pans with salt blocks that had been heated in the smokers. We cooked shrimp tableside on the hot salt blocks, and served them with (or without) my legendary cannabis curry sauce. The second course (my favorite) was smoked-duck ramen served in a martini glass with a daikon salad, noodles and a sous vide egg. The ceviche was served in bowls that were iced down, and the eggs were cooked and processed with the precision of a Michelin-starred restaurant. The health department had rules about not using those cooking techniques at Burning Man. We assured them that we wouldn't … and then we did anyway. "Sometimes it's better to beg forgiveness than it is to ask permission," Soss loved to say.

For the third course, also cooked tableside, we heated coals for five teppanyaki grills. We'd smoked some Wagyu beef rib caps to a rare temperature, and then chilled them. (Wagyu is the breed of cattle that the Japanese use for the infamous Kobe beef. It's the highest grade of beef on Earth.) We seared the rib caps on the hot grills to char the outside, and brought them up to temp. The smoke that they created filled the tent, and if anyone hadn't been crying about the loss of Soss, they were crying now. It was amazing to see the flames jumping up through the smoke in our little dining-room bubble. People laughed, cried and reveled in the fact that they were eating A-5 Wagyu beef in the desert at Burning Man. The flames and smoke added flavor and texture to an already visceral experience.

The next course was a whole pig that The Rev had cooked over coals in a sealed box. We broke down the pig, and people lined up to fill their plates. The final course of the night was dessert, nitrogen ice cream made tableside. The liquid nitrogen gave the course a very mad scientist sort of feel. We all told stories about our friend, and after the dinner we had a procession to the temple, where we hung a giant picture of him to add to the temple burn at the end of the week. I cried a lot from the time I heard of Soss's death to the Final-Q, which was fifteen months later. But I haven't cried about him since. His memory is a blessing.

Sometimes It's Better to Be Lucky, Than Smart

I've been both in this lifetime, but the greatest day ever was the day that I met Marsea. As I consider my life as a freelance chef, I am aware that it hasn't been the easiest path, or the path of least resistance. I wonder if I'd have made similar choices, had I not spent time in prison. Or had I been graced with a "normal" childhood. I still feel as I did in fourth grade … like an awkward, out of place kid who is bad at sports and has a dead mom. I have never felt like I "fit in" … but as I am maturing, I think I am realizing that this is a common phenomenon. Nobody is the cool kid that all the kids want to be. Nobody fits in.

Today cannabis is legal for medicine in more than half of the country, and recreationally in twenty-three states. Psychedelics are making a resurgence, and are gaining some acceptance as the powerful therapeutic tools that they are. Groups like MAPS (Multidisciplinary Association of Psychedelic Studies) have fought to legalize and research them. Marsea trained to offer psychedelic-assisted therapy, and she looks forward to participating in that work. One of the fathers of this profession, Stanislav Grof, once said that "Psychedelics … [will] be for psychiatry what the microscope is for biology or the telescope is for astronomy." I am certain that this will be the case.

The drug war marches on, continuing to destroy lives and costing taxpayers billions of dollars, but we are beginning to see signs of it crumbling. "Harm reduction" approaches provide safer methods and greater accessibility for drug users. Harm reduction embraces the fact that people will take drugs, and will engage in risky behavior, because that has been human nature ever since Eve allegedly bit into the proverbial apple. There is even a school of thought that says Moses and the burning bush may have been a DMT-induced hallucination. (For those who don't know, DMT, or dimethyltryptamine, is a powerful psychedelic with a long history of use in traditional South American shamanic practices.) That actually makes more sense to me than what appears in Exodus. In any case, my point here is that drug culture was, and is, everywhere.

Prohibition didn't work then, and it doesn't work now. Once the criminal element of drug use is removed, the inherent dangers decrease dramatically, as do drug-related crimes. These techniques have been proven effective in Portugal, which decriminalized all drugs back at the beginning of this century. Since then, drug use has fallen below their neighboring countries. People seeking treatment has increased by 60 percent, and the number of new HIV cases has fallen dramatically. In Portugal, drug-induced deaths have fallen from eighty in 2001 to twelve in 2012. More evidence of the effectiveness of harm reduction also lies in Christiania, Denmark, in Holland's well-regarded approach to soft drugs and prostitution and in Uruguay, which was the first country to legalize cannabis.

Depression still pokes its ugly head around me sometimes, but I am becoming better at recognizing it, acknowledging it and not letting it take hold of me for too long. I finally realized and accepted the fact that I am a trauma survivor. From childhood to getting tangled into the war on drugs, the trauma is real, and does not go away. What does go away is the feeling of helplessness that comes from not knowing how to deal with it. That has come from years of therapy and self-reflection, two things that my father didn't believe could help a broken little eight-year-old.

I still think back to when Captain Dave asked me where I saw myself in five years. I still don't want to commit to an answer. I prefer staying open to the great adventure that makes up this life, and I cannot wait to see what the future holds.

"Sure don't know what I'm going for,
But I'm gonna go for it for sure!"

—Bob Weir

Author's Note

I set out to write this book in the midst of the pandemic. I quickly realized that I had a lot to say and the stories I wanted to tell would fill more than one book. To those who've played a big part in my life and don't see themselves here, please understand that a lot more ended up on the cutting room floor than did in this book. I look forward to sharing more travel stories and strange tales of the pandemic, as well as more food and cooking stories, in the next book or, better yet, around a campfire that has yet to be lit.

Acknowledgements

Aside from dedicating this book mostly to my wife, Marsea, I also need to acknowledge how encouraging she has been to me. Your wife telling you your book is good is kind of like your mom telling you you're handsome. But she stuck with me in the three plus years this project has taken and has supported me through the entire process.

I also want to thank the good people at Iguana Books. In particular, Paula Chiarcos, Lee Parpart, Cheryl Hawley and Heather Bury. Your help and support has been invaluable and has left me with a book that I am proud of.

I am blessed to have way too many friends to list. So thanks to all those who supported me throughout this journey. See you in my next publication.

About the Author

Evan Marcus-Rotman grew up in Southern California and has traveled to nearly 50 countries. After cutting his teeth in restaurants and hotels and catering, he worked as a private chef on yachts, private islands, estates and on the road with rock bands before spearheading a successful private chef business in the Silicon Valley. These days he can be found cooking on the South Maui shores and is happiest when he's eating, dancing or 53 feet underwater breathing compressed air while neutrally buoyant.